'A witty, stylish and ente[...]f golf as it is played far fr[...]' *Observer*

'I enjoyed and was infor[...] book, and it leaves me itc[...]d play this maddening, addictive, alluring game' Andrew Greig, *Scotsman*

'[An] entertaining book . . . well worth it for any golf fan' *Sunday Herald*

'An easy read' *Daily Record*

'Well written [with] some amusing anecdotes and . . . oddball characters' *Sunday Times*

'[A] funny and fascinating journey' *Bunkered*

'It made me laugh' Robert McNeil, *Scotsman*

'[Chris Cairns] writes with a pleasing, light-hearted style which can have the reader ploughing through chapters wearing a permanent smile' *Yorkshire Evening Post*

'Great fun' *Nottingham Evening Post*

'[A] fascinating tale of golfing sub-cultures' *Golf World*

'Highly entertaining' *Liverpool Daily Post*

'A hilarious trip . . . round the municipal golf courses of Britain and a funny tale' *St Andrews Citizen*

'I'll say one thing for Cairns, he is clearly a man after my own heart. This delightful book proves that he is clearly besotted with one of life's supreme pleasures . . . the game of golf . . . I greatly enjoyed *No Tie Required*, Cairns has a nice eye for social and civic detail' *Scottish Review of Books*

Christopher Cairns is a freelance writer and journalist based in Edinburgh. Formerly a reporter and then environment correspondent for the *Scotsman*, his work has been published in several magazines and newspapers, including the *Sunday Times*, *Herald* and *Sunday Herald*. It would have been more, but he was too busy getting his handicap down from 14 to 9.

No Tie Required

How the rich stole golf

Christopher Cairns

headline

First published in 2005
by HEADLINE BOOK PUBLISHING

First published in paperback in 2006
by HEADLINE BOOK PUBLISHING

1

10-digit ISBN 0 7553 1379 8
13-digit ISBN 978 0 7553 1379 2

Text design by Design Section
Typeset by Palimpsest Book Production Limited,
Polmont, Stirlingshire
Printed and bound in Great Britain by
Mackays of Chatham plc, Chatham, Kent

Headline's policy is to use papers that are natural, renewable and
recyclable products and made from wood grown in sustainable
forests. The logging and manufacturing processes are expected to
conform to the environmental regulations of the country of origin.

HEADLINE BOOK PUBLISHING LTD
A division of Hodder Headline
338 Euston Road
London NW1 3BH

www.headline.co.uk
www.hodderheadline.com

To Mum and Dad

Acknowledgements

In absolutely no particular order, I'd like to thank the following people who, whether they like it or not, must share the blame for this book.

John Moreton, Karl Spracklen, Philip Knowles and John Burnett are just some of the historians and academics who were generous with their time and endlessly patient with a writer who only gradually came to realise he didn't have a clue what he was talking about. My special thanks, however, go to Dick Holt who provided not only guidance and valuable source material, but endless enthusiasm, encouragement, tea and biscuits.

Of those in the various associations, unions and other governing bodies, I am grateful to Ian Thomson, Kevin Stevens, Andy Salmon, Neil Hayward, Richard Flint and Norman Fletcher who took pains to guide me through the maze of golf administration. Meanwhile, Elizabeth Maxwell at SportScotland and Stephen Blake at the Golf Research Group ensured the book would contain at least some reliable facts.

At times in the research and subsequent writing – not to mention the journey itself – I seemed determined to head up blind alleys. Among those who took the trouble to get me back on track are Vivien Saunders, Herman Lewis, Ian Bogie, Willie Rusk and Peter Harrington. At Hodder Headline, I am indebted to David Wilson for his encouragement and diplomacy no less than for his editing skills, and to Bob McDevitt who clearly knows a bloody good idea for a book when he sees one.

It goes without saying that all of the above did their best to steer me along the path of accuracy and truth. Any digressions into complete nonsense are my responsibility alone.

To all my playing companions in this book, my grateful thanks for letting me join them on their golf courses, pester them with daft questions and write unkind things about their swings.

And to Marian, who has never once told me to grow up and get a proper job, all my love.

Introduction

There is not so much as a signpost. If you don't know where it is, it means you won't have been told and you are probably not welcome anyway. The approach to Muirfield, home to the Honourable Company of Edinburgh Golfers, is by way of an unassuming little road off the A198 between Gullane and North Berwick in East Lothian. The houses on one side of this road are comfortable, but only in keeping with an area generally well padded with nooks and fireside Chesterfields for Edinburgh's stockbroker and financial elite, nothing too palatial or noticeable. And that's probably just the way the members would want it. The field on the other side of the road, which doubles as a car park when the Open is in town, is equally unremarkable. It isn't long, however, before you notice some impressive wrought ironwork at the end of the road. These are the large, remote-controlled gates that lead into the grounds of the club proper, but they are not for the likes of you, me or anyone else for that matter, to drive their car through. Short of this entrance, you are directed off to the right to park in one of a row of tin-roofed sheds. Cars, it seems, will not be seen within a hundred yards of the clubhouse, even from the air.

I am more than usually excited by the round in prospect. Not only am I about to play arguably the best golf course in the British Isles, but in a semi-serious competition with proper rules, trophies and everything. I am a ringer – a late call-up to join a large party of Glasgow doctors who occasionally take their love of the game on the road round the finest courses in Scotland. Since they've been smart enough to wangle a prize fund from a drug company with an underspend on its PR budget and we're not sure how non-medics would look in the paperwork, this evening I am Professor Cairns of the Carntyne Acute Rectal Dysfunction Clinic, a bottom specialist without peer in the east end of Glasgow. My wife's cousin, Michael, who has drafted me in (himself a fictional surgeon who, when asked what sort, replies simply 'top') is nowhere to be seen as I climb out of my car and glance nervously at those already pulling golf bags and trolleys from their vehicles. I'm keen not to be the diffident outsider, but equally I can see the danger in attracting too much attention, easy familiarity and perhaps a tricky question about the latest thinking on irritable bowel syndrome before we've even teed off. I am opting for friendly aloofness and hope a combination of grinning constantly, but refusing to look anyone in the eye, will do the job.

We are obviously a cross-section of the medical fraternity. While slightly creased and care-worn looking GPs are fishing clubs out from under piles of PVC gloves and syringe packs in the boots of ten-year-old Toyotas, big-tied and chalk-striped consultants are taking theirs from the front seats of their mid-engined Italian sports cars, the boot space having been entirely used up with their shoes. It is 3.30p.m. on a warm summer's afternoon and, despite the fact that our tee-off for a group of around thirty is only half an hour away, we first half dozen are the early arrivals.

I had learned from Michael that part of the reason I was needed to make up the numbers was that the event had been something of a last-minute arrangement. Muirfield had had a late cancellation and contacted the medics, who'd played there before, to ask if they'd like to take the vacant slot. There being no question of them refusing, as many doctors as possible with the chance of a Thursday afternoon off had been scrambled in short order.

Once jackets are on and ties are straightened we make our way without further ado down through the gates and round the front of the clubhouse, the brilliant but strangely self-contained professor in the vanguard. Following my nose round the bay window of the members' lounge, I walk in the front door and head for the sign saying locker room.

'Excuse me!' The bellow from a room to the left just as I pass inside stops me dead in my tracks and I look round what turns out to be the doorway to the secretary's office.

'Yes?'

'Who *are* you?' roars a man at his desk, peering over the rim of half-moon spectacles.

Caught completely off-guard by this, and already feeling the strain from trying to look like a man of twice my intelligence, I begin stammering name, rank and serial number before he breaks through with, 'I mean, what are you doing here?'

That I am planning to play golf seems so obvious I don't answer for a second or two as I try to work out whether or not it's a trick question. At this point one of the party, which is now backing up at the door, introduces us as the group for the late afternoon booking.

'No, no, *NO!*' comes the response. 'You are *far* too early. You will have to leave.'

Stunned silence.

'Leave?' We all look at each other. 'What, you mean . . . go?'

The man at the desk sighs as if suddenly tiring of a whole day talking to half-witted oiks. '*Yes*. The afternoon party has not finished yet, so you will have to leave the premises. Do not come back until, oh, 4.15p.m. at the earliest.'

From the front door of the Muirfield clubhouse one can see not only most of the golf course, but also through the windows into the locker room. The course appears deserted apart from an elderly gentleman and his dog, while the late afternoon sunshine is glinting off rows of empty hooks and coat hangers inside.

'I – said – you – will – have – to – *LEAVE!*'

The walk back to the tin sheds and our cars is conducted mostly in silence as we wrestle with the conflicting desires to surgically insert his spectacles up this martinet's backside (I am suddenly unconcerned by my lack of genuine expertise in this area) and keep calm so as not to spoil the evening for the rest of the party. We stand around for a bit and check with each other that our senses are indeed in working order and that we have just been thrown off a golf course for being on time. No 'Sorry for the inconvenience, gentlemen – do use the facilities.' Not even a 'Please spend some time in our pro shop.' Muirfield doesn't have a pro shop. Muirfield doesn't have a pro.

Soon new arrivals, including Michael, are approaching and wondering why we're milling about. Incredulous of our story, they set off for the clubhouse, only to return a few minutes later with their tails between their legs and their teeth clenched in furious indignation. As our numbers swell, it's all getting faintly ridiculous – and late. Next, the ground staff leave in their vans from the staff car park with much condescending shaking of heads and tooting of horns for us to get out of their way.

'You should fucking turn up on time,' shouts one helpfully as he passes by. So much for proletarian solidarity.

Eventually our mob of well-dressed revolting peasants reach some kind of critical mass around the car park and, with fists and three-irons raised, we march on the gates of the palace . . . only to discover they've been locked and a sheepish-looking starter posted to keep an eye on us. It is ten minutes later, just as a half-hearted attempt at *We Shall Overcome* is emanating from the back, when the gates finally open and the 'afternoon party' that stretched Muirfield's resources to the limit leaves . . . with his Airedale and a caddie carrying his golf clubs.

With a supreme effort we suppress the urge to smash all the windows, drag out the staff, strip them naked and make them watch from the ninth green as we torch the place. Instead, like thousands before and, no doubt, thousands to come, we swallow our pride and try to make the best of the situation. Since we are half an hour late in getting to the tee, however, we are forced to start half the group on the tenth if there is to be any chance of us finishing in daylight. In fact, there's barely time for the

Honourable Company to extract its green fees and tell the only woman in our company she'll have to change in her car and under no circumstances is she allowed anywhere near the clubhouse.

Welcome to one of the 'best' golf clubs in Britain.

I

Two years later, I am once again on Honourable Company turf and playing with a couple of older members . . .

'Fuck me!' says Sandy. 'Ye'll no' want that one back again.'

'Aye, ye've got the hang of it right enough,' agrees his pal, George. 'That dinnae take ye long.'

They're right, of course. From all of 146 yards, I had traced that very fine line between a fade and a slice and sent the ball in a glorious parabola across the front of the green and into the right side bunker where it undoubtedly plugged. I'm pulling the tee peg out of the ground and mumbling stuff about 'just a fluke' and 'wait till you see the next effort', but the stupid grin on my face betrays just how pleased I am. It *was* a lovely shot. Considering.

Considering that exactly half an hour earlier on this grey July morning I had been asleep in bed, blissfully ignorant of the fact that the battery had popped out of the alarm clock again and I was not where I should have been. Considering that the previous day I had spent ten hours on my hands and knees building IKEA bedroom furniture and all my screwdriving muscles still ached.

And considering I had just hit a gutta percha ball with a hickory-shafted mashie and it damn near made the green!

'So how did it feel?' asks Sandy. I tell him the truth – it felt like one of the best shots I've ever struck. The reason for that, I reflect as we walk towards the green, is that whenever I have been lucky enough to hit an iron squarely on the meat, as Wodehouse puts it, the resulting shot has felt as light as a feather, as if not so much as a blade of grass, let alone a golf ball, has impeded the clubhead's progress throughout the swing. So it was with the mashie/guttie shot; the lightness of the hickory-shafted club and the, admittedly lucky, perfect connection combined to produce a stroke of beguiling beauty and ease.

As it turns out I am not in the bunker proper, but on the badly maintained rear face where collapsed ground and sandy footprints have stopped the ball rolling all the way in. One confident swing with the wedge-type affair I am carrying soon rectifies that, however, and in no time I *am* in the bunker proper. The next splash gets me out and on to the green some fifteen feet from the pin. Three straightforward putts later I am walking off with a triple bogey six and my enthusiasm for the task ahead undiminished.

The task in question is not only to finish this round before my stomach wakes up and asks where the hell the coffee and Sugar Puffs are, but to learn what I can of this course and the people who play it, and to convince myself I've found the right starting point for my journey. As perhaps you will have guessed, I am not at Muirfield – God doesn't make horses wild enough to get me back there – but at the old links in Musselburgh, a course the

Honourable Company of Edinburgh Golfers called home between arriving from Leith in 1836 and setting off for Gullane and their new course in 1892.

Sandy and George (or J'rge, as his companion calls him) have been good enough to let me join them for their regular early morning round. They are members of the Musselburgh Old Course Golf Club, a recently established club formed to promote and maintain the course, even though the land itself is in the hands of the local council. As starting points go for any kind of golf story, it would be hard to beat. It is, after all, the oldest playing golf course in the world, but for my own purposes it has a particular quality, namely that it remains publicly owned and provides affordable golf for local and visitor alike, as it has done for centuries. Of course, the fact that it's twenty minutes' drive from my home in Edinburgh also helps, especially given my problems with alarm clocks.

I'm on the first leg of a journey that I hope will take me to the real heart of golfing Britain – not the cosy bars and manicured lawns of exclusive clubs, but the Portakabins and divoted fairways of our public and pay-and-play courses. I will be on the lookout for cheap, but not necessarily bad golf, and courses that have an important story to tell in the development of public golf. I am in search of the good, the bad and the just plain weird. However, as my morning round with Sandy and J'rge in Musselburgh progresses, I realise the old place is setting the bar rather high on a number of those criteria and I'm worrying about the chances of any other course topping it for a) historical significance, b) value for money and c) oddity.

To take the first, well . . . where does one start? Actually, a pertinent question because no one knows for sure when golf did start on Musselburgh Links – it just always seems to have been played there. The scorecard eschews the usual list of dos and don'ts on the back page in favour of a blow-by-blow history of the site. While most older clubs might proudly boast of a founding date in the nineteenth century and perhaps a visit from the sports minister or someone who once managed third at Augusta, Musselburgh kicks off with, '1567: Mary Queen of Scots is said to have played on the Old Course prior to her surrendering to the Confederate Lords.' Beat that.

In fact, the early history of the course is like a who's who of sixteenth and seventeenth century Britain. Mary is followed in 1603 by James VI/I and fewer than fifty years later by Oliver Cromwell, who sadly declined the chance to squeeze in a round before sacking Edinburgh, choosing instead to camp his army on the links. One hopes they at least replaced their divots.

I stuff the scorecard back in my pocket and survey the second hole, a 348-yard par four, rather ominously called 'the Graves', which runs parallel to Linkfield Road, Musselburgh's main thoroughfare leading eventually into Edinburgh. With out of bounds therefore uncomfortably close on the right, and early evidence of acute fading (as we slicers like to call it) with these clubs, I aim well left with my whippy little brassie. To my delight, I hit another sweet shot that lands safely in some light, wispy rough. I shoulder the bag and march off with Sandy and J'rge, still glowing with pride at my instant mastery of hickory and pig iron.

I'm playing with the old clubs and the gutta percha ball out of curiosity more than anything else. Jim McGregor in the starter's hut will rent them out to anyone interested in getting a feel of what it was like in Musselburgh's heyday; the late nineteenth century when giants of the game such as Old Tom Morris and Mungo Park competed with each other for money and, once a year, for that new thing, the Open. I have a total of five clubs in my pencil bag: a putter, brassie, driving-mashie, mashie and the aforementioned wedge (a 'Hand-forged Dreadnought Special' according to the engraving on the back of the clubhead, but described by Jim as halfway between a sand wedge and a baseball bat). I ask Sandy and J'rge whether they've ever played with them.

'Och no. I've enough trouble with these things,' says Sandy, patting what appears to be a bowling ball on the end of a stick – his new driver. 'They're the best aero-dynamic technology has to offer and I can dae wi' a' the help I can get.'

Sandy is a retired fisherman who left school at fifteen, went to sea and for the next fifty years sailed out of Eyemouth to the North Sea sand banks, trawling for sand eels. He retired (reluctantly) at sixty-five and promptly took up golf. 'It gets ye oot the hoose.'

With most of the private clubs in the area either too expensive or with waiting lists too long for a man already retired, Sandy came to Old Musselburgh Links where East Lothian Council offers him unlimited weekday golf for the princely sum of £47 a year. He and J'rge, also retired, play three times a week.

'See they flats,' says J'rge, pointing across the road. 'There's a chap in there who's on the same old-men-and-boys ticket and he plays every day, Monday to Friday – wind, rain or shine.'

So, for the second of my criteria, value for money, I'm already sure Musselburgh leads in the clubhouse, having posted a score it will surely prove impossible to beat – £47 for five rounds of golf a week, fifty-two weeks in the year, works out at all of eighteen pence per round! Ah, but just because it's cheap, doesn't mean it offers value for money. Well, frankly, at those prices it could be crazy golf with windmills and seesaws and still be worth it. As it happens, however, Old Musselburgh is the real deal.

Originally a seven-hole course, the links had an eighth added in 1838 and a ninth in 1870. It meant that the thirty-six-hole Open, which was played there regularly until the Honourable Company moved to their new home at Muirfield at the end of the century, demanded four rounds of the course. Today, the 2,874-yard layout follows the same anti-clockwise path of the original and, although short by modern standards, it is tight, well-bunkered and provides a genuine challenge to just about every club in your bag. All five of them, in my case.

As we stroll down the second fairway, I'm about to ask my companions why this hole is called the Graves when I reach the high ground my ball has found and look down on a deep gouge in the fairway with two large bunkers in its shadowy depths. I've seen Iron Age burial chambers with more ambience. My own driver would have been able to reach this intimidating obstacle easily and I am grateful the brassie and guttie have taken it out of play. A shoved mashie right of the green, a dink with the Dreadnought and two putts gives me a bogey – an improvement at least.

In fact, my scoring continues in the right direction at the short par four third with a textbook par and I approach the tee of the fourth, the famous Mrs Forman's, with every hope of recording a birdie for the full set. To reach the green at this hole, 431 yards away, you must first hit a long drive over the race course, then place a precise approach on to a sloping green with deep bunkers at the front and a pub at the back.

You might want to read that again in case you missed something. This is the third criteria in which Musselburgh excels – oddity. The thing is, the golf course is in the middle of a race course. Sorry, did I forget to mention that? And not just any old abandoned track, but *the* Musselburgh Race Course, the one that hosts a full card of National Hunt and flat races throughout the year. When a race meeting is on in the afternoon, golf is suspended in mid-morning to allow the horses a chance to get a feel of the place without risking a crack on the fetlock from an errant Top Flight.

To complete a description of playing Musselburgh's opening holes, therefore, it is necessary to point out that you are in the shadow of large grandstands and enclosures and that the rail of the home straight runs down the right side of the fairways, between you and the road. This does not, as you might think, also denote out of bounds – the race course is an integral part of the golf course and the only allowance is the ability to move a club length no nearer the hole if the rail interferes with your shot.

'But it's grim, claggy stuff,' says J'rge of the lush grass inside the rails. 'Awfy hard tae get oot fae.'

With this in mind, the two old pals take me up to the ladies' tee, just short of the race course, as it makes a left-hander round towards the sea. J'rge, a retired plumber ('I was a plumber to trade,' as they say in these parts), has the honour, thanks to a lovely birdie at the previous hole, and he sends a drive straight as an arrow over the breadth of the race course and down on to the fairway on the other side. Sandy's ball makes it as well, although only ever managing to reach knee height, and then I beat them both with another bullet from the brassie.

I really am having a great time and it's not just because I am hitting the ball sweetly. The whole experience is reminding me that the game is essentially a very simple one. Unencumbered by an array of clubs, a trolley or scorecard holder, towel, clubhead cleaner, spare clothing, umbrella – tons of unnecessary junk – I am striding about the course with my hands in my pockets, the tiny tartan bag so light I forget it's there sometimes. With so few clubs to choose from I am also spared my usual opportunities to dither over yardages, wind direction and strength, slope, ground conditions and whether missing breakfast has taken a couple of yards off my shots.

While J'rge reaches the green with a tremendous four-iron, Sandy is struggling to make any headway at all and I pull a mashie way left, narrowly avoiding the wall of the eponymous Mrs Forman's – the pub. This ancient hostelry backs on to this far side of the course just behind the fourth green. At its corner nearest the green is a window, now blocked up, from where 'refreshments' used to be served to golfers in need.

During one famously tight and niggly challenge match between Old Tom Morris and local favourite Willie Park Senior, the St Andrews man simply walked in to Mrs Forman's after putting out, ordered a pint and refused to come out again, so angry was he at the partisan behaviour of the spectators. We don't know exactly what the locals were doing to put Old Tom off his stroke, but for players in those days used to dealing with crowds milling about the fairways and, indeed, other users of the links going about their business, be it drying laundry or grazing sheep, it must have been pretty bad. One shudders to think what a highly-strung modern golfing thoroughbred (it's the race course – it's getting to me) such as Colin Montgomerie would have made of it all. You have to suspect the huff would have preceded the desire for strong drink long before he got to Mrs Forman's.

By now Sandy is taking in the views and sampling the fresh air as if this was the real reason he came out this morning. After his pal easily wins the fourth, then birdies the next with a twenty-foot putt, he resorts to picking his ball up and marching to the next tee. 'We dinnae bother wi' scores here,' he says firmly.

As we head back across the race course, J'rge and Sandy are talking about a local golfing celebrity who played the course recently.

'That Alex Hay played here,' says Sandy.

'Oh aye?'

'Sounds jist like Peter Ellis noo, don't ye think?'

'Aye, he's been Englified aw right.'

Pause.

'He's no' very good,' says Sandy.

'Whit, at English?'

'Naw. Golf.'

The next hole sees Sandy go from bad to worse, finding one of only a handful of clumps of gorse on the course with his second shot. It might be my imagination, but I think I detect a little disappointment when I successfully locate it nestling in the heart of the thicket. He finally frees himself from the gorse, but he's not the only one that has lost count of his shots by then and J'rge and I easily share honours with bogeys.

On the way to the next tee, Sandy offers some explanation for his poor play; he holds up his left hand to reveal that his ring finger is completely missing. He reassures me it isn't left back in the gorse and that it happened at sea many years ago when he was trying to free a net that was caught on the drum. 'And thir wis a shuckle caught in a sheave,' he adds, as if to let me know the seriousness of the situation. He continues, with me nodding vigorously, not wanting to spoil the timing of a good gory tale by asking for a glossary of terms, but he throws in so much trawler jargon that the only bit I understand is that a cable suddenly freed itself and took Sandy's finger with it. I'm keen to go over it all again, perhaps with subtitles for the non-fishermen, but we've reached the seventh tee, J'rge has already hit off and he has the look of a man who's just heard the story once more than he ever wanted to.

J'rge's fine form continues to the end of the nine, while Sandy recovers enough composure to keep any more multiple bogeys off his card. My honeymoon with the hickory is coming to an end, thanks mainly to the weird-shaped putter and the guttie that pings off it like a marble, but I'm still willing to plug away for another nine. To my surprise, however, Sandy and J'rge announce that they only ever play nine holes and will be heading off for a warming cup of tea. I suppose if you're paying next to nothing for your golf you can afford to spread your rounds out a bit.

I thank them for their company and make a quick decision to dash into the starter's hut and swap the hickories for my own clubs – it will be interesting to see just exactly what a hundred years of advancement in golfing technology has achieved. I've shot twelve-over for the first nine – less than happy scoring for someone who has only recently achieved his lifetime's ambition of a single figure handicap (9.4), even with the clubs I was using. I will take Messrs Callaway and Ping out and see if they can repair some of the damage. While I'm in the starter's hut, Willie introduces himself and asks if he can join me for nine holes.

Willie is also retired, although from what I'm not entirely sure. He says something about the civil service to begin with, but a later explanation of his truly bizarre swing reveals he had a career as a painter and decorator. Willie has what can only be described as a three-piece swing – like a suite only not nearly as comfortable-looking. He begins by standing with the target so far over his left shoulder he is almost unable to turn his head far enough round to see it. The clubhead comes slowly back in classic style until about knee height, at which point he hefts it sharply out to the side and up to his right shoulder, as if swinging a particularly heavy sack of coal on to his back. There is a textbook half-beat pause at the top before he attacks the ball with venom, simultaneously performing the kind of hop and turn I thought only Morris dancers could master. This has him, for the first time in the entire procedure, perfectly aligned and a fraction of a second later he makes contact with the ball. More often than not, it then flies straight and true and Willie is left in something that looks remarkably like the correct follow-through position – proving there's more than one road you can travel to the right destination.

I hasten to add that I am not the type of fellow who pries uninvited into a fellow fellow's swing – it is Willie who offers both a critique of his unique action and an explanation. Not only does he have a shortened leg, but also an injured right shoulder that tends to pop out of its socket from time to time. Having already established that I'm not the prying kind, I nevertheless feel obliged to ask how he came to do such damage to his shoulder, hoping fervently there won't be any sheaves involved, shuckled or otherwise.

It turns out that he received his injury many years ago, painting a primary school. The huge stepladders and planking he and his colleagues were using began, for some reason, to topple over and Willie, who was on the ground, saw that they were falling straight towards a group of pupils. He ran at the nearest ladder and crashed into it with his shoulder, changing its direction sufficiently to miss the children. He relates all this in a simple, matter-of-fact manner, offering no unnecessary details or dramatic dash to the account. There was no fuss made at the time and I have the feeling that is exactly the way Willie wanted it. I'm playing golf with a genuine hero and I would like to believe his later work for the 'civil service' is the usual cover for derring-do on behalf of Queen and country.

Meanwhile, back at the golf, we've reached the second/eleventh and I play a delightful half wedge to a couple of feet from the pin, the kind of shot you want someone to see so you can accept their congratulations graciously, but with the air of someone who does that sort of thing all the time. I am disappointed to notice that Willie has been looking the other way but, just as I'm finally abandoning my finishing pose, a voice from behind says, 'No' bad son. Yon's no' easy.' I turn to see a man walking across the course, Tesco bag in his hand and a West Highland terrier at his heel.

'Er, thanks. Nice to have an audience.' He just smiles and carries on, heading, it seems, for the shoreline on the other side of the course.

I catch up with Willie and ask if non-golfers are still often found on the links. 'Oh aye,' he says. 'It's common land so you get all sorts here. You get picnics and everything during the summer. I've had to ask mothers if they could stop their kids playing in the bunkers while I play a shot. "Why?" they ask, "The bairns are enjoying themselves!" But I could hit them, I say. "Well jist make sure ye dinnae."'

A sharp attack of acute fading at the twelfth has me on the race course and facing the shot that only Musselburgh provides. I take the drop back from the rail and it is not lying too badly on the thick grass. I'd like an idea of how far I have to the pin, but the only marker I see informs me I have three furlongs to go. I hit sand wedge and it comes out sweet as a nut and close to the pin again, giving me a great opportunity to banish the memory of a missed tiddler on the previous green – which I do by making an even worse putt.

Willie, meanwhile, is flailing his arms and hopping about to useful effect – if he had any kind of short game at all, he'd be a lot better than the 20-handicapper he is. By the time we are back at Mrs Forman's, he's four over and they've all been dropped in and around the green. True to form, he hits two fine shots (this time we're playing from the proper tees) and is unlucky to have caught the front bunker. Three attempts later to get himself out, he picks up and heads for the next tee, a frown for once clouding the face of this good-natured old man. 'Ach, that's the greenkeeper's bloody hobby – building bunkers,' he says. 'Every year he sticks another one in. He won't look efter them properly, they're aw fallin' tae bits, but he just keeps sprinklin' them over the course.'

Despite Willie fingering me as 'a good player' and insisting I play off the medal tees all the way in, I somehow manage the right combination of bogeys, pars and birdies to finish level par for the nine. One up to modern technology, I'd say. As Willie snatches a quick hot chocolate before heading off for another nine holes, I settle up with Jim (£17 for eighteen holes, hickory club rental free in lieu of my noble purpose) and thank them both for their hospitality and company. I'd stay longer for a chat, but the stomach woke up an hour and a half ago and is insisting on nothing less than a substantial pub lunch. I think I know just the place.

Ever walked out of Shameless O'Parody's Irish Bar in Dar Es Salaam or wherever and wondered why there is no similar worldwide franchise of Scottish pub culture? Surely, you say to yourself, there is enough tartan flock wallpaper and phoney, framed Aberdeen bus timetables kicking around to fit out a few hundred homes from home for the Caledonian diaspora or anyone else looking for a little of that famous Highland hospitality? It's a nice theory, but I'm afraid such a train of thought would merely confirm that you had never actually set foot in a Scottish pub.

Drinking for the Irish – indeed for much of the civilised world – is a social activity. It goes hand in hand with 'the craic', singing, meeting new friends and generally oiling the wheels of life in agreeable company. Drinking in Scotland, however, is a much more serious business. It goes hand in hand with getting pished as quickly and as quietly as possible. There is an apocryphal tale of two old boys in a Scottish pub sitting side by side at the bar in total silence, supping their pints. As one nears the end of his drink, he signals to the barman for two more, then turns to his companion and asks him if he wants a bag of crisps. 'Are you here to talk or drink?' comes the reply.

Scottish pubs, therefore, tend to reflect this purposefulness with a distinctly functional approach to décor and layout – bar, floor, door, seats, bog. Perhaps the seats will be in leatherette, there may be a stretch of sticky carpet to denote 'the lounge' and occasionally the brewery will be experimenting with something other than fizzy beer or blended whisky, but these will all be minor variations. The Scottish pub, Manhattan theme-bar fantasies of Glasgow property tycoons aside, is a registered trademark, a guarantee of dinginess and gloom.

Mrs Forman's, therefore, is all that I expect a pub to be an hour after opening and before the lunchtime rush – if it ever gets one. It has yet to warm up – literally – and features two members of staff, one customer besides myself and a lingering whiff of Flash from the floor. It has a mixture of horse racing and golfing prints on the wall (shock), except for the far corner where a dart board covers the famous, now boarded up, window. The fixtures and fittings are late 1980s mock rustic, but still in good shape, and it's obviously not that long ago since the place was tarted up. In fact, I've been in a lot worse and am happy to order a pint of 80/- from the barman and the steak and ale pie from his colleague who, it turns out, runs the kitchen. There is no prospect of conversation with my fellow imbiber as he is far too busy losing his money to a fruit machine, so I repair to one of the tables, take out the scorecards and settle down to my usual post-match debriefing.

Since I began playing golf with any kind of regularity I have become addicted to tracking my progress against par, counting my putts and greens in regulation, drawing up bombing patterns for my approach shots and checking the percentage of fairways hit from the tee. I appreciate, of course, that not every golfer is inclined to reduce their game to an exercise in statistics; this is not cricket or baseball, for a full appreciation of which a degree in applied mathematics is required. It's just that, for some of us, there are few more satisfying postscripts to a round than the deduction from our GIRs that a solid perform-ance with the driver has not been wasted with sloppy iron play or that a hot putting streak has improved our up-and-down count.

I'm pretty sure it won't need a detailed analysis of the scorecards to identify a game of two halves this morning, but I'm settling down to the task anyway when the barman comes over and asks how I got on. Jimmy, it turns out, is a regular player on the old links and, although never having played with hickory clubs, he is able to provide an insight into why it was the putter that cost me most of my strokes on the first nine.

'Y'see, in the auld days the greens were shite,' he offers. 'Tae get the ba' anywhere near the hole ye had tae gie it a fucking great thump.'

And he's right. Before modern greenkeeping – before, in fact, the invention of the lawnmower – 'greens' were simply small areas of scythed and sickled grass where clumps, divots and weeds would still be left. I've often thought how frustrating it must have been for the nine-teenth century player to knock the ball close in perhaps only two shots, then spend the next half hour walking back and forth trying to get a lucky bounce into the cup.

Again, despite never having hired the hickories, Jimmy can identify with the freedom of a pencil bag, light with only a handful of clubs. Every Boxing Day, it seems, there is a charity match on the course when dozens of raging hangovers gather to play nine holes for a local good cause. 'Ye set off wi' a half set of clubs, aboot ten ba's and half a dozen cans,' explains Jimmy. 'Last year, I started wi' three birdies. Then the cans caught up wi' the drink fae the night before an' I wis fucked.'

We chat about the links and his struggles to reduce his 22 handicap before my lunch arrives and he leaves me to eat in peace. I've never worked out how to eat puff pastry in company while retaining any dignity, so this is fine by me and I resume my review of the morning's round(s). I have to be pleased – twelve over par for eighteen holes with the damage all being done on the front nine when I had the old clubs and ball and didn't know the course. I'm not demanding anything more from my game on this journey than that it stays in reasonable shape, doesn't embarrass me or cause any playing companions I may have to spend half their time answering stupid questions and the other half looking for my ball. Content I have avoided that pitfall, I give the cards little more than another satisfied glance before putting them away and pulling out a slim volume I bought back in the starter's box: *The Story of Musselburgh Links – The World's Oldest Playing Golf Course*. (By the way, the steak and ale pie – not to mention the pint – is absolutely delicious and I'm already feeling guilty about all the nasty things I know I will already have written about Scottish pubs.)

Unlike the lunch, however, the little book is something of a disappointment. Musselburgh Links is a site steeped in the history of the game, yet the authors chose to ignore many of the innovations and precedents it witnessed and instead fill fourteen out of twenty pages with the names and achievements of notable nineteenth and early twentieth century players – the Park and Dunn families, Ferguson, Anderson etc. – many of whom only had tenuous connections to the place. Now, I'm not saying the old boys should be forgotten, nor that their achievements are incompatible with an account of a course's history, but I do tire quickly of endless lists of championships and medals won next to grainy photographs of big beards and Norfolk jackets.

Especially when there is a much more interesting history to recount – one I have done a little swotting up on beforehand. For example, have you ever wondered why golf holes are the same size the world over and why that is precisely four and a quarter inches in diameter? Not likely, I admit, but it all stems from an implement for cutting holes in the turf invented in Musselburgh by one Robert Gay in 1829, which just happened to be that size. It gradually became widely used and eventually the R&A made it mandatory in 1893.

Another riveting fact given scant attention in the pocket history is the invention of the famous brassie – the equivalent of a four- or a five-wood with a metal plate on the bottom, of the sort I had used earlier in the day. Slicing, it seems, is not a new affliction for golfers and when players at Musselburgh did so on the first couple of holes of the old course they often had to play their next shots off the main road. (Obviously the concept of 'out of bounds' was not another

Musselburgh invention.) Anyway, the brass plate prevented the clubhead from disintegrating on impact with the road and adding to the player's embarrassment, watched, as he would inevitably be, by a handful of jeering passers-by.

Mentioned in brief on the scorecard, but omitted from the booklet altogether, is the fact that Musselburgh played host to the first ever official women's golf competition. It was held on New Year's Day 1811 and featured local fishwives. The records show that the doughty women competed for 'a creel and skull', which sounds ominously like a head in a basket.

Also missing is the fact that the guttie ball, a development that revolutionised the sport, was tested at Musselburgh. It had been invented some time in the 1840s by Dr Robert Adam Paterson of St Andrews who, either accidentally or deliberately, after a flash of perhaps divine inspiration (depending on which version you read), applied heat to some gutta percha packing he'd been sent and fashioned it into a ball. Out on the course, Paterson immediately saw it was superior to the established featherie, flying no further, but with greater accuracy and consistency. James Balfour tells the story in his *Reminiscences of Golf on St Andrews Links* (1887), recording that his brother-in-law, one Admiral Maitland Dougall, played with some of the first, smooth-surfaced examples one afternoon at Blackheath in London back in 1848. He observed that they flew better at the end of the round than at the beginning. This, it later emerged, was because the smooth surface had been cut by the various clubheads several times by then and the scratches gave it more lift and spin – the origin of the dimples now an integral part of all ball designs. Balfour himself sent for a supply (Paterson had sold the manufacturing rights to a firm in London) and conducted the definitive test on Musselburgh Links. The comparative study with the featherie was watched by John Gourlay, foremost manufacturer of that ball in Scotland, who quickly saw that his trade was doomed. He legged it back to his workshop and dashed off as many featheries to his customers as possible before word of the better – and cheaper – guttie spread.

My lunch finished, I emerge into conditions that have taken a decided turn for the worse; the wind has stiffened considerably and is now driving rain across the links and out into the Firth of Forth. Ah, summer in Scotland!

Before leaving Musselburgh, there is one last location I want to check out. It was Willie who had pointed to the building on Balcarres Road as we were nearing the end of our round. In fact, he'd done so to give me the line to the pin off the ninth fairway. The first in a group of three solid Victorian mansions, it had been, he informed me, the clubhouse for the Honourable Company of Edinburgh Golfers before they moved on to Muirfield. Since I'd had such difficulty getting into the current clubhouse, I am keen to at least see what has become of the club's previous home, so I drive back round the course, stop outside the building and, leaving the engine running, nip out to see if I can read the sign on the window above the door. I had planned to immediately dash back to the shelter of my car, but instead I find myself standing in the pouring rain, laughing out loud.

One of the many things the Honourable Company and its near contemporaries, such as the Edinburgh Burgess and Bruntsfield Links societies, are sensitive about is the extent to which freemasonry played a large part in their history. Robert Price, in his book, *Scotland's Golf Courses* (1989), bemoans the lack of written records for the early years of many of Scotland's great clubs and says this is probably due to the secret traditions of the controlling masonic members. 'Only when non-masons had joined the golfing societies in such numbers that the character of the clubs changed, were formal records kept,' he writes. John Lowerson, writing on golf in the book *Scottish Sport in the Making of the Nation* (1994), admits there is no direct evidence of masonic influence in the formation of the early clubs, but says such a connection might easily be deduced from a few shared characteristics – namely, heavy drinking, wagering, secretive selection and initiation procedures, and 'picturesque uniforms'.

What is undeniable is that many of the early office bearers of the first golf clubs were also prominent members of local lodges. Some historians, in fact, argue that freemasonry kept golf alive in the late eighteenth and nineteenth centuries, when the poor couldn't afford to play it and royal patronage was non-existent. By the end of the nineteenth century, however, modern freemasonry had spread its influence to the upper reaches of government and business on both sides of the Atlantic, was known to include high-ranking members of the aristocracy, and was generally viewed with a great deal of suspicion by the population at large. Masons themselves were becoming ever more coy about their affiliations while institutions, like the Honourable Company of Edinburgh Golfers, played down any suggestion they were overly influenced by the men in aprons.

It must be just pure coincidence, then, that the Honourable Company's old clubhouse in Musselburgh is now the Freemasons Hall.

2

It would be fair to say that, despite their historical connection, Muirfield and Musselburgh stand on opposite sides of the great divide in British golf. While one is the acme of exclusivity and privilege, the other maintains a tradition of accessible golf for anyone with the requisite number of clubs and a few quid for the green fee. While one, in my experience at least, demands that you leave your self-respect and dignity at the gates, the other asks nothing more than the usual courtesies and considerations on the course; repair your own damage and don't hold anyone up.

That this divide exists is universally accepted, although not always tolerated, within the golfing world. Its presence, however, is almost completely unheard of in non-golfing society (i.e. the vast majority of the population). The world of golf is a uniform one to most people, a place where there *is* only Muirfield and its evil spawn – the white, male, misogynist, middle-class stereotype. Society at large seems to hold that playing golf says absolutely nothing about your enthusiasm for exercise in fresh air, but everything about your attitudes to women, the level of inheritance tax and what should be done about asylum seekers. While golf, for golfers, is a game of maddening complexity and capricious whim, a sport that offers healthy pursuit long into old age, cama-raderie and competition, joy and despair in equal measure and a life-long, gloriously hopeless search for mastery and perfection, for many non-golfers, it is nothing more than a music hall joke involving arcane rituals and an unnatural fondness for cashmere.

Understandably, therefore, the sport has become a byword for all that is reprehensible and risible in middle-class Britain. A stand-up comedian or sitcom actor need only mention the word 'golf' to prime his or her audience for a gag on snobbery or off-colour attitudes to race and gender politics. Sadly, it is not just what we might call the low-brow media that perpetu-ates this conception. When Robert Kilroy-Silk aired his peculiar views on Arabs in a tabloid newspaper column, they were described thus by an editorial in the *Observer*: 'They are crass, racist and ill-informed – the kind of stuff heard at the nineteenth hole from people who drink too much pink gin . . .' The writer of this did not need to elaborate. He or she knew their readership would get the point – bigots play golf. Now, I believe that this is a distortion, that the game and the vast majority who play it are unfairly maligned by an igno-rant media and public too lazy to look past the cliché. But am I right? I cannot, after all, argue with the fact that hideous golf clubs do exist and that they are well-stocked with reactionary old gits – Muirfield is not the only place I've been made to feel as welcome as a cock-roach in a curry. The question is whether these few laagers of Edwardian attitudes should continue to monopolise golf's image.

Most clubs, of course, are perfectly reasonable institutions going about their admissions, competitions and
club functions in a fair and equitable manner. But there
are more than two million public-course golfers in Britain
– double the number of club members. Surely the best
way to seek out viable golfing life beyond black balls
and easy prejudice is to go in search of the game this
vast majority of golfers play?

To that end I am venturing into a world popular culture
would have it does not even exist; a world where people
of all ages, colours and income brackets play golf. This
is where you don't need to know the steering committee
of the local rotary club just to get on the first tee, or re-
mortgage your house for the privilege, where the eleventh
green might more often command views of the rendering
plant and M62 than Elysian fields, but where no one is
likely to ask what school you went to before inviting you
to join their four-ball. It is the world of low-cost, non-
restrictive, pay-and-play – usually municipal – public golf.

My aim is to visit just a tiny fraction of the many
hundreds of courses that would fit into this category and
to tell something of the story of how and why golf came
to be a game of haves and have-nots. I hope that I will
be celebrating the discovery of hidden gems in picturesque corners of the country played by stout men and
women of plebeian birth, but honest and upright views,
but I am sure there will be more than a few blasted
heaths and ignorant fools along the way. It will be enough
that I see golf's 'undiscovered country' for myself and
find out if it is as inoffensive and wholesome as I'd like
to think, or whether it is my own notion of a noble sport
cruelly misrepresented that is the distortion.

*   *   *

Before getting too far down that road, I feel a little light history is called for. Nothing too taxing or comprehensive, of course – heaven knows there are enough golf histories knocking about. Indeed, at the risk of offering what might appear to be an invitation to shut this book right now and go off and do something more rewarding, one could argue there is more than enough already written about the infernal game . . . 'I have serious misgivings as to the propriety of inflicting another book on golfers already satiated with the literature on the subject.' So wrote the American HSC Everard in a foreword to his own work in 1896, one year after the very first book on golf in the United States was published. If he believed he was about to pen the last word on the subject it's as well he didn't live to see the current publishing industry surrounding the game, where books on everything from what your left knee should be doing halfway through the backswing to Tiger Woods' thoughts on carbohydrates is pushed on an eager golfing public.

Nevertheless, for my own purposes, I believe some of the early back-story of golf should be told, if only in an effort to discover just when and how that great divide between the haves and have-nots first opened up. This, of course, presupposes that at one time golf was an entirely egalitarian game, played by humble shepherds and belted earls alike, often on the same links at the same time, possibly even in the same four-ball, better-ball. It is what is known as the 'myth of democratic golf in Scotland'. The extent to which such familiarity actually happened, certainly on a regular basis, is open to debate, but there is at least one recorded episode of hands across the class divide – not, in this case, involving a shepherd and an earl, but a cobbler and a future king.

In 1681, James, Duke of York, was loafing around playing golf in Leith when he was challenged by a couple of English noblemen to an England v Scotland foursome match (interesting, is it not, that almost eighty years after the Union of the Crowns the royal family was still regarded as essentially Scottish). Showing either an admirable common touch or a seething, burning desire to rub the Sassenachs' noses in it, James stunned his coterie of ennobled hangers on by choosing as his partner one John Patersone, a local shoemaker who actually made more money betting on himself at golf than he did in his workshop. Not surprisingly, James and the cobbler ran out easy winners. The duke was so pleased with the result that he gave Patersone half the winner's purse – more than enough money to allow him to build a house in Edinburgh's then fashionable Canongate.

Of course, the duke went on to succeed his brother, Charles II, and become James II, one of this country's least popular monarchs, ramming Roman Catholicism down everyone's throat, levying customs and excise duties off his own bat, suspending Acts of Parliament and generally doing anything he could to overturn the constitution and rub people up the wrong way. Since the only way to get rid of the blighter was to draft in William of Orange in the so-called Glorious Revolution of 1688–9, a watershed in British history that led to, among other things, centuries of civil war in Ireland and the Hanoverian succession, we can reasonably assert that James was ultimately responsible for all that flowed thereafter, including the late Queen Mother, Ian Paisley and Rangers fans revelling in being 'up to their knees in Fenian blood'. No one said all golfers are perfect.

The myth of classless golf in Scotland runs deep in the

national psyche and was, for a time at least, accepted unquestioningly by the wider golfing world. Take this from the February 1927 issue of *Golf Illustrated*: 'Democratic as it may have been in its indigenous Scottish soil, where the duke stood aside for the dustman on the dustman's medal day . . .' We'd all like this vision of matey egalitarianism to be true, but, like the notions that the Scots have a superior education system, are more racially tolerant than the English, invented just about everything of use in the modern world and can all hold our drink, it does not really bear much scrutiny. You need only look to the first ever historical reference to golf – the famous edict of 1457 by James II of Scotland in which he banned the citizenry from playing the 'unprofitable sports' of golf and football, which were to be 'utterly cryit doun and not usit'. Instead, the king wanted the populace to spend more time practising their archery and other martial arts in preparation for fighting the English. What is seldom mentioned is the fact that the ban only applied to those of humble birth; the nobles and lairds were free to continue playing golf and football to their hearts' content. From the very earliest, therefore, golf can be said to be synonymous with a degree of class distinction.

It is also the case that prior to 1600 Scottish golf took at least two forms. There was the 'long game', played on links land by those who could afford the time and the purchase of clubs and balls, and the 'short game', which was played on town streets and in church courtyards using cheap balls or even pebbles with old bits of stick as clubs. The latter bore a striking resemblance to the game of *colf*, played in the Low Countries.

So, to get back to the Great Divide Question, one would

have to conclude that golf, like all sports at all times in history, has never been immune to political and social forces. The game will always have reflected the nature of society beyond the course perimeter . . . and since, to my knowledge, Scotland has never been a utopian socialist state, we must conclude that, to varying degrees, greater spending power, education or accident of birth have always affected the pecking order on the links.

Leaving the matter of expense aside for a moment, it will not have escaped the observant reader that so far there has been no mention of golf played anywhere in the British Isles outside Scotland. This is for the very simple reason that, prior to the mid-nineteenth century, the only golf south of the Border was being played by handfuls of exiled Scots, starting probably with members of James I (and VI)'s court in London from 1603 onwards. Another incursion was in the Manchester area in the early 1800s, when large numbers of Scottish entrepreneurs moved south to set up and run new steel mills and manufacturing plants. Indeed, it can be argued that there was no such thing as 'English golf' until the Royal North Devon club was founded at Westward Ho! in 1864. This was the first club established by Englishmen for Englishmen, although even here the idea came from a General George Moncrieff visiting from St Andrews and the course was designed by Tom Morris.

For centuries, golf in England was viewed with either complete indifference or suspicion by the general population. Much of this is undoubtedly due to the fact that it was played by immigrant Jocks. As late as 1885, Horace Hutchinson could write that golf in England was 'an eccentricity affected by the few'. And yet curiously, England has a claim to being home to the oldest golf club in Britain and therefore, naturally, the world. Royal Blackheath was the venue for those aforementioned courtiers of James I; indeed the man himself was wont to smack a ball or two on the heath. The Royal and Ancient Handbook lists its founding date as 1608 and the present clubhouse certainly dates from that time, but even the club admits it is a little difficult to substantiate this as the beginnings of a club as we know it today. In fact, there appears to be little evidence of a formalised club until at least 1745, which would actually make it the second oldest in the world. Or the third.

The debate on the relative antiquity of certain clubs, an arcane one to most people, is nevertheless the cause of occasional port-fuelled controversy in the smoke rooms of Edinburgh gentlemen's clubs to this day. If we dismiss Royal Blackheath's 1608, our old friends the Honourable Company of Edinburgh Golfers (at the time known as the Society of Gentlemen Golfers) have the most widely respected claim to the title with a founding date of 1744. But they have never been able to completely sink the challenge from the Edinburgh Burgess Golfing Society (now the Royal Burgess Golfing Society of Edinburgh), who claim to have been up and running long before that. There is, unsurprisingly, no definitive answer to the question; it depends on what criteria you set for the formation of a club.

The Burgess boys claim that, as one of many groups of citizens who played regularly on Bruntsfield Links to the south of the city centre, they formed themselves into a bona fide club in 1735. However, Edinburgh and Leith had dozens of groups of friends and loose associations playing regular golf together, many of which later claimed club status. It is accepted by most historians that the date of the first formal golf competition should be taken as the founding date of the particular club – hence 1744 for the Honourable Company, when they played for a silver club put up by Edinburgh councillors. The Burgess 'club', meanwhile, seems to have been happy spending its time in casual bounce games and hanging around the Golf Tavern (a hostelry that in one guise or another has sat next to Bruntsfield Links since the 1400s), because they didn't get organised enough to hold an official competition for another twenty-nine years.

Whatever the truth of the matter, it was the staging of 'official' contests and the formation of clubs proper that heralded the beginning of the end for any form of 'democratic golf' that ever existed in Scotland. It was not only that the new clubs began to take up more and more time on the common links, it was also that they asserted control over the very nature of the game.

Take the rules, for example. Until the Honourable Company wrote down on paper thirteen rules to govern that first competition in 1744, golf was more of a general idea open to local interpretation. Different groups of golfing friends and different courses had conflicting ideas on what constituted an unfair lie, say, or how many strokes penalty you incurred for hitting a passing sheep. The travelling golfer would have to learn more than just the layout of a new course; he'd also have to acquaint himself with the local rules before he even teed up.

Geoffrey Cousins, in his by turns fascinating and outrageously patronising history, *Golf in Britain* (1975), explains that since the new clubs were invariably peopled by the professional classes, they had a further advantage when it came to arguing over the interpretation of the rules: 'The lairds, the landed gentry, lawyers, clergymen, doctors, professors and officers were well qualified by birth, education and circumstances to be accorded not only priority when playing golf, but also deference to their decisions affecting play.' So, a hundred years after a future king could happily team up with a cobbler, the toffs were busily carving up not only access to the links, but also the rules to suit themselves.

The one laudable aspect of golf in pre-industrial revolution Scotland that can be safely asserted is that it was universally free of charge. Even on golf's holiest of holies, the Old Course at St Andrews, green fees were not introduced until 1913. But, of course, that didn't mean those of higher birth could not secure an advantage in the matter of expense. Although originally a pretty basic game involving sticks and anything round(ish) to take the role of the ball, golf has always been subject to technological advancements. And just as today the purchase of the latest whizz-bang driver with revolutionary tri-metal, forged titanium, down-the-middlium and kryptonite head with a sweet spot the size of Kent can not only improve your game, but ruin your bank balance, so it has been throughout the game's history that an edge on the links comes at a price.

Before Dr Paterson's guttie ball, you played with a featherie (a top hat's amount of feathers stuffed inside a small leather pouch) or not at all. These were laborious and dangerous to make – workers used a press strapped to their chests, which caused many injuries, and feather dust damaged their lungs. The gentry could afford as many as they liked, but at a whopping five shillings each as far back as the seventeenth century (a week's wage for an artisan) they successfully priced many ordinary folk out of the game. Even those who did scrounge enough to play found themselves at an ever-increasing disadvantage compared to their professional and noble betters as the original stick evolved into a purpose-built club, then clubs (plural) as specialist implements for different type of shots began to appear.

Cousins notes that distinctions in the level of the sport enjoyed by opposite ends of the social scale grew wider with each technological innovation. He then adds a typically unnecessary and glib assertion that all is now fair and tickety-boo in the wonderfully socialist world of golf in modern Britain: 'Distinctions of that kind [between the lower orders and their superiors], sustained from Stuart days to the mid-Victorian epoch, are now blurred almost beyond recognition. Those that survive in an emphatic form do so by tacit mutual tolerance and arouse neither comment nor rancour.'

Aye, right.

For all of these differences between the game played by ordinary men and women and that of the moneyed and professional classes, there was still the common links land that bound them together. That was until golf became so popular that it outgrew the land available for play.

The Honourable Company's move from Leith Links to Musselburgh in 1836 was only partially successful as it wasn't long before other golf clubs followed suit – at one point it was estimated that sixty golf clubs without premises of their own were playing on Musselburgh Links. Eventually, in search of that exclusiveness and privacy for which golf clubs were becoming synonymous, the Honourable Company moved from the soon-to-be home of Musselburgh Freemasons and settled in a marshy stretch of land near Archerfield Wood outside Gullane, an unpromising and featureless few acres that

Tom Morris was to transform into one of the best courses in the world.

By the 1890s, however, England already had more golf courses than Scotland – and, like Muirfield, they were private, fenced-in courses for members only. This was to be the shape of things to come as golf boomed in Britain and began its inexorable journey from quaint Caledonian pastime to multi-billion dollar international business featuring currently the most recognisable sportsman on the planet.

The late nineteenth century more or less shaped the game we know today. The formation of clubs and the establishment of private courses, the availability of affordable equipment bringing golf once more within the reach of ordinary men and women, the inauguration of club and international competitions, the rise of the professional, and many more features now considered intrinsic to the sport all date from that golden era. It was also, as a necessary concomitant to the new trend in course-owning private clubs, when specific provision for the general public had to be made – it was the dawn of municipal golf.

While there may be contention in golfing circles over which private club can claim to be the most venerable, the question of which is the oldest purpose-built public course in the country barely registers as an afterthought. The Bolshevik in me would like to assert that this merely typifies the golf establishment's lack of interest in the great unwashed, but I would have to admit it is probably due in no small part to the infuriating difficulty of actually trying to find the answer. Forget foundation dates and first competitions. The search for the oldest purpose-built public course (i.e. not evolved common links courses such as Musselburgh and St Andrews) requires the negotiation of a labyrinth of half-truths and conflicting claims, involving clubs acting as de facto public providers, compulsory purchases and shifting definitions of what a truly accessible 'public' golf course is.

Some historians, for example, casually observe that there were only two municipal courses in all of the British Isles by the end of the nineteenth century – Braid Hills in Edinburgh and Bournemouth. The former, built by the town council to accommodate the hundreds of golfers bumped from the overcrowded Bruntsfield Links, was opened in 1889. Bournemouth, on the other hand, was little more than a marketing wheeze by that up-market resort, aimed at attracting a better class of holidaymaker. Although municipal in the strictest sense, being conceived, built and administered by the local council, the course that opened in 1893 charged a green fee deliberately high enough to keep the scruff at bay and allow plenty of room for the minor aristos who were indulging in the new fashion of spending at least a few weeks of the summer by the sea.

Several other courses which could lay claim to the title are not helped by the circumstances of their foundation and/or conversion to municipal status being lost in the fog of Scotland's peculiar feudal system of land tenure and more than a century of local government re-organisation. Take, for example, Portobello. Any records of this nine-hole course's early history have long since been shoved in an old shoe box and lost in the transfers from town to city council and now the imaginatively named Edinburgh Leisure, the semi-autonomous body charged with administering the city's sports and recreation facilities. This is particularly annoying because, according to SportScotland (the re-branded Scottish Sports Council), Portobello has the oldest founding date of any public golf course in the country – 1853. Now, on the face of it, this knocks Braid Hills and Bournemouth into a cocked hat, but the strong suspicion is that this was one of those cases where an existing, private course was bought by the town council and run on behalf of its rate-payers. Trying to establish this one way or the other, however, let alone the date at which a transfer might have happened has, I'm afraid dear reader, proved beyond my own meagre talents as an investigative historian.

SportScotland's information came several years ago from a research unit at Edinburgh University that has since disbanded. Approaches to the council, the Museum of Scotland, several historical societies and local amateur historians all drew a blank, as did a trawl through the extensive archives in the city library. There is an Ordnance Survey map dating from 1896 which clearly shows the course as part of a 'public park', but earlier surveys of the city that might have been able to provide a Braids-busting date did not extend as far as Portobello.

The most obvious potential source of information was the Portobello Golf Club now based at the course and the fact that it had celebrated a centenary in 1956 naturally encouraged me to think I was on the right track. Alas, like many custodians of club traditions, particularly those now attached to municipal facilities, the good men of Portobello were embarrassed to admit the ancient history of their institution was as much a regrettable mystery to them as to any outsider.

I was, however, generously allowed to read the club's minute book, a magnificent leather-bound tome, but this only dates back to the early 1900s and, in any case, the Portobello *club* did not play the Portobello *course* until after 1927. This was when Musselburgh Town Council began charging for play on the club's preferred venue of the old links and the members were forced to move to the inferior golfing turf of Portobello.

Nevertheless, like all golf club records, the minute book makes fascinating reading. Among many historical gems is proof that surely the least able player ever to darken a first tee anywhere in the world did so at Portobello. I give you Mr J Shepherd.

The entry for 12 March 1930 kicks off with a breezy account of the by now traditional start to the golfing season at Portobello – a matchplay game between the captain and vice captain, the above mentioned J Shepherd. This was played over one round of the nine holes, but this year, as the minute book records, '. . . unfortunately, the captain was unable to be present through illness.' The absence of an opponent, however, was not enough to prevent Shepherd from only managing to win the match five and two.

The minute book itself was 'lost' in a vault of the Bank of Scotland during the Second World War and didn't resurface until 1951. But in neither the early entries nor those recording the club centenary in 1956 is there anything that sheds light on the nineteenth century history of the site. Now, of course there will be a record of exactly when Portobello's nine holes were laid out and by whom *somewhere*, and I'm sure there are those skilled at poring over land registers and tracking title down through the ages who would be able to provide the definitive answer, but they are hunched be-spectacled creatures of the half-light with prison pallor and disturbing hobbies. I am a normal person with better things to be doing . . . like playing the bleedin' course itself.

*   *   *

Were this any other part of the country, I would have spent the night after my round at Musselburgh in some modest hotel or guest house and have an amusing tale to tell regarding its nylon sheets or way with poached eggs for breakfast. However, since my own hearth and home is a few miles up the road, I didn't. Instead, I am arriving at Portobello after an evening with Marian, my confused wife, who is wondering when this odyssey is finally going to get going. Not that she's keen to be rid of me, she says with a straight face.

Along the way I pick up my pal Denis, who hails from Belfast and was for a time almost a colleague of mine, working as he did on a sister paper while I disgraced the pages of the *Scotsman*. He has since gone on to much bigger and better things in Fleet Street, but is back in town for a visit and suddenly interested in golf. Having lived for years in Edinburgh, where you are never more than twenty feet from a testing pin position, Denis has apparently waited until he is ensconced in darkest Hampstead before deciding to take up the noble game.

Despite having played only three rounds of golf in his entire life, it turns out that one of them was on Portobello a few months earlier, and Denis is keen to see if the handful of lessons he's had since on a north London driving range will turn the unsightly threshing of that performance into the controlled athletic game of his dreams. He has no clubs, no golf shoes or waterproofs, on another typical July day that threatens rain, and comes out to the car from the friend's flat he is staying in still munching a slice of toast and with a mug of coffee in his hand. Preparation, he tells me with his mouth full, is over-rated.

Once on open ground to the south of Portobello, the

course is now sandwiched between the main railway line from Waverly Station and the A1 east out of Edinburgh. Making up the square on one side is a post-war council housing estate of the variety you just know they will tear down in the near future to make way for another ill-conceived and jerry-built attempt to accommodate the low-paid and unemployed, and on the other by a row of modest yet solid Victorian mansions. I know that the original site of the course was on the other side of the railway and can now see over the back of the old clubhouse, that it is a railway marshalling yard and depot. We haven't booked a tee-off time, but the guy in the starter's box to the front of the clubhouse says it's no problem, takes our £6 each for nine holes (let's not commit to eighteen just yet – call me overly cautious, but watching a man plough up parkland in driving rain might be fun for only an hour or so) and off we go.

Denis, built like a lamppost, is a good six inches taller than me, but he still manages to squeeze into my spare waterproof jacket and strut up to the first tee looking the part with my dad's half set of clubs and trolley. No sooner have I teed off, however, than he is dashing back to the clubhouse to use the 'facilities' ('Too much of the Devil's brew last night, Chris'). Eventually he comes bounding out again, picks up the first club he comes to in the bag, gives it an experimental swish, then sends a very impressive shot 150 yards or so just off the fairway to the right.

'Great shot,' I say. But it is obviously not up to the required standard.

'Ach, sure it's not even on the fairway,' says Denis. 'And yours is much further.'

'Yes, but I used a driver and you used . . .' I check his club, '. . . a six iron. What do you expect?'

'Harrumph.' And so the theme is set for the day.

I would be lying if I said Denis had a classic swing or that he hit every shot out the middle of the club, but for a man who has only just taken up the game, he does not do too badly at all. Denis, however, is impatient. He has always maintained he is accomplished in a number of other sports (although the qualification, 'You know, stuff with bats and that,' is hardly convincing) and he does not like being so obviously unskilled at golf. For a good hour I try to persuade him to be patient, that he has good hand-to-eye coordination, a natural athleticism, long arms – anything to keep his spirits up. But he is determined to be dissatisfied and eventually I give up and leave him to his self-loathing.

I suppose his naturally competitive mood is not helped much by the fact that I am clearly playing a blinder. Thanks to a chip in at the third and some miracle putting on what are easily the most rutted and potholed greens I have ever seen in my life, I complete the front nine in two over par. Portobello is not the longest course in the world – 2,210 yards for nine holes – and most of the time a drive and little more than a wedge is enough to find the green. The fairways are generously wide as well and where the rough hasn't been trampled flat it is only a few inches long. But even so, two over . . .

The course dots back and forth across only the northern half of the already small Portobello Public Park, the rest of which comprises a couple of football pitches and some meagre plantations of underfed trees. I remember from the minute book reading about the club's repeated efforts to persuade the council to expand the course, at least in the summer, but, apart from being allowed some minor tinkering of the running order for the holes, the club has been thwarted at every turn. It has always been particularly concerned about the eastern end of the course, close to the housing estate – an area frequently used for walking the 'bairns and dugs' during the day and pursuits of a nefarious and probably unhealthy nature during the night. Playing the short par three in that corner, we can see why – apart from well-worn paths criss-crossing the course there is a scattering of empty beer cans, the remains of bonfires and who knows what lurking under the bushes. We have plenty of time to take in the views as we are forced to wait on the tee while what looks like a fifteen-year-old mother shoves her child in a pushchair directly over the green before heading out moodily across the rest of the course. I am confident she can only have improved the state of the green and my chances of a putt that runs true.

Denis finishes the nine with a total of 54 (he insisted on counting every single swipe and air shot) and is enthused with the prospect of beating this on the second circuit. The rain has held off and, since I am in such hot form myself, I agree and give Denis my £6 to pay the starter on his way to his third pee of the round so far. Shortly after embarking on the 'back' nine, however, I am reviewing the wisdom of that decision. The first/tenth hole is a reasonable 382-yard par four with not so much as a dogleg as a kink left halfway along. I pull both my drive and approach with a five-iron left, leaving me with no more than twenty feet to the pin, but with a massive bunker in the way. It is time for my patented lob wedge routine; a couple of masterful practice swings, setup, backswing, second thoughts, deceleration on the downswing, strike ground behind ball, flop into bunker.

At the annual general meeting of the Portobello Golf Club in 1972, it was agreed that members should be allowed to smooth out the sand in bunkers and replace the ball in the original position. This, of course, is because Portobello has no rakes (one suspects they wouldn't last long round here and you can't exactly chain them up to a post). The bunkers are, as a result, more like small opencast mines than sand traps. To make matters worse my ball is nestling in what looks suspiciously like it might have been dog shit at some point in the last five years and I decide to forego the option of picking it up and cleaning it. Instigating, instead, a new local rule on the spot, I salute another fallen soldier, cover it up with sand, drop a new ball and play out to the middle of the green, then two-putt for a double bogey. Meanwhile, Denis's resolve to improve on his front nine has also hit the buffers early with a seven compared to the six he had first time around. Is it too late to get the six quid back?

Over the next few holes, I give in to the repeated requests to explain to my playing companion where he is going wrong. This is not a step to be undertaken lightly. Advice given on the golf swing, particularly while on the course and even when asked for, is rarely an instant success. When the player concerned has barely got past the lesson entitled 'Now hold the rubber end' it is even more of a dangerous task. I have heard of rock solid marriages that have crumbled like a Cadbury's Flake shortly after she asked him: 'Why don't you teach me how to play golf?' There is something about the golf swing – in reality several of the most unnatural things you can do with muscles and limbs all rolled into one – that makes the novice think it's a doddle. When they find out it isn't, it won't be their lack of coordination or suppleness they'll blame – it will be you.

But Denis is clearly suffering and Portobello's uninspiring up and down, dead flat course wasn't much of a diversion even first time around, so I put on my best bedside manner and try to break it to him gently. The first thing you need to do, says I, is have the ball somewhere close so you can hit it. Denis's stance is such that the ball is actually several inches forward of his leading foot. This requires a weight shift with the hips only a pre-Vegas Elvis could have achieved if there is to be any chance of the club meeting up again with the ball. Sadly, Denis is doing the complete opposite – he is suffering from that common complaint of the new golfer, reverse pivot.

Luckily for him I am an expert in reverse pivot, having myself been afflicted at the outset of my illustrious golfing career. It sounds like something wrong with your steering column, but is in fact the transfer of your weight during the swing from your front foot to the back, instead of the other way round as it should be. It is the natural consequence of trying to scoop the ball into the air (something most beginners believe the golf club is for) and it is very easy to spot since the sufferer will end his or her follow-through on their back foot as if reeling from a particularly hurtful insult. It does not guarantee every effort will be mishit (see Denis's opening tee shot), but decent contact with this swing is mere happenstance. Knowing the problem in a golf swing, however, is nowhere near halfway to solving it; the brain's got the message, but the rest of the body – you know, the smart bits like the elbows and buttocks – think they know better and simply refuse to cooperate.

I inform Denis of my diagnosis, prescribe an improved setup and commencement of the downswing and wait, in absolutely no hope whatsoever, that a cure has thus been effected. This insures me against the disappointment of watching him continue to assault the ground six inches behind the ball while falling backwards – but it does nothing for his own state of mind when this is exactly what happens. 'Give it time,' I offer weakly, then rush off to my own ball before he can think of the appropriate profanity. There's something about hearing swear words in an Ulster accent that is particularly scary. Remarkably, a few holes later he manages to move everything in the right direction and there is the unmistakeable sound of a correctly struck ball – it flies twice as far as anything he's hit before and he finishes in classic style; weight on the outside of the left foot, belt buckle facing the target, big cheesy grin on his face. I'm back on the Christmas card list.

Shortly afterwards I discover that not paying too much attention to your score can do wonders for your game. To my great surprise, I am standing on the last tee needing a par for a three over total of sixty-seven. To achieve this, however, I have to negotiate Portobello's tough ninth/eighteenth hole, the one hole that would grace any championship course. It is a 193-yard par three up to a raised and wickedly sloping green surrounded by intimidating bunkers and playing today is into a stiff easterly wind. Denis is also all of a quiver because a quick calculation on the tee has told him that a double bogey will be good enough for a back nine total of 53 – one better than his earlier effort.

Up first, I somehow manage to put a five wood on to the green, but it's right at the back – a good thirty feet *uphill* from the pin. Denis duffs into the front right bunker, barely scrambles over the top lip with his next and chips quite close with his third. It is now me to play and I can see no way of hitting the putt hard enough to negotiate the bumps and hollows of the green, but soft enough not to go careering off the front edge and into the bunker Denis has just emerged from. Hey ho, I give it a lash and sure enough the ball is hurtling downhill, taking blows from all sides like the *Millennium Falcon* going through an asteroid belt, when it hits a particularly large crater, jumps up several inches and skids to a halt less than a foot from the hole. I take the 'gimme' from Denis and pick it up before it starts moving again. He then nudges up holeside quite nicely for an easy five and we both walk off the course entirely satisfied with our morning's efforts.

'So, where to next?' asks Denis, lifting a hair of the dog to his lips. We're having lunch in the bar of the Café Royal, one of my favourite pubs in Edinburgh, and my Scotch pie and his veggie burger arrive just as I'm telling him that the plan is to make a vaguely clockwise circumnavigation of the country and that I shall, therefore, take the road south to the Borders and Northumbria beyond.

'Not many famous old links round there is there?'

The point, I explain, is not just to play historical public courses – I'd be stuck in the east of Scotland half the time if that were so and Marian would be wondering if she'd ever see the back of me.

'So, you're just going to play anything you come across?'

'There will be a dash of *ad hoc* to the carefully organised itinerary, yes.'

'Well, if it's all going to be like Portobello then I take back what I called you the other day.'

'What was that?'

'I said you were a skiving bastard.'

'And now you can see what a testing, yet necessary and admirable venture this is?'

'No, I just think yer off yer fuckin' head.'

3

Maybe I could accept that a caravan is overtaking me if it was being towed by an over-engined Volvo or a Merc. But a Land Rover! Even on their own these bloody things are so slow I usually have to brake or make a nifty dart into the outside lane to avoid rear-ending them. Now here I am admiring its photos of German shepherds in the window and reading that fox hunters 'do it side saddle' as it edges past, the unmistakable hum of its thick tyres on the tarmac only inches from my right ear. And, oh God, no – it isn't a caravan. It's a horse box!

I know that sometime soon there must be a downhill to this uphill and I will have the chance to get back in front, but what would be the point? The embarrassment would only have to be endured all over again on reaching the next incline. Better tuck in behind and pretend at least that I know these people, that we're in some kind of convoy and the only reason they are in front is because they know where we're going.

After my lunch with Denis, I am at last on the open road, heading south on the A1. The plan is to reach Tyneside by late afternoon, locate the course I want to play the next day and then find somewhere to lay my weary head. At this rate, however, I will be lucky to get out of Scotland before it gets dark.

Having been 'persuaded' to leave our own car at home for Marian's use while I am off on my travels, I rashly accepted an offer from a friend who runs a garage on the outskirts of Edinburgh to use one of the cars he gives customers while their own are under the knife. Only half jokingly referred to as the discourtesy car by Andy and his small band of mechanics, this twelve-year-old grey Toyota Starlet boasts such traditional features as manual window adjustment, individual door locking and power-less steering for that work-out-while-driving experience. If it were a pair of jeans from Gap it would be called 'authentic', 'original' or 'classic' – i.e. it is bog standard. It has a five 'speed' gearbox, manual choke and an engine from a perfectly good Kenwood Chef. By the time I reach Berwick I need a shave.

One of the most dramatic of rail journeys, the east coast line through the Borders and into Northumberland clings to the edge of red sandstone cliffs and soars over the Tweed estuary and countless windswept bays. The equivalent by road, however, is not nearly so engaging. The A1, as it runs a few miles further inland, offers nothing but farmland and count-less entreaties to slow down, followed by a list of the number of recent fatalities. Much as I'd like to comply, I have little scope left for slowing down short of pulling on the handbrake and nipping out to stretch my legs. Still, one of the car's better anachronisms is a radio *cassette* player, which has prompted me to dig out a selection of old tapes I haven't listened to in years. Before long I have settled quite happily into this more sedate pace and am pootling along memory lane, my reverie fuelled by the sounds of Love and Money, Hue and Cry and Prefab Sprout.

At least an hour later than I had planned, I am nearing my destination. The combined effect of two wrong turnings off the A1 and then the A19 cancel each other out and before I know it I am driving past the gated entrance to Backworth Golf Club in the early evening, unsure whether I am a navigational genius or just jammy. The area itself is unpromising on the guesthouse front – a succession of post-industrial villages connected by round-abouts and bypasses. But I notice signs for Whitley Bay only a few miles down the road and, resisting the temptation to linger in downtown New York (a village that clearly inspired its American namesake to invest in those icons of the Manhattan landscape, street lights and a bus stop) I decide to check out the delights of summer at a northern seaside resort.

I would imagine that from a distance Whitley Bay is quite stunning. It has an enormous sweep of beach to command and some of the late Victorian and Edwardian grand hotels set back from its promenade are as large and imposing as any I've seen in Brighton, Eastbourne or any other more up-market resort. The close-up view I get as I drive into town looking for a place to stay, however, is a little less impressive. Although more concerned with trying to fathom a one-way system clearly devised by someone with an anti-clockwise fixation, I can't help but notice that there is rather a lot of peeling paint and broken glass in this town.

The shell-suited proprietor of the Cherrytree House B&B, a hundred yards or so off the seafront, apologises that he can only offer me a double room for £30. Not only is this well within my price range, but I spot some golf clubs propped up in the corner of the hallway and am more than happy to accept the hospitality of this kindred spirit. On showing me to my room, however, the kindred spirit promptly grabs the second pillow on the bed and says firmly, 'You won't be needing that.' Is he merely performing the equivalent of removing the second setting of cutlery for the single diner or is he delivering a subtle hint that no matter how lucky I get in my evening's trawl of Whitley Bay's fleshpots I will not be allowed to bring my catch back to the room? Since I'm only in the market for a square meal and an early night it makes no difference, but I set off for the town centre a few minutes later with renewed anticipation.

'It's so . . . so bare.' Not, alas, a comment on the general state of undress to be found in Whitley Bay's pubs and clubs, but an observation overheard in the street after I am a good half hour into my search for something open on this Sunday evening. The American mother of two who spoke has such a pained expression on her face her words are unnecessary. Her children are clearly chilled to the bone as a cold wind off the North Sea pushes them uphill, but, more than that, they look bored out of their minds. Meanwhile Dad – whose idea this obviously was – is trying to look brave, while forlornly scanning the horizon for something, anything, to justify his stupid decision to risk terrorist attack and lousy restaurant service, fly the Atlantic and visit Whitley Bay. They trudge wearily up South Parade, all dressed in the same navy blue windcheaters and heading, unfortunately for them, towards the town centre of boarded up shops and rough-looking pubs that I've just been through.

I don't know when the summer season officially starts in these parts, but I would have guessed that a weekend in July, even an overcast one like this, would generate some level of activity. The only things moving in South Parade once the Americans have passed, however, are a swirl of litter in the middle of the road and the odd bouncer shuffling from foot to foot outside half a dozen or so theme bars. Banana Joe's, the Hairy Lemon (fruit has always been associated with exotic pleasures by the British) and several others are flashing their neon lights, playing summer hits through open windows and advertising their desperation with offers of happy hours that last a week and signs like 'Motorcyclists welcome'.

Just when I'm beginning to fantasise about the Bourbon biscuits next to the kettle back in my room, I stumble across Aldo's International Restaurant. How it is more international than any other Italian restaurant I'm not sure, but I'm not going to quibble. I get a table for one and order the prawn cocktail and chicken cacciatore. For the next half hour or so I join my fellow diners – a family of six and a lone French cyclist studying maps and trying to work out how the hell she got here – in appreciation of Aldo's Americana décor (all newspaper cuttings on Al Capone and 'Old Glory' mirrors) and selection of easy listening.

The most infuriatingly catchy tune in the history of music has to be *Magic Moments* as performed by Perry Como. Once in there, it can be a bugger to get out of your mind and you can find yourself dee-dee dee-dee dum, dee-dee dee-dee dumming the opening bars for days on end. Towards the end of my meal, therefore, I am more than a little alarmed to realise that the CD playing in Aldo's is one we used to have at home before

I accidentally laid it at an angle on the bottom step and broke it under my heel. I know that unless I can get the bill and out of here before the Wichita lineman stops bleating about needing you more than wanting you and wanting you for all time, then Perry will strike and I'll have that cursed tune going through my head for a fortnight. I think I leave far too big a tip, but I'm not about to hang about for my change. I successfully get out of earshot in time and stride out along the promenade looking for somewhere for a nightcap.

It is not to be. Whitley Bay, it is true, has become a little more animated during my meal, but boy racers cruising the streets in souped-up Nissan Almeras and Ford Fiestas is not my idea of a thriving café culture. All along the seafront, huge hotels and tearooms lie dilapidated with the evidence of several failed attempts at revival – all easily dated to the 1970s, 1980s and 1990s – visible in their smashed windows and faded signage. One edifice in particular catches my eye.

The Avenue's most recent comeback must have only just ended in tears because the signs and paintwork around the boarded up windows look very up to date. Beside the entrance there is one of those long-winded plaques you find in places of historical significance and I begin to read: '*Walter Scott esq sold the land at the foot of Park Avenue to the builder Thomas Patterson in 1901 . . .*'

It goes on in exhaustive detail to reveal the frankly dull story of the building's construction. By the time we get to prominent members of the Whitley and Monkseaton Urban District Council who were present at its opening on 24 June 1907 my interest is definitely on the wane and I'm beginning to wonder if anything of significance ever did occur here. But then the last paragraph delivers its devastating news: '*In January 1914 there was a fire in the hotel caused by Newcastle United FC leaving their jerseys to dry around a stove in the basement. Luckily there was very little damage.*' Phew.

Suitably underwhelmed by this window into Whitley Bay's past, and still unable to find a likely prospect for a quiet *digestif*, I conclude there is nothing for it but to wend my way back to my solitary pillow and reflect on why I am in Tyne and Wear in the first place.

It has been my experience that the English are more class-conscious than Scots. There's a statement to provoke wounded indignation and derision in equal measure, but I stand by it. Of course, there are all the social strata you could want in Scotland, from the congenitally unemployed in council housing schemes in Paisley to the toffs in their Perthshire estates. And there are those across the country who take great care to monitor their lives and everything in it from cars to weekend pursuits to make sure it maintains a high degree of middle-class purity. But it is the *importance* of class, the frequency with which it crops up in conversation and the accepted relevance of it in any description of a third party that I notice in England. Not that it is always used pejoratively – far from it. It is simply that where you come from, what your parents did and what kind of school you went to seems to be of more interest to folk south of the Border.

A good friend of mine from London established all these facts on our first meeting many years ago and then asked, 'So, would you call yourself working class, then?' He was not trying to wind me up, he was genuinely and innocently interested in what passed for working or middle class in Glasgow, a place he'd never been to. I remember telling him, in all honesty, that I had never before given it a thought, but that I was probably working class. Did this mean I had lived a sheltered life to that point, surrounded only by my social peers and therefore unknowing of the ways of the world? No. It is just that where I come from we have our own 'cultural' pre-occupations and view the world as being composed of essentially two types of people: Celtic supporters and Rangers supporters – or Tims and Huns as they are more commonly known.

There are also, to my mind, only two sports worth bothering about: football and golf. Somehow, I just can't seem to get worked up about rugby (how can you get excited about a game when the better team *always* wins?), tennis (far too much standing about tugging at sweaty clothes), cricket (just far too much standing about) or athletics (I don't care what anyone says – running round in circles is not a spectator sport). It might appear that my choice of sports is proof that I was indeed nurtured in a uniquely classless environment, but with football and golf I have a foot in both camps, even though the latter – on municipal courses more akin to the assault variety than the golfing – would scarcely be recognisable to the average member of Wentworth or Royal St George's. But there is the rub. I won't delve back into the hoary old myth of 'democratic golf', but it *is* the case that in many places in Scotland – Glasgow among them – golf is, and always has been, played by all. Not so in England.

The whole notion of class and sport dates in large part back to the late nineteenth century, when games and outdoor pursuits were actively encouraged by a bourgeoisie that was in a rising panic over rumblings of discontent among the lower orders. Afraid of either a Paris-style revolution after 1848 or the widespread acceptance of new and dangerous notions of socialism being dreamed up by that Marx fellow in London, the upper and political classes thought it would be just the thing if the workers were given the opportunity to let off a little steam now and then. However, it would be the following century before Alister Mackenzie, the brilliant but barmy golf course architect, would advocate municipal golf as a capital way of preventing the working classes from taking up Bolshevism and Communism. In the meantime, golf was definitely not what was on offer to the restless proles.

What was on offer was many of the sports that have since become quintessentially working class; boxing, rugby (league) and soccer, indoor pursuits like darts, and opportunities to chuck hard-earned money away by gambling on dog and pigeon racing. It was all part of the development of what became known as 'rational recreation', a programme of investing in sporting facilities as well as providing parks, museums, public baths and libraries, all designed to soothe the savage breast, combat urban radicalism and restore the right and proper subservience to Church and state that had served Britannia jolly well to date, thank you very much.

Peculiarly, there were – and are – sports that developed a pan-class appeal, most notably cricket and horseracing. And then there was the whole issue of broken time payments (small payments made to working class sportsmen to allow them to miss work to compete) and the great divide these helped create between the increasingly well-off and upper class amateur and the professional sportsman, a split that led, among other things, to the separate development of rugby league and rugby union.

Golf, of course, was only just beginning to spread into England and it was not the chimney sweep or the factory worker who was playing it. The history of how, where and why private golf clubs spread across England is interesting in itself, but for the moment I'm concerned with why the English middle classes took to the game at all. John Lowerson is one of the few academics who has delved into this aspect of golf in recent years. In his contribution to *Sport in Britain: A Social History* (1989), he spells out why he thinks the middle classes played the game.

Firstly, he argues, it provided exercise away from the office. It also allowed ex-public school boys to extend their indoctrinated notions of 'manly athleticism' into middle and later years. Indeed, the sport could be played at almost any age, anywhere in the country and any time of the year. Golf was not (initially at least) 'tainted' by the presence of women, while the scoring, involving handicaps, bogeys etc., was mathematical and appealed to the commercial and professional classes. Lowerson also describes golf as a 'singularly personal game', well suited to the consciousness of 'inner-directed individualism'. Like I said, he's an academic and they say stuff like that all the time. I think what he means is that the late Victorians put great store by self-discipline and regulation. The man who could take the slings and arrows of unlucky bounces, dodgy lies in the semi-rough and opponents fluking holes in one with nary a twitch of his upper lip is obviously the sort of stout fellow you'd want running the Foreign Office or, for that matter, accounts and billings at Smither's Stopcock & Flange.

More importantly, of course, golf offered the opportunity for social differentiation, for pursuing a pleasing rural pastime in the company of those of a similar background and outlook. As Lowerson puts it: 'Clubs which were instrumental as syndicates in acquiring land to build the course were also devices for excluding people who would not fit, for encouraging emulation and the necessary degree of deferent patience which would prompt an urge to join.'

Meanwhile, back with the workers, rational recreation was having its greatest impact through the formation of sports and social clubs. Many of them were associated with local churches – from such clubs the likes of Aston Villa and Everton grew. Others, particularly in the industrial towns and cities of the Midlands and the north, were work-based and it was from these that more famous names in British sport were to emerge, among them Wigan and St Helens in rugby league and Liverpool, Manchester United and Bolton Wanderers in football.

For the most part, however, the sports and social clubs stayed small-scale and served their local communities. Clubs, in fact, like Backworth Colliers Miners Welfare in north Tyneside, which drew its members from the local colliery, also known as Eccles, and the pit at Bates in Blyth. Like similar clubs in the area and across northern England, it offered a selection of sporting pastimes, including cricket, bowls and darts. In 1934, however, the club was made an offer by the ninth Duke of Northumberland of eighty-five acres of parkland and the magnificent Backworth Hall, built in 1780, all for £8,500. The club registered as a charity, raised the cash and moved into its impressive new home. And, as if to confirm that Britain between the wars was no longer the country of sporting apartheid imposed in Victorian times, one of the first things the miners did with their slice of Northumberland was lay out a golf course.

I sleep well enough at the B&B. That is until 4.40a.m. when the Saturn V rocket strapped to the foundations is ignited and its eight massive H-1 engines, each delivering 200,000lb of thrust and burning more than 2,000 gallons per minute of liquid oxygen fuel, slowly pushes the building up into the early morning air, heading for the upper atmosphere.

At least that is my reasonable assumption given the almighty roar and shuddering that engulfs my room and has me bolt upright in bed, watching stuff fall off the sideboard and wondering if I might catch a last glimpse of the British Isles far below if only I had the guts to look out of the window.

Turns out the man in the next room has flushed the toilet.

Three hours later and still unnerved by the rude awakening, I head downstairs for breakfast, somehow manage to find a seat in a dining room obviously dedicated to one family's passion for the car boot sale and order the full English. Not only is it cooked to perfection, but the lovely chatty woman who serves me asks what I am doing in the area and then declares that I must be 'reet clevah' to be writing a book. I leave the Cherrytree with more warm and fuzzy thoughts than I'd thought possible at five in the morning.

Backworth Hall is accessed through a dingy gated entrance darkened by massive horse chestnut trees opposite the Backworth Club public house on the road between the village and Shiremoor. At first glance, even from the side, it is an impressive building. But the moss on the walls from blocked guttering, the weeds around the paths and the conspicuous lack of jobsworths demanding money before you park your car tells you this is no stately home. Around the back there is an unsightly jumble of outbuildings and rusting fire escapes and, set a little way off, a tiny hut of the variety usually seen presiding over seaside crazy golf courses.

Nodding good mornings at a couple of guys chatting in the driveway, I walk over to the hut and ask the chap at the door if he can point me in the direction of John Robertson. He does so right over my shoulder and I turn to see that the secretary/financial officer and general factotum of Backworth Golf Club is one of those I've just walked past. John remembers our brief chat on the phone a week or so back, but apologises that an electrician needed to check on their alarm system is calling that morning and he can't join me for a game. Instead I am introduced to Eric and Peter, two early morning regulars and, after a bit of confusion in the hut over whose guest I was going to go down as, I pay my £9 for eighteen holes (it would have been £13 as a normal visitor) and we head off for the first tee.

On the way, we conclude the introductions and I ask about the pits nearby that supply the members of the club. The lads (a generic term used by us sporting types that can include even this pair of forty-somethings) confer but struggle to name anything beyond those I already know about. Eventually they simply agree that there used to be 'loods of pits roon heah'.

It turns out that neither of my playing partners is a former miner – in fact only a tiny fraction of the members have ever seen a coalface. Ex-miners still get subsidised membership, but the Eccles pit closed in 1980 and Bates in 1986. Now it's the unemployed like Peter – looking for work in a local shipyard after failing a medical to get back out to the rigs in the North Sea – and the self-employed like Eric, a landscape gardener, who make up the bulk of the membership.

The tight little course has just the nine holes laid out on land facing the main entrance to the hall, beyond not only the formal gardens but also the bowling and cricket grounds. These are two of the other sports still offered by the miners' welfare club (archery is another), although the croquet was stopped through lack of interest a few years back. The first tee is slightly off to the side among mature woodland and starts you off on a short par four – only some 240 yards off the yellow tees. The green, slightly downhill, is clearly drivable, but there are bunkers guarding its approaches and Eric, up first, takes a fairway wood for position and planks his ball nicely on the fairway. Then Peter, who's only recently taken up the game, makes an awkward, stiffish swing and finds the light rough down the right side. My three-wood thankfully goes nice and straight and we set off for our morning's round.

Inspired by my experiences at Musselburgh, I am only carrying a half set of clubs over my shoulder. Peter, a tall, fit-looking guy I can't imagine failing any kind of medical, has a full set on his back, while Eric, built a wee bit more for comfort, is shoving his clubs along on a three-wheeled trolley. Again, the weather is grey and threatening, but with only a slight breeze, and every now and then it's warm enough to remind you it's July. While Eric and I chip on and two-putt for our pars, Peter fluffs his first effort at a pitch out of the rough and has to settle for bogey. We saunter over to the second tee and I ask why they've joined Backworth and not any other club in the area.

'Well, there's plenty of what we call cliquey golf roon heah,' says Eric. 'Reet snobby places you wouldn't want to play in, to be honest. But the craic heah's great.'

As if to illustrate the point, Eric and Peter then get involved in a lengthy bout of badinage with another group just walking off the eighth/seventeenth green, the thrust of which seems to be taking the piss out of Peter for missing a tiddler of a putt in the medal at the weekend just past. I'm conscious there is the danger of caricaturing every accent I come across in this journey, but I must say that I understand practically nothing of what is being said. It is obvious, however, that Eric is enjoying it a great deal more than Peter.

Distracted by the encounter, I don't pay close enough attention to Eric's advice over the next tee shot and send a drive straight as an arrow into a large fairway bunker guarding the turn in this slight dogleg left. The other two are safely off to the right. Although there is no rake in the trap, there is precious little sand either and I easily knock my second out and advance a fair way down the, er, fairway. Eric is quick with advice for the next shot and tells me I only have an easy wedge in to the flag. Being the expert, however, knowing the course better than him and figuring there is at least 120 yards to go, I hit a full-blooded nine-iron that sails past the pin still rising and ends up in a ditch under a hedge. I play the vast majority of my golf on coastal links and rely quite heavily on yardage charts – flat parkland courses with trees everywhere really screws up my already shaky grasp of perspective – but even that is no excuse for ignoring yardages from a guy who, by his own admission, plays here up to three times a week.

Sheepishly, I drop out for four, dunch my first chip into the fringe of the green, clip it on and then two-putt for an impressive quadruple bogey eight. Eric, an eleven-handicapper, makes a regulation par. Peter, who plays off twenty-two, bogeys again and so the pattern is set for most of the front nine. I veer from solid to woeful play, Peter occasionally manages at least two clean contacts in a row to scramble a par and Eric cruises along in seemingly complete control, not looking even capable of dropping a shot.

Many of the holes afford attractive views of Backworth Hall's impressive Georgian façade. Seen from a distance, and on the other side of parkland and those gardens, it really does look like a baronial seat, or at least a comfortable country house hotel – the perfect spot for some corporate schmoozing. No wonder, I am told, the present, twelfth Duke of Northumberland, would like to re-acquire the estate. 'Oh, he'd love to get his hands on it,' says Peter with a smile. 'He keeps making offers, but he's no chance. We're staying put.'

Striding down the par five seventh fairway with an extra spring in my step, having just birdied the par three sixth with an exquisite wedge to three feet, I ask the class question. Golf, they agree, has a reputation for snobbery and privacy, but not (here it comes again) 'roon heah'.

'There's some clubs that get themselves all worked up aboot politics,' says Eric.

What, party politics? I ask.

'No, man. Internal politics. Who's in, who's oot and the like. I canny be doin' with that.'

Neither of them, they assure me, have ever experienced any funny reactions from non-golfing friends or neighbours because they play the game. Some clubs in the area might have a middle-class image, but the game itself does not.

'There's places in Tyneside we've played in club matches you wouldn't want to go back to. Fookin' awful they were,' says Peter. 'All "Don't do this, don't do that," y'know?'

But mostly its 'ordinary folk' who play the game, he says. Not that that means you don't get the odd bandit (a golfing term for someone who plays a lot better than their official handicap) and he jerks a thumb at Eric, currently one *under* par and pushing his trolley along with his belly while rolling a cigarette. Before long more good-natured abuse starts flying about.

'He had a partner in Saturday's medal,' says Peter, 'but he bunked off cos he couldn't take any more of his fookin' shite. So he ends up with us.'

'Aye, just in time to see you miss that fookin' putt, ya wanka.'

It is the third or fourth time the subject of Peter's ignominious performance on the seventeenth green that day has cropped up, so I nervously ask for the full story.

Peter, it seems, had been playing a blinder. His net score was looking like it would be in the middle or even low sixties and should have been easily enough to win the medal. His approach to the green was excellent and had left him with around ten feet for birdie. Ignoring Eric's advice to simply roll it up and make sure of par, Peter went for glory and sent it a couple of feet past. Still, an easy par putt . . . only he lipped it out. And that would have been bad enough, but Peter then walked up in a rage to tap it in, hit the ball with the sole of this putter and failed to make enough contact to send it the remaining two inches into the hole! Shell-shocked at turning a decent birdie chance into a double bogey, Peter crumbled and dropped two more shots over the closing hole. He limped in to discover he'd lost out on winning the medal by *one stroke*.

To be honest, the slagging he is getting this morning from Eric and everyone else who comes within shouting distance has more than a little compassion to it. If taking a deep breath, cupping your hands over your mouth and shouting 'dozy twat' from 200 yards can ever be called supportive, I think the lads at Backworth are managing it. Much worse, I think, for Peter would have been everyone avoiding eye contact and insisting on discussing the weather all day. Eric, in particular, seems almost as concerned by his friend's game as Peter is and offers advice on a regular basis, especially when his swing gets too fast and jerky. 'Ha'way, mate. Sloo it doon,' he tells him.

A chip and putt secures par for me, while Eric birdies with a four. The eleven-handicapper is now one under par for seven holes. Meanwhile, Peter is going from bad to worse. Having shanked his first drive into the woods, the best he can manage is an eight.

The eighth hole starts off from the furthest corner of the course and has dense woodland – and out of bounds – all down the left, an evil little bunker at driving distance and more trees down the right. Only when I approach the green, my ball having caught the thick fringe and failed to run on, do I realise that this is the infamous hole itself – the eighth doubles, of course, as the seventeenth. Perhaps that is why Peter's swing has deteriorated so badly. By the time he reaches the scene of Saturday's calamity, he's topped it twice, missed it once altogether and is lying four. But, in a show of quite remarkable mental fortitude, he then single putts for a bogey five.

Before we leave the green – Eric having at last dropped some shots (three of them, in fact) thanks to driving out of bounds, and me chipping and putting for a bogey – the three of us stand looking down at the in-filled hole location from the weekend medal, while Eric tells the story once again, this time with actions and expressions. I've heard so much about this double bogey by now I am almost surprised there isn't a plaque – another local sporting tragedy to rank alongside the great Slightly Burnt Football Jerseys Disaster of 1914.

The second nine sees a reversal of fortune for everyone. Knowing now where to hit my drives on this deceptively tricky little course, I manage to steady the ship with a string of pars. Peter, perhaps content at having laid a ghost to rest on the eighth green, also begins to strike the ball much better, while Eric shows signs of indeed being an eleven handicap player with some wayward tee-shots. Even the straightest drive here, however, can land you in trouble, because the course is obviously built on ancient farmland and undulations left over from the high ridges once used for growing crops are evident all over it. There are many golf courses in Britain built on such land, and I've played on a few, but the ridges have usually run across the line of the hole. The way Backworth is laid out, they run like giant corrugations straight down most of the fairways, meaning the bounce can either flatter a bad drive by kicking it towards the middle, or just as easily take a good one and throw it off into the semi-rough. The other consequence of the ridges is that the ball usually settles in the hollows, greatly increasing your chances of ending up in someone else's divot. This is exactly what happens to me on the eleventh, but I punch a low seven-iron out of the hole and nicely on to the green, then two-putt for par – a lot better than the eight I racked up here first time around by landing under a hedge.

Peter has also hit a lovely approach and at least a par looks certain until he sends his first putt way past the hole. Far enough past, in fact, for him to hear from Eric the words every golfer dreads: 'It's still thee.' He three-putts for a bogey, as does Eric, and I head to the tee of the par three twelfth, set deep inside the trees, with the honour. There, I have no hesitation in choosing a pitching wedge of the variety that secured me a birdie on the front nine and I hit it easily as well as I had only an hour or so earlier. I have no doubt it would have settled just as close to the pin . . . had I hit the shot on the correct bloody hole! Unfortunately, the third/twelfth hole looks remarkably similar to the sixth/fifteenth, but is almost forty yards longer. Not only can I not count, I can't judge distances through trees very well either (as I've already established) and it is only when my ball lands way short of the green that I realise I've made yet another embarrassing error. Bogey.

Eric is now matching Peter's score and swings between double bogeys and pars. Approaching the fourteenth green, the mobile phone strapped to his belt goes off, but he doesn't answer the call, just switches it off.

'I hate this fookin' work sometimes. People think they can just phone up anytime and you'll drop everything to come and do their job right away. They think you've nothing better – *Aye, just leave the pin in mate, I'm off the green* – to be doing than running after them.'

So, is this a day off? I ask after he's putted out.

'No, no. I'll probably get started this afternoon. There's a couple of jobs I've to do estimates for.' Then he stretches and takes a thoughtful draw from his roll-up. 'Naw, I think I'll just stay in the bar. Let the bastards wait.'

Over the closing holes I ask them about the costs of playing at Backworth. The green fees I mentioned earlier are certainly cheap enough for visitors and they are only restricted on weekend mornings when there are club competitions. Both Eric and Peter are members, of course, and they pay around £250 a year in fees. Eric has worked out that, given the number of games he plays there each year, his golf costs him on average twenty-five pence per round. I have the distinct impression that he believes playing this amount of golf and therefore getting such value for money in some way compensates for him not putting the hours in at work. There's a logic to it, I must admit.

We finish with bogeys all round, the thoughts of lunch in the bar already crowding out any concentration over our putts. I quickly change shoes, throw the clubs back in the discourtesy car and follow them up the front stairs and through the main entrance to the hall.

Inside, the building is even less like a stately home. If the linoleum flooring and yellowing paintwork don't give it away, the dirty great marching banner at the head of the stairs should do it. Proclaiming, 'Backworth Federated Group of Miners' Lodges Welfare Scheme', and picturing all the activities on offer above the slogan, 'Education, Recreation', it would surely have had a nineteenth century upper class paternalist beaming in satisfaction. If ever there were an illustration to encapsulate the theory of 'rational recreation' then this is it.

The bar is off to the side and John Robertson is there ready to buy my lunch and pint of lager, despite my protests. The large, Newcastle-shirted barman, known simply as Shrek, gives me an odd look when I ask for a couple of cold filled rolls, as if to say he wouldn't have been so modest in his order if someone were buying *him* lunch, and I follow John to a seat in the corner.

Like the course itself and the rest of the hall, there are no airs and graces in here – the décor is mostly cartoons, posters and club notices, the furnishings of the low-maintenance, wipe-clean variety, and the entertainment, this and every lunchtime, is coming from Norman with the gold chunky necklace at a badly out-of-tune piano. Gershwin and Cole Porter standards have rarely sounded so odd; he's hitting all the right notes in the right order, but they're not quite coming out that way. Besides, I don't think *It Ain't Necessarily So* was meant to be played as a polka. Thankfully, Eric tells me, he is refraining from favouring us today with his equally unique singing voice.

While Eric and Peter throw themselves into the general hubbub of jokes, news from the course, anecdotes and insults (mostly directed at Norman) flying around the room, John fills me in on his task to try and bring a little bit more money into the club.

'I don't really have a title as such,' he confesses. 'I'm kind of the secretary, but I do the financials as well. I'm trying to get more business into the hall – weddings, conferences and the like – but it's a bit tricky.'

Just as I'm asking why, my lunch arrives and I realise I have misinterpreted Shrek's expression. So large that they have to be brought separately to my table, the slabs of 'stottie cake' either side of my ham salad and tuna fillings look more like sofa cushions than bread. I all but dislocate my jaw to take a bite out of one and John continues.

'It's the "miners' welfare" bit,' he says. 'We've found that it can be a bit of a problem marketing the hall to businesses. Once they're here and can see what we can provide, they're happy enough. But some people think it's a bit down-market or out of date.'

It will never be enough of a problem, however, to make them change their name. There may be only a handful of miners left in their ranks, but they are proud of their heritage. Indeed, John then tells me of their plans to arrange regular matches with Musselburgh Golf Club (separate from the old course I played) and any other clubs they can trace that were, like them, founded by miners' welfare societies.

I can understand why Eric is tempted to spend his days in this friendly, inclusive little bar. Norman has finally finished at the piano and is off back to work. His 'threat' never to play for this bunch of ingrates ever again is greeted by a cheer and a round of applause. Several of the regulars, meanwhile, are chatting to me about their favourite courses in Scotland. One chap, on discovering that I live in Edinburgh, decides to check a copy of the R&A's *Golfer's Handbook* and let me know the names of all the local courses in the city. It is, of course, a bizarre and completely unnecessary favour, but I am touched nevertheless. Then another asks me if I know 'the one next to the motorway' that he and some friends played last year. I tell him he'll need to be a wee bit more specific and he says it begins with a 'B'. As I think of possible candidates, the keeper of the handbook chides his pal for being so stupid, because (he's just discovered to his astonishment) there are no fewer than twenty-five golf courses in Edinburgh.

I run through the Babertons, Bruntsfields and Bonnyriggs, but it is not ringing a bell with my inquisitor. In exasperation he goes out to his car and brings back his collection of ball markers – a plastic bag of crested discs he then pours out on to the table. A few minutes of careful sifting later he holds one up in triumph and shouts, 'Balbirnie Park!' I confess I've never heard of it and immediately Handbook Man picks up his trusty tome again and goes to work. The insults really begin to fly when he discovers it's in Glenrothes in Fife and not Edinburgh after all.

'Do you not remember going over the fookin' Forth Bridge, y'twat?' says one.

'Eh, no. Must've been asleep,' says the other, shovelling his hoard of markers back into their bag.

My lunch over (I am forced to take the second roll in a doggy bag), I thank John, Eric and Peter for their hospitality and head quickly out to the car. It is already past 2p.m. and I've just remembered that I'm in North Tyneside, that I had planned to get to Essex by the end of the day and that I am not driving a Ferrari.

4

Eleven out of fourteen fairways, ten greens in regulation and thirty-four putts for a round of seventy-nine – nine over par. Scorecards, as the old saw goes, paint no pictures, but if this is only a sketchy outline of my round at Backworth it is still a pleasing one. OK, it wasn't the toughest golf course in the world, but I'd never played it before (the first time around at least), the standard of greenkeeping was acceptable without ever straying anywhere near good, and I'd only a half set of clubs to choose from. Playing to my new handicap – especially in view of that quadruple bogey – is therefore very satisfying. As indeed is this pint of something called Butcombe Blond Bitter I am enjoying in the Lord Burghley pub as I review this morning's performance.

Having managed to find my way through the Tyne Tunnel and back on to the A1, I had settled to the task of reaching Essex or at least somewhere south of Cambridge by nightfall. For the thick end of five hours, with occasional breaks at wonderful greasy spoon cafés, I drove through what I can only describe as bog standard farmland. Much as I would love to be able to evoke the transmutable landscape of my journey in the style of proper travel writers – how the sweeping plain rises gently into foothills, primeval forest is finally tamed by the axe and plough, that sort of thing – I confess a drive down England's right flank provides little in the way of raw material for such prose.

No doubt the Friends of Cleveland, The Vale of York Rocks Society or Lincolnshire's Flat Earthers will think me some kind of dullard for failing to appreciate the 'unique' prospect of their respective counties. But I'm afraid that Tyneside to Rutland, for this observer at least, provided all the ever-changing novelty of a slow ride through the Russian steppe. As Robert McNeil (newspaper columnist and close personal chum) would say, it all looked like Englandshire to me, but thankfully the infinity of not quite flat fields rolled by at a fair pace, the discourtesy car having reached a respectable cruising speed by about Darlington. Nevertheless, it was not long before I realised my goal of reaching somewhere vaguely East Anglian was way too ambitious. By early evening the combined effect of my traumatic 5a.m. wake-up, the round of golf and the soporific scenery had me looking for the next likely location for a meal and a bed.

Right on cue, Stamford appeared off the port bow, hazy sunshine lighting up what I later discovered was the old Lincolnshire limestone of its town centre nestling round a hill in the distance. It looked like a wee bit of Bath lost in the East Midlands and was certainly the most inviting place I'd seen for about four hours. Exhaustion is the only excuse I can think of for deciding to stay in the first place I came to as I drove into town. That and a very impressive sign hanging from gallows spanning the main road proclaiming, 'The George of Stamford'.

My suspicions that I had moved up in the world since Whitley Bay were first aroused in the car park as I squeezed in between one of those Porsche 4x4s and a 7-series BMW.

A walk past posh shops – sorry, boutiques – selling original paintings, cashmere sweaters and toiletries you don't find in Boots took me into a fantastic oak-beamed reception area that creaked agreeably underfoot and was filled with the gorgeous scent from several vases of freshly cut flowers dotted about the place. Needless to say 'England's greatest coaching inn' cost a tad more than the Cherrytree B&B, but I was in the mood for lavish.

Thankfully, they had a single room and I filled in the registration form, near the bottom of which it asked for the licence plate of my car. When I confessed that I didn't actually know what it was, the girl said the make, model and colour would do. She scanned the details and handed me my key. Perhaps it was the fact that no one was called to help with my bags, but I detected a sudden aloofness in her manner.

'I've left golf clubs in my car. Will they be alright there,' I asked. She looked again at 'Toyota Starlet, greyish' on the registration form and there was a pause as we both imagined a car thief making a beeline for its boot, ignoring several hundred thousand pounds worth of German automotive engineering in the passing.

'Yes, sir,' she managed to say without sneering. 'I'm sure they will be quite safe.'

The room was at the end of a series of corridors on a rollercoaster of ancient floorboards, connected by a succession of dimly lit corners and evil little carpeted steps up or down. I tripped twice in broad daylight and stone cold sober. The room itself was bijou to say the most, but comfortable and quiet. I dumped my bags and left before the bath and bed could seduce me into skipping food and drink. Sadly, the hotel's restaurant required a jacket and tie – items I had taken deliberate care not to pack on this trip – so it was off on weary legs into the beating heart of downtown Stamford.

A short walk over the River Welland and up into the town centre took me to the Lord Burghley, the only pub I could see not already infested with what appeared to be at least a couple of legions of Italian students filling the old place with excitable Latin babble and laughter.

'Any of your beers local,' I asked the surly-looking barman.

'No,' he said flatly.

'OK, I'll have the one with the nice picture on the hand pump.' And so I sit here in this peaceful, if a touch unfriendly, pub, supping on Butcombe Blond and annoying the barman and his equally miserable assistant by writing tiny numbers on a scorecard and making satisfied little noises to myself. I'm contemplating the wisdom of having another and taking my chances with the George's wacky flooring on a couple of pints when the Italians arrive.

'*Bella bassa beedledeedley rrrappa massa montewonty!*' a thin boy in a figure-hugging shirt bawls to no one in particular as he walks in ahead of a troop of effortlessly stylish young teenagers.

'*Trreppi franti ladossa insifaconni!*' a gorgeous young woman replies at the top of her voice, arms going like a windmill. In any other language this volume could only be the prelude to a fight and the police would have already been called. Instead they smile as if having shared some high decibel intimacy and begin ordering diet colas for thirty from the now suicidal looking bar staff. It is time to leave.

My short walk to the pub had revealed plenty of huntin', shootin' and fishin' shops, Jaeger outlets and places to blow ten grand on an antique bed pan, but nowhere likely for a modest evening repast. Nowhere, at least, save for a Pizza Express across the road from the George, tastefully done up in sandstone and buff colours – presumably to make it look like it's been there since Dick Turpin dropped by for a Deep Pan with extra cheese. In keeping with the Italian flavour of the night, not to mention my inability to pass up pizza under any circumstances, I decide that what I need most just before going to bed is an American Hot with pepperoni and jalapeño chillies. What the hell – I have Rennies and I'm not afraid to use them.

That the game available at Backworth fits into my loose definition of 'public', accessible golf is beyond question. It is cheap, asks no questions of status or ability and is only off limits to someone walking in off the street for a few hours at weekends, to accommodate competitions – exactly the same regime as applies at any municipal course. And yet it is a private club.

To refine my earlier rant about the misrepresentation of golf, it would perhaps be more accurate to say that it is the perception of the golf *club* that is responsible. From *Terry and June* to the advert informing us that pompous twits play golf while cool, sophisticated types drive Audis, the golf club has been the very embodiment of the sport's awful image. And while it would be grand to be able to say that Backworth represents an equally vibrant yet wilfully overlooked strand of golf club history, it is not so.

Middle-class golf clubs dominate the picture, quite simply because most private golf clubs are (or, at least were) middle class. How could it be otherwise? The whole notion of social or activity-specific clubs is largely a middle-class invention after all. They date from the mid-eighteenth century when the middle classes as we know them – educated *middle*men who didn't get their hands dirty, but didn't own the factory either – first appeared across rapidly industrialising Europe. Shunned as much by their high-born betters as their resentful minions, they sought out each other's company and before long began establishing all manner of forums for their get-togethers – debating and political societies, art clubs, philosophical talking shops and, in Scotland, golf clubs. Add to this the fact that for most of its history golf has been a relatively expensive pursuit and you have all you need for a sport to be dominated by one social class.

Another reason for drawing a distinction between the club and the game itself was that it was the lure of the clubhouse, not the links, that actually fuelled the astonishing spread of the sport through England in the late nineteenth and early twentieth centuries. And it was astonishing. Before 1879 there were only twenty golf clubs in England, but in the next decade more and more began to be established. By 1890, the trickle had turned into a torrent and in the next twenty years no fewer than 512 new English clubs were founded.

Yes, there was an agricultural depression that made land cheap, but hundreds of square miles of rural and suburban England would not have been turned into golf courses if something had not driven this mania. Those hallmarks of the game that were to appeal to the middle-class male mentality – the athleticism into old age, the emphasis on self-discipline and the lack of 'burdz' – were, of course, already established features, but they were attractions that only gradually became apparent to the many. Remember that in 1885 golf was still being described as 'an eccentricity affected by the few'.

What made golf boom in late Victorian England was the realisation by the middle classes that golf clubs gave them exactly the right environment in which to indulge all their favourite fantasies. The move from common land to private, purpose-built courses (as demonstrated by the Honourable Company in Edinburgh and many others) was only partly about ensuring tee-off times. It was also about providing room to express themselves – something the new wave of course-owning parkland clubs were to demonstrate.

The freedom the golf club afforded the members to mix with others of their own class – or better still, a class they aspired to – should not be underestimated. The modern industrial metropolis with its clear definition of workplace and dormitory, inner city and suburb, was only just emerging. There were many professionals, small businessmen and managers who, in the 1880s and 1890s, still lived next to or on top of their place of work. As Cousins puts it: 'The tradesman lived over his shop and the doctor over his surgery. The banker went upstairs from his counting house after locking up the safe and sending his clerks to their attics. The merchant slept almost within reach of the bolts of cloth he handled during the day.' Where better to escape this twenty-four-hour world of duty and responsibility than on a golf course or in the clubhouse? Where else could the Victorian husband and father let the starch out of his collar for a few hours and shoot the breeze with his pals? The upper classes had their private, West End clubs and weekends in the country. The workers had their pubs, social and sports clubs. And so the middle classes claimed the golf club for their own. Even later, when the suburbs spread their mock Tudor and neo-classical little mansions and semi-detached villas over the land, the golf course became the focal point for many developments. Builders and land agents often planned the course first to offer as an inducement, then sold the plots round about.

(Exactly the same practice still goes on today with expensive, up-market housing developments helping to pay for the new, private golf club on their doorstep.)

In London, the turn of the century saw a rapid spread north and west into previously rural Middlesex and golf clubs played an important part in the suburbanisation of the likes of Stanmore, Mill Hill, Edgware and Pinner. New branch lines and the London Underground were crucial; it was important that the professional classes were within striking distance of their place of work and the Metropolitan and Bakerloo lines ensured that was the case. An interesting measure of the spread of suburban London is that the number of golf clubs within fifteen miles of Charing Cross increased from nine in 1890 to eighty-nine by 1910 – almost a 1,000 per cent increase in twenty years.

This, then, was the fertile soil on which the seed of golf fell – mile upon square mile of suburbia heaving with class-conscious, upwardly mobile men and women with a new-found sense of their own identity and the wealth to be able to enjoy time away from the office. The inspiration for Sir John Betjeman's *Metroland* series, this was a new kind of urban landscape with a new set of social mores and nascent prejudices stalking its drawing rooms, church socials and, in no time at all, clubhouses. The sports historian, Richard Holt, has written extensively on middle-class England and its relationship with sport. In his history of the Stanmore Golf Club, as well as later essays on golf and the English suburb, he lays bare the extent to which the late Victorian and Edwardian generation more or less invented the golf club as we know it to suit their own, class-conscious agenda. At Stanmore, for example, the combined entry fee and annual subscription of ten guineas was set deliberately high enough to price out manual workers and even lower middle-class clerks and shopkeepers. However, he notes, 'Money was not the only obstacle. Simply being able to afford to join was not enough. The bourgeoisie was a socio-cultural not just an economic category. A minimum level of funding had to be accompanied by a certain degree of refinement. Like at most clubs, a candidate at Stanmore needed two proposers from within the club who could vouch for that mixture of family connection, education, occupation and income which was required.'

A place to relax among like-minded chaps, the golf club was also an opportunity for the suburbanites to indulge their passion for aping the upper classes. You only have to look at the houses they built for themselves. All porticos, pillars and porches, they are like little stately homes. The larger ones had rooms for scullery maids or housekeepers, and common street numbers were even eschewed in favour of faux country house names. The people inside these houses knew exactly what they had to do to achieve, and then maintain, the desired social standing: attain the right position in the local church, give parties to the right guest list, be 'at home' to callers on certain days . . . and join the right clubs. It was all a simulation of the life they imagined the toffs were enjoying on their estates and in their London residences.

And just as their home lives had pretensions to the upper-class world they envied, so their golf clubs became substitutes for that exemplar of high society, the country weekend house party. If you weren't posh enough to be invited down to Blandings for a shoot with Lord Emsworth and his guests, then you could always turn up at the golf club (many of them actually built on land sold by debt-ridden country estates, complete with converted mansion houses) and pretend. Even the garb preferred by the Edwardian middle-class golfer – the universal Norfolk jacket and breeches – had more to do with looking like you were about to bag a pheasant than dressing comfortably for three hours of swinging a golf club.

Finally, and not unrelated to this fascination with the landed gentry, the golf course became the perfect expression of late nineteenth century ideas on taming nature and the idyllic landscape. With an eye more to Capability Brown than Old Tom Morris, England's parkland courses were not really laid out with the demands of the game in mind. As Holt says, 'Golf offered a new version of the pastoral, an older aesthetic updated, with wide fairways fringed by trees leading to that supreme object of suburban veneration: the perfect lawn in the form of a green.'

Of course, most, if not all, were designed by old Scottish pros turned golf course architects, but they gave the clubs what they asked for, and that was scaled-down country estates, not recreations of wild Scottish links. Golf, then, was a means to an end for middle-class England, not an end in itself. It was the enclosure, the privacy it provided for indulging in social politics and pretension, that was important, not the opportunity to play the game. Conclusive proof of that can be seen in the records of many clubs from around that time where scores of non-playing members are listed and almost as much ink is devoted to dinners, dances and other functions as to medal scores.

Was it so different in Scotland? To begin with, yes. Since the clubs evolved out of a centuries-old tradition of playing the game, they were more concerned with organising golf matches than cheese and wine parties. But Scotland had its middle classes too and the same financial and social imperatives when it came to founding private golf clubs. Despite a wider public, municipal base than in England, the march of private clubs across Scotland was swift. By the 1890s, Glasgow only had two municipal courses (with twenty-seven holes between them), but no fewer than twenty private clubs. And existing clubs had already begun to crack and split under the strain of middle-class social rigidity. At Carnoustie, for example, the town's golf club 'invited' its more plebeian members to leave and form their own club. By the end of the century, Carnoustie had the original club, now populated exclusively by professionals and the gentry, the Dalhousie Club for the 'nouveau riche' businessmen from Dundee, a ladies' club, the Mercantile Club for men on a lower occupational rung, and finally the Caledonia Club, presumably for the real scruff who couldn't get into any of the others.

It is little wonder, then, that the clubs came to symbolise the snobbery many outside the sport associate with golf. But is it fair, more than a hundred years later, to tar all clubs with the same brush? After all, is this odyssey not about uncovering the reality of golf in Britain, looking beyond generalisations and lazy assumptions? I may be concentrating on low-cost, non-restrictive golf and the ordinary men and women who play it, but that does not mean I have to demonise all private, more expensive clubs in the passing.

It is easy to deride Stanmore or any other old golf club for the attitudes and behaviour of its founders, but at least it has had the courage to allow a full and frank account of its history to be written. Many clubs still frustrate sports historians and enthusiastic members with the time and energy to write their histories by refusing to cooperate and hand over the minutes, afraid of what their mad old non-PC members in 1900 might have gotten up to. Yet what club, sporting or otherwise, should be held responsible for its affairs in another age? No organisation dating from the nineteenth century would be able to say its membership policies or employment practices have always been up to twenty-first century standards. The important question is surely what are these clubs like now?

As I said at the outset of this journey, stuffy old repositories of Victorian attitudes still exist, but the fact is that the archetypal exclusive middle-class golf club is in decline, and has been really since the end of the First World War, when the first blow was dealt – a shortage of male members of the right social calibre, too many having been killed in France. Throughout the rest of the twentieth century, the gradual usurping of class distinctions by hard economic realities forced more and more clubs to relax membership criteria and cast their nets wider to ensure there were enough fees in the kitty and money behind the bar to pay for the upkeep of the clubhouse and the course.

It might be accurate, therefore, to say that all bad golf clubs are private, class-ridden institutions full of self-important gits who care more for social climbing than playing golf, but it certainly cannot equally be said that all private clubs are bad. Apart from anything else, the situation today is much more complicated than a simple split between the public and private sector. Not only are private clubs constituted in a variety of ways – Backworth Miners' Welfare, for example, is a non-profit-making charity – but there are clubs attached to council-operated courses, non-course-owning clubs, clubs within clubs, artisan clubs (more on them later) and, of course, that new phenomenon, the proprietary pay-and-play courses . . . with their own clubs. It is the latter that perhaps represents the greatest current threat to the traditional private members golf club. And one of them is next on the itinerary.

5

I've daydreamed about this moment for years. It's the B1024 and I must be getting close to the entrance on the left pretty soon now. I slow down and look around, trying to find anything familiar, a landmark of some sort, but this is deepest rural Essex and one field of wheat or oil seed rape looks pretty much the same as the next. Moreover, although I'm still in the slightly flat corner of Englandshire, I can't see very far, on account of the hedgerows (I thought there was supposed to be a shortage of these things) that are so high I can barely make out anything beyond the road.

At last, there it is – a sweeping, landscaped entrance to *the Essex*? Wait a minute, I thought it was called Earls Colne? And where did the big security gatehouse and barrier come from? Oi! Who moved the aerodrome? I thought it was over there. Come to think of it, where's the golf course? It should be right in front of me, but I can't see a thing because somebody's planted a bloody great conifer hedge in the way. OK, don't panic, all I do is follow the road round to the left here and, yup, there's the driving range and over here should be . . . that can't be right. The clubhouse was never *that* size. It's huge.

Honestly, some people have no respect for a person's memories.

It was ten years ago and I was plying my trade with the *East Anglian Daily Times*, living in Colchester and filing copy for the Essex edition. My golf to date had been limited to boyhood nine-hole rounds with my dad's old bats at Alexandra Park, the local municipal in Glasgow, and later excursions with mates down to Troon's excellent public courses (tee-off at nine, finish the round by midday, put clubs in the station's left luggage, embark on a ten-hour pub crawl, then catch the last train home, hopefully not being too bladdered to remember the clubs). Oh, and the occasional, wistful trip to a driving range off the A40 in the two years Marian and I lived in London. We moved out to Essex and there I had access to a number of golf courses, a set of fifty-year-old blade and persimmon clubs inherited from Marian's aunt and the sudden desire to play the game properly. Not wishing to be left out, the aforementioned significant other decided to take up the game as well. Colchester Golf Club was too expensive and, anyway, had a long waiting list, and the only other possible venue in the town was a little place called Birch Grove.

This was a really attractive nine-hole course, quite close to where we lived, but, again, it was a private club and, although the green fees for visitors were reasonable, it was neither the friendliest nor the most liberal of establishments. Marian, a corporate lawyer in the City given to working for days on end with only coffee and a change of pants to keep her going, arrived for a game with me at Birch Grove one Saturday and was promptly refused entry on the grounds that she was 'a woman and the course is reserved for those who work during the week'.

I fancy nipping over later today to see if the dent made in the door by the back of the secretary's head is still there.

And so it was to Earls Colne, a new pay-and-play golf complex half an hour's drive away, that we went to take some lessons and hack, slice, hook and dunch our way through those painful early days of trying to play the game properly. It had only been open a couple of years before we got there and, in truth, was not in the most attractive of locations, stuck between a small industrial estate and an aerodrome. But it didn't charge the earth and had a friendly, welcoming air about it. It boasted a driving range, nine-hole course, with more under construction, and the full eighteen-hole 'championship' course, as well as other activities I only vaguely remember. There may have been a gym and a tennis court but, not being interested in such fripperies, I can't be sure.

For two years, I slowly but surely graduated from the range to the nine-hole to the eighteen-hole course. More than happy to play on my own and avoid inflicting my rudimentary skills on anyone else, I stole down here at every opportunity my shifts on the paper allowed and have very happy memories of making my first decent contact with the ball, beginning to sink putts and, ever so slowly, lowering my scores – all the while with an English summer sun beating down on my back. (That last bit can't be true, but you know what fond memories are like.) Nevertheless, the eighteen-hole course is, or at least was, a monster full of lakes and punishingly long holes. I lost any record of what my personal best here was, but have long dreamed of coming back with a game honed and matured on the ancient links of East

Lothian to show my old stomping ground what I can do now.

As I try to find somewhere to park, it is obvious the place has gone from strength to strength (part of my justification for coming back to investigate) because the car park is packed – and this is lunchtime on a Tuesday. James Gathercole, the smart young golf operations manager, meets me in the bustling reception area-cum-golf shop and apologises that we won't be able to have that chat we'd arranged until later in the day. In the meantime, why doesn't he try and squeeze me in for a round with someone teeing off in the next half hour? Squeeze me in? I used to turn up here unannounced and walk on to the first tee with just about the entire course to myself. I resist the urge to say, 'It wasn't like this in my day, y'know,' and get my clubs out the car. I'm walking to the first tee when James heads me off and informs me that the front nine is now the back nine and vice versa. 'It wasn't like this in my day, y'know,' I tell him.

The course is playing host to a corporate bash sponsored by a local MG Rover dealership and a few of their latest models are parked on the lawn in front of the clubhouse bar and restaurant. When I reach the tee, James introduces me to Sean and Mike, who are just about to head off for their round. They are more than happy to have me tag along. It turns out that neither are attached to MG Rover, indeed Sean is scathing about their cars and has to be shushed by Mike as he cracks loud jokes about the winner getting a new Rover, second place getting two, third three and so on. The handful of sales reps near the tee are clearly no strangers to the gym and are scowling under their brutally gelled hair. Like Mike,

I am relieved when we finally get teed off and under way.

The tenth – sorry, first – at Earls Colne – sorry, the Essex – is a 547-yard par five that doglegs right uphill with a lake and trees on the left and out of bounds and an even bigger lake on the right. It has a huge bunker in the middle of the fairway just at second shot range and plays to a small, raised green well guarded by more bunkers. It is not one of the more difficult holes on the course.

At last summer has arrived and it is warm and sunny with only a slight breeze. I've slapped on the factor eight and am really looking forward to a great day on the sun-baked fairways of my golfing youth. I hit my first drive and decide the sun-baked semi-rough will have to do for the moment. I'm off to the left, Mike is safely on the fairway and Sean has sliced his into the lake. They are sharing a buggy, while I am pulling my clubs in a trolley so, between them being on one side of the fairway and me being on the other, and Sean driving like Schumacher even when we are within a few yards of each other, it is only when we reach the green that there is any scope for conversation. Mike, in his late fifties, hails from Hartlepool, while Sean, in his thirties, is a local lad. Sean is engaged to Mike's daughter and the prospective in-laws are down for a visit. It is clearly not their first trip south and I am relieved to see that they are more than comfortable in each other's company – no 'I think we can give you that putt, *Dad*', 'Well, thank you my boy – y'know our kid didn't make such a bad choice after all.'

In fact, it isn't long before they are effing and blinding like a couple of old pals and, although I have never quite gotten used to inter-generational swearing, I realise I could've done a lot worse for a pair of playing companions.

On in regulation, I then three-putt for a bogey six while Mike makes a tidy par and Sean records a double bogey seven. I put the putter back in the bag and turn to pass on some inane memory of the last time I played that hole, but all I see is a cloud of dust as Sean floors the throttle and speeds off to the next tee. Eh . . . ah, right. This happens throughout our round, but my annoyance doesn't last that long. After all, what's the point in hiring a buggy and then crawling along at walking pace? I am the one who has gate-crashed their two-ball and it is up to me to make sure I keep pace.

Mike and I play solidly to the green of the next, a shortish par four, while Sean, again, has sliced and hooked his way down the hole. I think it's his fifth shot that finds a bunker to the left of the green, from where he makes two hopeless attempts to extricate himself. Mike has seen enough and gives him some tips about opening the blade of his sand wedge, taking sand before ball etc. And, as if by magic, Sean pops his ball out of the bunker . . . over the green and into the bunker on the other side. As if to prove that was no fluke, he then gets out of that bunker in one go. Armed now with a reliable bunker technique, he is well equipped to get himself out of the original bunker again – and this he does, taking great care not to return once more to the second bunker. Which would be his fourth, if you follow. Unfortunately he achieves his goal by flying over both the green *and* that bunker and landing under a bush with absolutely no shot whatsoever. My admiration for him grows when he nevertheless takes a few more swipes, manages to get the ball out, chips on to the green and two-putts for something closer to the par for the entire front nine, rather than just that hole.

On the next tee I decide to take Sean's mind off his troubles by asking about his job. Not the usual tactic, I grant you, but I figure there surely can't be anything in his life that gives him more grief than his golf game. Besides, he's wearing a gold, jewel-encrusted watch and is constantly pushing buttons on one of those Blackberry mobile phone/email things. He has to be good at something. Thankfully, my guess is right and the enquiry makes him beam as if suddenly lit from within. Out puffs the chest and he's off. 'Run my own software firm . . . technology . . . niche market . . . great team . . . automotive industry . . . interesting meetings with Ford coming up . . .'

Sean rattles all this off as if we've just met at some conference somewhere and we're networking with name badges on our lapels and glasses of warm Soave in our hands. I'm sure he's delivered exactly the same instant verbal CV a hundred times and he is clearly chuffed by his success. For a precious minute or two, we escape the harsh reality of a day off to play golf and chat happily about intellectual property rights and the importance of brand recognition in a congested market place. Mike, however, is a hard man and calls time on our wool-gathering by driving off and splitting the fairway at the next.

The third hole is a brutal par four of 450 yards that always plays longer, being into the prevailing wind and slightly uphill. You can also touch the trees on either side of the fairway by just holding your arms out. This is where Sean loses his second ball of the round and almost his third, after his drop and shot takes him from trees on the right to rough on the left. Eventually we find his ball about twenty yards back from where he said he hit it – a scenario that is repeated several times during the round, Sean always adamant he's hit it a lot further than he actually has.

This part of the course runs alongside the access road and was always a particular trial for a beginner like me. Drivers would stop as I prepared to tee-off or hit from the fairway – whether out of courtesy or an unwholesome interest in watching people screw up I don't know, but it was enough to put me off. I have vague memories of some spindly little twigs running down the edge of the road and, though I accept *leylandii* is not the most popular plant in England, I would guess golfers at the Essex at least are grateful for its remarkable vigour. Those twigs have grown in ten years into the thick, twenty-foot hedge now separating the road from the course.

The hedge, of course, is not the only thing planted in what was previously a potato field and, before that, a Second World War American airbase. In those first few years, I may not have been crowded off the course by fellow golfers, but I could usually rely on having to stop at least once to let Eric and whatever tree he'd decided to shift pass by. Eric Hobbs, the farmer-turned-golf course proprietor who had owned the land since 1965, had a new toy – a large orange tractor with massive hydraulic arms designed to tear trees out of the ground and re-plant them in the new desired location. The big stuff had already been done; the old runways had been broken up and used as hardcore for the Kelvedon by-pass, fourteen lakes had been dug and something like 100,000 tonnes of topsoil shifted to create hills and valleys. Eric had also stuck in forty miles of drainage pipe and planted around 6,500 trees. Now he was fussing over the final touches. Like a butler straightening napkins and dessert spoons before a banquet, Eric spent weeks roaming round the course planting a pine here, moving a willow from there to there, standing back for a look, then changing his mind and shifting them back. It was never wise to take your yardages off a particular tree – it probably wouldn't be there the next time you played the hole.

I also seem to remember something about the amount of stones and boulders removed to make the fairways – and thinking it wasn't nearly enough. If truth be told, all Eric's money and effort had gone into building a pretty grim golf course. Not only did it look like some hasty bit of landscaping designed to make a new airport runway acceptable to the nimbies – the aforementioned lakes were little more than big, muddy puddles and the trees were all scrawny saplings – but it just didn't play properly. I had liked it well enough but, at such a formative stage in my game, I would have liked anywhere that didn't charge much and provided the seclusion to perform my grotesque interpretations of a golf swing in privacy. Better golfers I invited along were uniformly unimpressed and, even as a high twenty-odd-handicapper, I had to admit the clay soil fairways lurched from mud bath in rain to concrete in dry.

It is bone dry today, as the amount of dust Schumacher is kicking up with his buggy testifies, and it hasn't rained, I am told, for more than a week, yet the fairways are quite giving to the club. I also haven't suffered a weird bounce or an elbow-jarring strike off a stone just under the surface and I am beginning to suspect the changes effected to the course in my absence have been more than cosmetic. We've reached the seventh tee, Sean having lost his third ball at the sixth and me having racked up a triple bogey thanks to pulling my approach and having to drop out from under a bush.

While Sean batters out an email with one finger and explains to someone back at the office that he can't be in four places at the one time, I grab the chance to chat to Mike. A toolmaker who worked his way into management, Mike's fortunes took a turn for the worse some years ago when his company folded and he lost his job. After a spell on the dole he accepted an offer to go back on the shop floor and he's been there ever since, operating a lathe and counting down the years to his retirement.

'I suppose I've gone full circle,' he says. 'I'm grateful for the job, but to be honest I'm just serving my time until when I can afford to retire.'

When, no doubt, he will be able to improve an already very tidy golf game. Can I assume that a toolmaker from Hartlepool would share the views of those at Backworth that golf is no longer an elitist sport – if it ever was one?

'Oh aye. There's all sorts play the game now,' he says. 'It's not as expensive as it used to be – the clubs and that are much cheaper, if you go for decent second-hand stuff, and there's places like this that let you in no matter how badly you play.'

I haven't paid for my round yet, since I was viewed as a guest of management by the staff and there was a bit of a rush to get me on the first tee, and Mike can't tell me the cost of golf here because he's always been a guest of Sean's. I think of all the gyms, swimming pools and indoor tennis facilities I caught glimpses of as I arrived and wonder if I am perhaps straying a little off the right-eous path of cheap and cheerful I had pledged to follow.

It certainly all looks a deal more expensive than anywhere else I've been so far, and certainly more up-market than when I was here ten years ago. Sean arrives on the tee, but he has a determined air about him and I decide questions about how much money this torture is costing might not go down too well.

I don't know whether it was that phone call or the last lost ball, but he stares down this par three with a steely gaze and a set jaw. A fresh ball is placed on the tee, an eight-iron is pulled from his bag and he sets himself up with a lot more care over grip and stance than I've seen previously. As he slowly takes the club back, I am wondering whether I should tell him it isn't his honour when suddenly the earth shakes, there is a 'wump' like the sound of distant artillery and Sean's ball is arching high towards the green.

'Shot,' say Mike and I in unison, with perhaps a touch more surprise in our tone than Sean would've liked. He's still holding on to the finishing pose, largely because the ball is still going up. And up. When it finally does come down it is well past the green, dangerously close to some trees. I double-check the yardage – 156 – and I reckon he's flown it nearer 170. With an eight-iron. This isn't lost on Sean, either, and he shows absolutely no concern at having missed yet another green and possibly losing another ball. He leaves the tee with the satisfied smile of he who has just had his manhood tested and not been found wanting. I'm sure if he thought it appropriate at this point he would deliver a growl. Thankfully, his ball is not lost – but he still racks up another double bogey – while Mike uncharacteristically three-putts and I recover from a shoved tee shot (I'm not saying what club I used) to save par.

Everyone has a disaster at the next. I take five to get on to the green of a par five and then give myself a ten-foot putt for bogey simply because I am in a hurry to catch up with Mike and Sean, who are already heading through the trees to the next tee, having both lost balls and given up on the hole. The ninth is scarcely a happier event, Sean's mobile going off at the top of my back-swing causing me to yank my drive left into the lake, while my playing partners sclaff and scuff their way rather absent-mindedly down the fairway and almost casually putt out for varying degrees of bogey. I'm prepared for them announcing it was a nine-hole round today, but to my surprise they charge on past the same collection of MGs and their attendant sales reps towards the tenth tee. Right, I say to myself, let's make this a game of two halves. As it turns out, that is precisely what I have – but I hadn't planned on the front nine being the better of the two.

A triple bogey eight at the tenth sets the tone for a couple of hours of frankly awful play from me. I am already hot and footsore from yomping after Sean and Mike's buggy. The tuna sandwich I had in a pub not far from the course was clearly not enough and I am feeling decidedly hungry. And let's not forget the sleepless fallout from my scientific test to see if Rennies can dowse the flames of pepperoni and chillies – they can't. That's all the excuses I can muster, but it still doesn't ease the pain of turning back the clock to the days of my golfing apprenticeship in more ways than I had anticipated. I'm back where it all began for me – and I'm back playing like a beginner.

On the thirteenth, Schumacher takes a detour to the tee and tries to run down a small flock of Canada geese gathered by a pond. 'You have to be careful with these things. They can really go for you,' says Sean, as he speeds off leaving me, on foot, to deal with a collection of pissed off looking geese. I make the same soothing (I hope) noises I use to pacify dogs and small children, give them a wide berth and make it safely to the tee. I ask through gritted teeth whether Sean has a particular interest in geese.

'Only to shoot them, and they take a lot of killing, those things,' he says, shouldering the head of his driver and taking imaginary pot shots. 'I shoot game mostly – pheasant, partridge, that sort of thing. I'm quite a good shot.'

'Just as well,' says Mike, 'cos you don't shoot any birdies on the golf course.'

This is true of all of us as the back nine, which is even longer than the front, unfolds. It has three par fives and specialises in demanding drives over switchback lakes and bunkers placed helpfully in the middle of the fairways. Slowly I realise that part of my problem is that many of these obstacles are now in range. Whereas in yesteryear all I could manage was playing short of them, hopping over or around and banking on a single putt for par, today I have probably been in more sand and water than I had in all my previous rounds here put together.

By the time we reach the seventeenth, Sean has lost a ball on each of the previous three holes and is watching as I tee up my trusty Titleist Pro VIx.

'Ever used the Srixon?' he asks. I say no and he pulls a fresh one from his bag (it must be like the Tardis in there) and urges that I give it a go. As I hesitate, he launches into an impassioned and technically detailed paean to the humble Srixon – how it flies just as far as the Callaway, has the drop and spin of the Pro VIx, the durability of a Top Flight and so on and so on. This from a man who rarely plays with the same ball two holes running. Still, I give it a crack and, sure enough, it flies pretty straightish and farish down the fairway. When I get to it and am about to pick it up, Sean zooms by and shouts, 'Keep it,' over his shoulder.

'Are you sure you can spare it,' I say under my breath as he heads off into the trees to look for the latest victim of his slice.

Remarkably, he finds it. Then *I* find it after his first attempt to get out of the woods fails. Mike keeps an eye on the ball as Sean's next effort gets even more snarled up in the trees before his fourth, in keeping with the Second Law of Lousy Golf, finds a tiny gap in the foliage, crests a huge greenside bunker, takes one bounce and lands on the top tier of the green, three feet from the pin. (The second law, by the way, is the one that explains the persistence, not to say masochism, of bad golfers. It states that not long before the end of a particularly painful round, when thoughts of giving up the game for good begin to press themselves upon a chap, he will execute a miraculous shot of such beauty and precision that he will be reassured he can play after all and only needs to come back for a little practice.)

Even this immutable law, however, is surely tested by Sean's performance on the eighteenth, a sweeping, snaking par five downhill, with trees, then water, on either side. At a rough estimate, the average golf hole should take about ten minutes to play. For a three-ball playing a par five, let's be generous and say fifteen minutes. The tantalising sight of the clubhouse in the distance only makes the 25 *minutes* we spend playing this hole looking in turn for three of Sean's balls – plus one of Mike's – almost unbearable. In inverse relation to his game, Sean has a particular dislike of losing golf balls and will take as much time and cover as large an area of wooded wilderness, standing water and bog as possible before abandoning one. By the time I stagger off the final green (with a par!) I am not only exhausted, hot and hungry, but wet from the knees down, covered in seeds and grass, and bleeding from a thorn wound on my left arm. As for my feet? It has been five hours since we teed off at the first and my dogs, as the Americans say, are barking. Sean and Mike apologise that they have to rush back for a dinner with their ladyfolk and can't stay for the traditional post-round pint. I hope I manage to sound disappointed.

I say that in all honesty because, despite sounding like every golfer's idea of the playing partner from hell, Sean was actually a really nice bloke. I admit his grasp of golf rules and etiquette was tenuous, to say the least (I haven't even mentioned his habit of talking while you're putting or his peculiar method of marking his ball on the green), but Mike never pulled him up about it and I didn't think it was my place to. I conclude that his golfing gaffes were through ignorance, not indifference to our sensibilities. Moreover, Sean always displayed courtesy when he thought it was called for, was generous in his comments and never let his obvious distress at his own game sour his mood and spoil the afternoon for everyone. Besides, it does us golfers good every now and then to be reminded that propriety and effectiveness on the course is not the be all and end all in this life. As the Oldest Member in PG Wodehouse's *The Heart of a Goof* says to his incredulous listener over a lemonade on the clubhouse veranda, there are 'men who have never broken 120 in their lives and yet contrive to be happy useful members of society'.

Over a refreshing lemonade of my own a little while later, I am reading the 7 June 1944 edition of *Stars and Stripes*, the American forces newspaper, and, not for the first time, wishing I had worked in the days before editors decided intros had to be short and to the point. *'UNLEASHING the full fury of Anglo-American air power, Allied aircraft yesterday bombed and strafed mile after mile of French beaches, seizing undisputed mastery of the air and heaping record-breaking tonnes of explosives on Nazi coastal installations in providing the greatest umbrella in history for the invasion force,'* the front page story begins breathlessly. Splendid stuff. As, indeed, is the rest of the memorabilia collected by Eric Hobbs and others at Earls Colne, now preserved in a large, bound album recording the history of the site and development of the course.

I am flicking through the pages and chatting with James Gathercole in a café overlooking a luxurious indoor pool. Earls Colne was opened as a military airfield in 1941 and taken over by the USAAF a year later. Everything from Flying Fortresses and Liberators to Marauder bombers and Mustangs flew from this corner of Essex to 'kick ass' over the Channel. Thanks to its one and a half mile-long runway (now supporting the A12) it was a crucial base in providing air support for the D-Day landings and subsequent push towards Berlin. Notable visitors (before today) have included Bob Hope and Glenn Miller.

Apart from the Second World War stuff, there are some more recent clippings from the *East Anglian Daily Times*; indeed from an old friend and colleague, Danny Wheeler. Never one, I remember, to undersell a story, Danny had gotten hold of some stats from the English Golfing Union in July 1991 about what needed to be done to satisfy the projected demand for golf in the county and informed the *EADT*'s no doubt outraged readership that 'Essex is in danger of being overwhelmed by fairways and bunkers'.

In fact, Essex, like the rest of the country, did experience a boom in golf course development in the early 1990s. Figures from the Golf Research Group show that between 1991 and 1995, a total of 434 new courses were opened in the UK – that is almost a 400 per cent increase on the previous four years – and all but a tiny handful of those were proprietary pay-and-play operations such as Earls Colne. A 1989 report from the R&A, *The Demand for Golf*, was partly to blame. It had predicted that 691 new golf courses needed to be built before 2000 just to satisfy demand and planning authorities came under pressure not to stand in the way of this expansion of 'vital' leisure facilities. Crucially, however, this analysis coincided with the wholesale withdrawal of many EU agricultural subsidies, forcing Eric Hobbs and hundreds of farmers like him to look for other ways to turn a profit from their land. Yet the fact is, most schemes foundered at the planning stage and of those that did eventually see the light of day, the vast majority (I've read up to 80 per cent) went bankrupt within the first few years, the result of either having been poorly built or simply located in rural areas that were too remote from a large enough customer base.

My memories of playing on the muddy/concrete fairways of Earls Colne, next to an industrial estate that this city boy at least considered to be the middle of nowhere, made me curious about how it had managed to avoid being one of those casualties. It turns out that Eric sold the ninety-nine-year lease in 1995 to Eddie Shah (the would-be newspaper magnate) who, at the time, was a shareholder in Wentworth and was acquiring a chain of new golf courses across the country. Shah renamed the course, revamped the clubhouse, adding a new gym, pool and tennis courts, and built the hotel that now sits behind what used to be the old first tee. He, in turn, sold it in 1999 to one of the biggest chains of pay-and-play golf courses in the country, Clubhaus, which promptly ripped the place apart again and updated the gym and spa. More importantly (from my point of view), it also brought in a new greenkeeper who was given the job of turning the course I remember into one that is actually half decent to play on. James couldn't recall the guy's name but, whoever he is, he did a hell of a good job. The quality of the turf is far better than it was and the greens have all been completely rebuilt and now drain well enough to allow play in all weathers, at all times of the year.

That, in a nutshell, is how Earls Colne survived when so many others of a similar breed fell by the wayside; it was bought out, re-branded and turned into a proper sports and leisure complex. And far from being in the middle of nowhere, James was quick to correct me it is close to not only Colchester, Coggeshall and Halstead, but also Braintree – for the last three years, Europe's fastest growing town (no doubt something to do with Stansted being built just up the road).

As for prices . . . well, I have to admit, it's all a wee

bit more expensive than I would've liked. A visitor turning up for a game will be charged £25 during the week and £30 at the weekend. For that reason alone, the Essex shouldn't really be included in a tour of low-cost golf courses. (Hey, but tough. I've already played the bloody course, it took me five hours, my playing partners lost a total of fourteen golf balls – all of which, of course, had to be hunted for before being abandoned – I played crap and am currently in pain from my throbbing feet to my stiff neck. *It's staying in.*) Far more reasonable are the packages on offer to members: £78.50 per month gets you a golf club membership that allows unlimited access to both eighteen-hole courses (the old nine-hole beginners' course was expanded) and any and everything else – gyms, pools, tennis etc. But who, today, I wonder, is the typical golfer at the Essex?

'If I had to generalise I would call him the modern dad,' says James. 'He, at least, is the guy who is joining the club. The pay-and-play market is much the same as it always was and, if I were to be honest, I don't think the top golfers are coming here.' The modern dad, he explains, is one who wants his weekly round of golf, but is not prepared (or allowed?) to leave the wife and family behind for half the day. The Essex, I am told, is a 'one-stop leisure destination for all the family', the type of place where the kids can be put in a crèche, leaving modern dad free to play golf, while modern mum has an affair with the tennis pro.

Although there are still memberships available, business is booming. In a curious reversal of the usual story of technological innovation, the Essex unplugged its computer-operated booking system and went back to biros and timesheets – and has increased efficiency so much it is filling 80 per cent of available tee-off times, as opposed to the 40 per cent it once did. It's something to do with hooking people up so there are more four-ball matches and fewer singles or even two-balls taking up tee-off times. (I'm sure that makes financial sense for the Essex, but if it means more five-hour rounds like the one I've just had, I'm glad this isn't my local course any more.)

Then James informs me that Colchester Golf Club, like most in the county, has scrapped its waiting list. 'Private clubs are waking up to places like this,' he says. 'The old days of clubs looking for the right sort are disappearing. Basically, if you have a golf handicap and two arms and two legs, you can join them.' The unfortunate implication of discrimination against amputees aside, it is a point well made. The explosion in proprietary golf courses at the tail end of the twentieth century has delivered perhaps a fatal blow to the restricted world of private golf clubs, a large proportion of which were founded in the last great wave of development exactly a hundred years before.

The mental effort involved in adding up the score, counting putts – even remembering the individual holes – is almost beyond me. I just manage to concentrate long enough to work out that I shot 89 today – sixteen over par and not far short of twice my handicap – before I drop the card in the remains of my chicken and black bean sauce and take another slug of warm beer. It is over three hours since I left the Essex and I am not where I expected to be.

Continuing the memory lane theme of the day, I took the road from the course back through a string of quaint little Constable Country villages towards Colchester. Once there, and having driven round for a bit, checking out our old house and some familiar landmarks, I started looking for a hotel or a B&B. Half an hour later and on my third sweep through the town on its truly infuriating one-way system, I had to admit defeat. I had caught sight of one hotel on the High Street, but a new road layout narrowing it to one lane made it impossible to stop, especially with a queue of petrol heads at my back all gunning the engines of their luminous banana yellow Golfs and hot rod Escorts.

Out of town would have to do and I headed east vaguely thinking of Clacton or Frinton, but the first mileage sign reminded me of just how far away those places are and I was already seriously tired and hungry, so I ducked off the A133 and drove down to Wivenhoe, a pleasant wee village I remembered on the estuary of the River Colne. Half an hour later, having negotiated several sets of roadworks going in and coming out, I had learned there is nowhere to stay in Wivenhoe (nowhere, at least, that cares to advertise its existence with so much as a sign) and no one even on the street I could ask.

I headed back towards Colchester, but took the A12 and resigned myself to another expensive night, this time at a Holiday Inn I knew near Stanway, but it was full, and so was the other big hotel I knew at Marks Tey, further down the road. By now I was well on my way towards Chelmsford – ah well, I thought, I know I'm going to London sooner or later, I may as well head in that general direction.

If Colchester's one-way system is confusing, at least it's slow. I had absolutely no chance of keeping an eye open for accommodation in Chelmsford, because its dual carriageways and roundabouts, especially at that time of the evening, are clearly reserved for local racing drivers, trainee stuntmen and the suicidal. At one point I made a split-second decision not to carry on round a particular roundabout and turned left instead to come off at the next exit. At that exact moment a motorbike shot straight across my bows and beat me to it. Had I not turned the steering wheel a nanosecond earlier, he would have been pureed all over the road and, more importantly, the discourtesy car would have lost its offside front wing.

I got out of there as fast as I could, missed the sign for the A12 and found myself on a little road heading for Margaretting. OK, I thought, a village inn or B&B will do. Only Margaretting doesn't have one. Neither does Ingatestone or Heybridge or Mountnessing. I found my way back on to the A12 and decided one of those ubiquitous chain travel inn, lodge-type places would have to be the last resort. And, sure enough, I came across two of them as I sped ever closer to London. And both of them were full.

By now it was after 9p.m. and I was inside the M25. Essex had one last chance to provide me with a meal and bed for the night – the Premier Lodge in Romford.

'Sorry mite, we's full up,' said the girl behind the desk. I must have visibly crumpled before her, because she took pity and offered to see if the Travelodge in Ilford had a room for me. I dragged a smile up from somewhere and she went on the phone. 'Allow bibe, 's'availability innit,' she said to someone who presumably understood what that meant. Yes, the Travelodge had a room and 'bibe' was going to keep it for me. Hussar!

Armed with the girl's directions involving the A18 and

the A136 – neither of which I was soon to discover actually existed, at least anywhere near there – I nevertheless followed my nose and found my way to Ilford. I say 'followed my nose' advisedly because the High Street, I saw to my delight, is an Aladdin's cave of kebab shops, Chinese takeaways, Indian restaurants, burger bars and every other kind of savoury delight you can imagine. It was now almost eleven hours since that tuna sandwich and as I drove down the street with the window open I was drooling so much my lap was getting wet.

But no bloody Travelodge! I filled up with petrol at a garage and asked the guy behind the desk for directions and he drew a map on the back of my receipt that was simply unintelligible. I made one more mouth-watering pass of the High Street, then back out the other side to where I had seen one or two less than salubrious-looking establishments on the way in.

The chap at one of these hotels said he could give me a room for the night and only imminent collapse prevented me from hurdling the desk and showering him with kisses. Obviously able to spot a starving man at twenty paces, he then delighted me by saying that once I had selected what I wanted from the menu, 'they' would bring it to my room and I could also get a drink from the bar. I honestly didn't think it looked like the kind of place that would still be serving food at that time, nor that it would have room service. And I was right.

The menu in question was from a Chinese takeaway and 'they' delivered it to my room only after I'd ordered more food than I wanted just to get it over the minimum charge. The drink from the bar (a desolate room that tried for that continental *al fresco* feel by allowing the punters to drink straight from the can), I got for myself –

two warm bottles of Budweiser was the best it could offer – and now I am sitting on the floor of my room. That is because the room features three beds that take up almost the entire floor space, a TV high on the porridge-coloured walls, but no table or chairs. To add to a dozen aches and pains, my bum has just gone numb, I have a crick in my neck from craning to see the telly and am getting gas pains from the egg fried rice and beer. It is time for bed.

The boy racers are doing speed trials outside my window and the 'reassuring' huge metal plate and double lock on the door fails to keep out the noise of men and women involved in who knows what kind of negotiations on the landing. Meanwhile, TV sets are blaring and doors are slamming all over the building, but I only hear it all for the half a second it takes for my head to hit the pillow.

6

After a few minutes of general milling around the putting green, meeting old acquaintances and swapping business cards with new ones, we all begin matching up and making our way down to the starter's hut. The IT manager shakes hands with the police superintendent who, in turn, greets the systems and information manager, and they all welcome the journalist on to the first tee to make up the four-ball. Summer is still struggling to assert itself and a warm sun occasionally lights up the course, but it's the wind that's concentrating our minds. Strong and gusty, it is roaring through the poplars and silver birches, bending their heavily leafed branches alarmingly and covering the fairways with an almost autumnal harvest of leaves and twigs. More ominously, the forecast suggests it will be pushing in heavy rain from the west and we know there is no guarantee we will finish our rounds before it hits.

But, it's a day out of the office and everyone is determined to make the most of it. Wyboston Lakes lends itself to this kind of golf society networking. A little over half an hour's drive from London up the A1, it is not unlike the Essex, being a modern pay-and-play venue with plenty of facilities for conferences, other sporting pursuits or just relaxing off the course in nice bars and restaurants. Although privately owned, it is listed as 'public' in the *Golfer's Handbook* and is a deal cheaper than the Essex, with a weekday round costing just £14 – or less if you take one of the many corporate/society packages on offer.

The first is a par five dogleg right at ninety degrees around one of the eponymous lakes. Remarkably, only one of our number finds the water, but it is still a tough opener and I'm pleased to sink a long putt to save par. There is a bit of a wait on the second tee and I get chatting to Herman, the systems and information manager, who, after explaining exactly what he does for a London borough's housing department (all of which goes right over my head), looks me squarely in the eye and says firmly, 'But I'm not a techie.' Obviously the land of computing is experiencing some tension between the tribes of technicians, programmers and managers; fine lines to be drawn, differentials to be defended. I give him a look that says, 'Of course you're not a techie, old man. Why, the very cut of your jib would make such a presumption laughable,' and he seems pleased enough.

So we chat on for a bit about his golf and how often he gets to play (the answer, of course, is 'not often enough') and what he likes about the game.

'I love the challenge of golf,' says Herman, 'but the best thing is it takes up three or four hours of the day. I know that's why some people *don't* play it, but I just love getting away, out of the house or the office, for that length of time.'

A short par four at around 340 yards, the second hole nevertheless has an interesting defence for its green – two enormous, mature trees growing side by side right in front. I belt a splendid drive as far as I can and that leaves a bump and run that I can send in under the branches. My playing partners, however, are in several types of trouble. Ray, for example (he's the cop), has pulled his drive into the trees on the left and is in a horrible lie. He has a number of options, it seems to me, but even before I have begun to compile a mental list, he has a club out of his bag and is hacking and thrashing away in increasing despair. Since Ray is a very, *very* big man with more muscle on his arms and shoulders than I have ever seen on anyone outside of a boxing ring, this makes for a compelling, but still frightening, spectacle. From his first lash, the three of us start backing off to give him all the room he wants. Eventually it pops out on to the fairway and Ray offers a weak smile and marches after it.

Keen to sound supportive and encouraging, I compliment the strapping twenty-five-handicapper on his impressive power off the tee as we are walking off the green a little while later.

'I'd swap for your short game any day,' he tells me as we head down the path towards the third. 'I don't know what goes wrong the closer I get to the hole.'

He is looking enquiringly straight at me and I realise with a shudder that this is a question that he wants me, the better golfer, to answer for him. This, however, is not Portobello and man mountain here is not my harmless pal Denis. Although I am to discover in the course of the round that Ray is a genuinely gentle giant, at this moment I am not prepared to start offering swing tips to a policeman who looks like he could snap me over his knee at the first sign of my advice being in the slightest bit duff.

'What was that, Herman?' I quickly shout over Ray's shoulder. 'Yes, a four for me. Now let's see, what did you get . . .' And I hurry over to immerse myself in an intense study of our scorecards.

The third is only 110 yards long and today is downwind. This is where we are playing for that mainstay of the golfing society outing – nearest to the pin. Although extremely short, the hole is far from toothless; the small green rises beyond a pond after which there is a thin stretch of rough and then more water. I have the honour and try to massage a wedge to the right distance, but just succeed in finding the front edge of the green. I suspect only the strong tail wind is stopping it from rolling back down into the water and I start cajoling everyone else to play their shots quickly, so I can race round and mark my ball. The ball, however, does not seem in any great hurry to move, which is fortunate as several minutes later I am still standing by the tee trying to mask my anxiety over its fate with concern and sympathy for my three playing partners, every one of whom has just plopped their first shots into the pond.

'Maybe nearest to the pin was a bit ambitious,' says Ray. 'We should have had a nearest to the green competition.'

Three off the tee, then, for everyone and, by the end of the hole, only Donovan, the fourth member of our match, has managed to squeeze so much as a double bogey out of it. I have parred again and am beginning to feel quite friendly towards my game once more, after it let me down so badly at the Essex. No doubt subconsciously scarred by the experience of trailing after Sean and Mike all that day, I have gone against one of my most dearly held golfing tenets of faith and accepted Herman's offer to join him in a buggy, but as we head down the winding path to the fourth tee, I get out to stretch my legs and chat with Donovan.

He is an instantly likeable, slightly built guy who laughs at his own game (he was the one who splashed into the lake off the first and celebrated this by high-fiving with everyone on the tee) and offers words of encouragement, congratulation and commiseration at each and every turn. However, as an IT manager for a major bank, I have the strongest suspicion that he might be 'a techie'.

'I'm supposed to be working today, but my mate's covering for me. I'm still on call, but it's OK, the mobile's on vibrate,' he says patting his pocket.

His job appears to involve, among other things, ensuring that all the bank's ATMs remain up and running. Something, he tells me with a trademark grin, they failed to do a few days ago. A brief description of what had gone wrong and how they'd fixed it convinces me that Donovan is indeed a techie and – I admit to absolutely no expertise in these matters – probably a bloody good one.

Like Ray, however, this twenty-four-handicapper has fingered me as the golfing expert. We meet up a few minutes later after my drive at this tight dogleg right has found position *a* (of course) and everyone else is scattered to the left and right.

'Do you have to be actually over the line to be out of bounds?' he asks me.

'I believe so, yes.'

'And what if your ball is in a hole a rabbit made?'

'You get relief.'

'Ah. Looks like I could've saved myself a few strokes back there.'

I defy any other golfer to be told he's just taken at least three unnecessary strokes on a hole and grin as good-naturedly as Donovan does. I can't make my mind up whether he's got the perfect temperament for golf . . . or just doesn't understand the bloody game.

Back in the buggy I take the chance, while Ray and Donovan struggle to reach the green, to bring up the issue that prompted me to gatecrash their golf day in the first place.

'Oh, I think it's still a problem,' says Herman, 'but it shows itself in different ways. To be honest, it's probably a good few years since any of us felt a bit apprehensive on the first tee. Y'know, kind of self-conscious. And maybe even then it was just a little paranoia.'

Over four weeks in 1960, the *Jewish Chronicle* ran an investigation into discrimination against Jews in golf clubs. While discovering that the majority of clubs across the country operated no official policy of barring Jews, there were plenty that did – and few of them were in the slightest bit abashed about it.

'We haven't any Jews. If a Jew applied it is likely he would be refused. Once you let them in they'll control the club,' said one club secretary.

Other enlightened comments included: 'The general view is that Jews have their own club. The feeling among our members is that Jews would not be welcome' . . . 'We would not say we bar Jews. We just prefer not to take them' . . . 'A golf club is the extension of one's home; the election of new members is purely a domestic matter' . . . 'To do business with Jews is a necessary evil, but there must be some place where one can be free of them.'

And all of this just fifteen years after the horrors of Auschwitz and Belsen were broadcast to the world. What is worse, perhaps, than the bigotry displayed by individual clubs is the fact that one of those quotes, the one about membership being a purely domestic matter, came from Captain WGL Folkard, then secretary of the English Golf Union (EGU). Like the rest of the sport's administrative bodies at that time, the EGU did not actively support discrimination – but it was determined to do absolutely nothing to stop it.

Needless to say, Geoffrey Cousins takes a patronising, not to say insulting, view of the matter in his book written a further fifteen years later: 'One of the difficulties in the past has been the conflict between the flamboyant and luxurious tastes of Jewish golfers and the comparatively conservative attitude of gentile club members. Having visited many Jewish clubs over a period of many years, I know that generally they are run more efficiently than the majority of other clubs. This is not surprising given the keen business instincts of Jews ... *It follows that any gentile club admitting Jews in large numbers would be likely to find life more difficult and more expensive* [my italics].'

The issue of expense refers to one of the more intriguing criteria often cited for preventing large numbers of Jews joining a club; they don't drink as much as we do. The 'logic' went like this – Jews, because they are culturally indisposed to knocking back too many whiskies at the nineteenth hole then driving home over the limit like normal people, do not spend enough money at the bar. Since most clubs rely on bar takings to keep themselves solvent, they would be forced to find other sources of funds and that would probably mean increasing membership fees. A sterling defence of the indefensible there; we're not racists – we're piss-heads.

John Lowerson, writing in *Scottish Sport in the Making*

of the Nation (1994), reveals that anti-Semitism was just as prevalent in Glasgow golf clubs (as well as that peculiar West of Scotland fondness for excluding Catholics) and that Jewish golfers finally formed their own club at Bonnyton. 'Then [the club] added insult to injury by instigating an open admissions policy.' Jewish golf clubs, in fact, began to spring up across the UK wherever there was a large Jewish community. Although keen to integrate themselves into 'normal' British suburban society, all they really wanted was the same as any club member – the chance to play the game and socialise at ease with their peers, and if they have to be all Jews, then so be it.

Even forty years ago, however, many Jews were unhappy at the attention being drawn to the issue, believing it would only serve to fan the flames of intolerance. Today, the suspicion among academics is that a low level of discrimination against Jews still stalks the members' lounges of some British golf clubs, but the Jewish community itself seems even more determined to either deny or dismiss it. Indeed, my enquiry with the Jewish Council for Racial Equality was met with some derision.

'If you want to know about racial discrimination in golf today, look at the blacks and Asians,' said the woman on the telephone. 'What we experienced in the past is probably what they are going through today.'

And that is why I am here at Wyboston Lakes with Herman Lewis, founder of Unitee Golf, one of three golfing societies based in London aimed mainly at the Afro-Caribbean community. Herman, whose parents came from Jamaica (and, in fact, have recently returned), is not convinced, however, that exact parallels can be drawn between the experience of Jews forty-odd years ago and that of ethnic minorities today.

'For one thing, I think the country is far more aware of the whole issue,' he says. 'People of colour still encounter racism from time to time, but the opportunities to actually discriminate are not what they were years ago.'

In the real world that may be so, but some golf clubs – the truly private ones which do not permit any access to members of the public – inhabit a manufactured little world of their own, a controlled environment where they have not only created a cosy retreat of manicured greens and leather armchairs, but where even certain laws of the land don't apply – like the Sex Discrimination Act of 1975. As private membership clubs, while they still must operate an equal opportunities policy for hiring staff, they have an exemption under the Act when it comes to electing their members. So long as their written constitution says it is a single sex club, they can keep the memsahibs out with impunity. Contrary to popular opinion, however, the same does not apply with regard to the 1976 Race Relations Act. The only private clubs that can deliberately remain all-Anglo-Saxon or, for that matter, all-Afro-Caribbean or Serbo-Welsh, are those with memberships of no more than twenty-five. This is hardly the basis for a financially viable as well as racially 'pure' operation, yet it remains a fact that there are far more all-white golf clubs than all-male ones. A formal, written policy of discrimination would be illegal, but the suspicion lingers that in more than a few cases this mono-chrome membership is no mere happenstance.

'I wouldn't know about club membership, because I'm not a member of a club myself and have not applied to join any,' says Herman. 'I don't think I'd get much from the social side of being in a club . . . I mean, it's all about feeling comfortable isn't it? OK, most of the clubs I've been to are perfectly alright, but some of them . . . y'know, it's just not going to be worth the hassle, is it?'

The Unitee event today, like the other summer days out Herman organises, is a stableford competition. I'm only playing as a guest and not eligible for any prizes, but my scoring is something like eleven points for five holes. Just in case it keeps going, I begin to prepare my argument for Scots being a racial minority in England. So far, however, most of the holes have been downwind and none of them have been terribly long. Waiting to tee off at the sixth, I ask Ray how he came across Unitee Golf.

'It was by accident. I happened to be at my club when these guys had arranged one of their events. I went into the clubhouse and saw all these black faces and I thought *alright* – this is great!'

Was it so unusual?

'Yeah. Well, of course we have some black members,' he laughs and points at himself, 'but I had just never seen so many black golfers in one place before – there were dozens of them. I could see they were attracting attention and I just thought this was a great opportunity to break down some social barriers, so I signed up.'

And with that he belts his fairway wood high over the trees of this dogleg right and lands in the perfect spot just short of the green, about 250 yards. I do my best to follow with my driver – taking the more conventional route round the corner with a slight fade – but I am still nowhere near his ball.

'You want my short game and I want to be able to hit a three-wood like that,' I say.

Immediately Donovan starts laughing. 'That's a nine-wood, man,' he says delightedly. 'That's all he needs.'

Ray smiles shyly and offers the sole of his club for confirmation. 'I can't hit a three-wood.'

The rest of the front nine features another nearest-to-the-pin competition on a much longer par three with a vicious crosswind – which Herman and I nevertheless manage to tame in some style (Herman goes on to win that prize) – and a couple of uninspiring par fours. I'm still playing steadily, but I confess to being a little distracted. Thinking back to what Herman and Ray had to say, I remember my own behaviour when I turned up at the course earlier in the day. Walking towards the pro shop I'd seen a black guy on the path and asked him if Herman had arrived yet. I was right that he was part of the Unitee Golf group – but I hadn't even asked. I had made an *assumption* because he was black and because you don't often see coloured people at golf courses. Even the starter, I had noticed, was automatically treating every black golfer there – very courteously, of course – as if they were part of the Unitee society. Nothing terribly wrong with that, except that it confirmed Wyboston Lakes probably doesn't see many non-white golfers.

Over the start to the back nine, Donovan, who runs his own golf (mixed race) society for men and women, tells me how he got started playing golf. He admits this 'white middle-class sport' was not something he and his mates in Catford were brought up with.

'It was a friend, a guy at work, that took some of us out for a round and we were just hooked. It wasn't like any other sport we'd played, y'know football or basketball. It was so hard to learn,' he breaks off to laugh at his own early experiences with the game.

'But now we're better at it and it's great taking other guys out and teaching them how to play – and how to behave, that's real important.'

Again, the preference is for a golfing society rather than a club.

'Yeah, well, it's cheaper if you don't get to play all that often,' says Donovan, 'and we get to play lots of different courses, mostly down Kent and Surrey way.'

I have a bit of a slip up at the tenth when I pull my drive into the water, but I fish it out and manage to escape with a bogey. Generally I am doing OK, but a glance at the clock as we reached the turn back at the clubhouse has shown that I am heading for another four-hour-plus round. Thank God I have some interesting guys to talk to, because it has to be said that, apart from perhaps the first two or three holes, Wyboston Lakes is one seriously dull golf course. Oh, it's got plenty of trees, lakes and ponds, but somehow the course designer has managed to get the very least out of these features. Not once in the round do you stand on the tee and feel inspired by the hole in prospect, faced as you are every single time by a flat, wide fairway between plantations of trees and the red stakes of lateral water hazards. Despite the rush of the gale blowing in the trees you can also hear the A1 as it runs down the course's western flank. It's in perfectly good nick – most of the bunkers have rakes and the greens are reasonably true – but even halfway through the round, when someone recalled something that happened at the fifth or the seventh hole, the rest of us would be struggling to remember what that actually looked like.

At the eleventh hole, Ray tears himself away from an explanation from Herman about how totally non-techie systems and information management is and booms another nine-wood past my best drive. Noticing that he hasn't used a tee peg, I rather peevishly point out that this is not only making his shot harder, but dishonouring the memory of George F Grant. Ray frowns for a second and I am suddenly uncomfortably conscious of the fact that he has arms as thick as my golf bag. Then he breaks into a knowing grin. 'I'm sure he wouldn't mind,' he says. 'I just find it easier this way.'

George F Grant, according to the blurb on Unitee's website, is the black American dentist who in 1899 invented and patented the wooden tee peg. For that reason the black tee is Unitee's logo. The website, in fact, is very professional – not unconnected to the fact that Herman is a systems and information manager, I suspect – and keeps the members up to date with their scores, handicaps and the events calendar. It also has a couple of snippets of interesting history.

Like that of George Simkins who, with his equally black friends in Greensboro, Georgia, liked to play a weekly game of golf on public courses in the area. Unfortunately, one day in 1955, they decided to play a course called Gillespie Park which, although owned by the city, was leased to a group of white citizens, thereby allowing the municipality to circumvent a Supreme Court ruling that public golf courses couldn't operate a colour bar. Simkins and his party were told they couldn't play, but they left their green fees on the counter anyway and went off to play their nine holes. After which they were promptly arrested, charged with trespassing and given a thirty-day jail sentence. An appeal to the Superior Court was lost and in the Federal Court a judge ruled in their favour. The order was given for Gillespie Park to be opened to all races, but before that could be enforced someone broke into the clubhouse and burned it to the ground. The city refused to rebuild it and shut the entire course down.

I suppose, it being a story from the Southern States before the equal rights movement got going, we are lucky it didn't end with Simkins and the rest of his four-ball being lynched, but I ask Herman whether, apart from being excluded from certain clubs, blacks and Asians in this country suffer from any racism, any abuse, either on or off the course.

'You might be surprised by this, but discrimination doesn't really come up as a topic for discussion among us,' he replies. 'I, myself, have only really had one bad experience. I'd walked on to the first tee ahead of another group by mistake and one of the guys shouts: "In this country we queue." But like I said, it's getting better. We're not feeling so different any more.'

It begs the question, then, why have a golf society for people of colour in the first place?

'Why does any group have societies and clubs?' responds Herman. 'We find that we have a lot in common. There's a shared experience in our upbringing – we're all mostly second generation immigrants – and, even if we've never met before, we find something that binds us together.'

By the time we reach the thirteenth, however, the binding is a little loose for Herman's liking and he is glancing behind him anxiously. We are the second four-ball out and there are supposed to be another seven behind us, yet we haven't seen anyone following on for about an hour now.

'There was that tricky bit when the path crossed over with the one we were on in the front nine,' he says. 'Do you think maybe they're all playing the same holes over again?'

We reassure him that, despite the fact it might be hard

to tell on this boring golf course, nobody would be that stupid – and certainly not all twenty-eight of them. But it doesn't stop Herman behaving like a mother hen who's lost her chicks for the next few holes. Not that it's affecting his play. A seventeen-handicap with a solid swing, Herman has improved as the round has gone on and is now finding every fairway and green, making the putts and recording par-net birdies for an impressive late burst of stableford point scoring.

I, on the other hand, am definitely tiring; my drives are all getting a bit pullish and my deft lag putts are now accelerating as they pass the hole or stopping yards short. I've three-putted twice in the last few holes and I tell myself the only way I am going to avoid total collapse is by pulling my socks up over my girded loins and eating that melted half of a Mars bar in my golf bag.

As we head down the par five seventeenth, we feel the first spots of rain in the wind. Then someone looks at their watch and calculates we've been out for four and half hours – and we're not finished yet. The news hits Donovan badly. Twice he slices into the trees, then fights his way down the right-hand semi-rough, unable to muster the strength in a single shot to get himself out.

'I definitely need some food,' he says. 'Or lager. I can't decide which.'

Although Herman and I have scooted about all day in a buggy, the eighteenth cannot come soon enough. The smell of cooking wafting from the clubhouse does not help our concentration and we all make a hash of trying to get in that last flaming hole. Eventually the final triple bogey putt drops, we shake hands and head for the bar in a cross between a stagger and a dead run.

*   *   *

'Black people are passionate people, y'know? This is just the way we talk – we're full on and we're loud. We tend to get noticed.'

Coming from a guy with a huge leather Rasta cap covering his dreadlocks, his beard tied to look like a boy scout's woggle and a voice that could herd cattle, this statement is somewhat unnecessary. Leo is in expansive mood in the clubhouse. Wiping the froth of a Guinness from his mouth, he is keen to explain why he thinks coloured people draw attention to themselves in the otherwise peaceful surroundings of clubhouse bars. And, in doing so, does just that.

'We went into this clubhouse once, right? There were a load of us and we all goes in laughing and talking,' he grins and his eyes open wide. 'The club called the police! They thought we were going to start a fight and that it was going to kick off any minute. I mean, we were just having a good time, y'know? I think they weren't used to seeing so many black men and they were intimidated.'

Most of the racism he's encountered has been subtle – a funny look here, a first tee that suddenly becomes full or an official taking offence at their clothing. He points to his cap.

'Look, I'm a Rastafarian and I wear this because of my religion, right? But you wouldn't believe the comments I get about it every single day. And when I go to a golf course . . . man, you can just see them itching to tell me to take it off.'

Maybe you should have 'PING' on the front of it, I say, and Leo screams with laughter.

'Yeah, man. I'm not sponsored – that's my problem.'

He is still chortling away when the swarthy catering

manager comes over to ask when we think all the groups will be in and they can serve the dinner. A time is agreed and then Leo says, 'South America?'

'I'm sorry?' says the manager.

'It's alright. I'm from Grenada, man. You're from South America, right? What is it – Venezuela? Colombia?'

'Eh, no. I am not from South America,' says the chap, warily.

'OK, it must be the Mediterranean, then – Morocco, Libya . . .' Leo snaps his fingers. 'Lebanon. That's it, isn't it – you're from Lebanon?'

'No, I am not from the Mediterranean at all.'

'So where *are* you from?' asks Leo, clearly irked.

The manager draws himself up. 'Austria.'

A few minutes later, Leo is still shaking his head, a map of the Niederösterreich quickly drawn as proof on the back of a table plan by his side, while the manager heads off to ask a friend if he thinks he looks Colombian.

'Austrian? I mean, *Austrian*?' says Leo.

Maybe only a black guy would've been able to get away with that. Then again, maybe I'm being hyper-sensitive. All Leo did was enquire, albeit in a rather forthright manner, as to the man's origins. If a whitey in here had asked you where you came from, I ask him, would you take offence?

'No,' says Leo indignantly. 'That's not being racist. That's just being curious and friendly. It's not the same as, as . . . look, the worst that's happened to me was when I was standing on the tee of this course at a bit where there were a couple of tees and greens all next to each other. A three-ball comes up to this green and one of the guys shouts, "Hey, you got any gear, man? You got an ounce or two I can score?" and then he and his mates have a big laugh. I mean he's shouted it right across the whole golf course and everybody is turning round to look. I tell you I tore into him – only verbally, of course – but it ruined my day. I couldn't play a shot from then on in.'

I tell him about the past experience of Jews and ask if he thinks there are any similarities to how ethnic minorities are treated today.

'To tell you the truth I've had grief off Jews as well,' he says. 'But no, I don't think it's the same. For one thing, I've had golf clubs begging me to join them. Seriously. I don't know whether it's just cos they want to be seen having black members and I'm about as visible as you can get, or what.'

But you like playing with Unitee Golf instead?

'I don't like this – I *love* it,' Leo says with feeling. 'Coming to places like this and seeing all these black and coloured faces everywhere. I love it.'

His first experience of the game was the same as Donovan's – in fact just like Ray's and a couple of other of the guys I've asked; he was introduced to it by a friend and was instantly hooked.

'I'm a plumber and that can be a really shitty job – if you'll excuse the pun. I love getting out on the course – the trees, the fresh air, it's great. And I love the game, I love being able to play it properly – when I can – the skill, the challenge, even the rules, the etiquette – everything!'

And so, happily off the subject of race and discrimination, many more round our table join in with their own enthusiasm for golf, how they got started, best and worst scores, favourite courses and all the usual nineteenth hole chatter.

Eventually, the rest of the matches – most of which have had much more trouble with the lakes than we did – make their way into the clubhouse, much to Herman's relief, and everyone starts drifting towards the restaurant. I am staying for a few days with my friends David and Louise in Battersea and have a dinner date with them this evening, so reluctantly I must pass up the chance to join everyone here for their post-match meal and presentations.

I catch up with Herman as he is heading for a table and introducing himself to a new member. '. . . but I'm not a techie,' he is saying just as I get within earshot. We shake warmly and I get an open invitation to any Unitee matches whenever I am in town.

'The guys in Unitee have all had different experiences, but they all have one thing in common,' he pauses. 'OK, two things – but one of them is that they love golf.'

A recent survey by the EGU (based on 54 per cent of the English golf clubs which responded) showed that 96.4 per cent of golf club members are white and British. With fewer than four per cent from the ethnic minorities that make up 13 per cent of the total population (according to the latest census information), it is obvious golf has a way to go before it can claim to have a representative social and racial mix. Similar figures for non-club member golfers who use municipal and other public courses do not exist on an English or UK-wide scale, but some years ago Birmingham surveyed all those leisure cardholders who play on the city's municipal courses and found that almost 20 per cent were from ethnic minorities. In a completely unscientific and not-for-quoting way, it does tend to back up the consensus I got from the guys from Unitee Golf – that proportionately more black and Asian golfers will be found on public courses than on private. If they have to join something to get handicaps and regular competition, they would rather it was a golfing society and not an established club.

The most obvious explanation is that since a high percentage of Afro-Caribbean and Asian citizens are still among the lower and under classes, the very few golfers among their number will go for the cheaper, public option. But there are wider implications for the game itself, as Neil Hayward, assistant secretary of the EGU, recognised when we spoke on the subject:

'To be honest, there are many in here who are questioning why we are having to do this, to admit we have a problem when we don't feel that we actually do have a problem,' he said. 'The vast majority of golf clubs have always been open to all races, but that is obviously not what some people think. We have a job to do. We have to make people understand that anybody in this country . . . can join a club and take part in this wonderful game.'

What the game's administrators and academics agree upon is that in the issue of race, golf is once again falling victim to perception; the population at large sees it as expensive, exclusive, male *and* white. To make matters worse, that perception is becoming self-fulfilling. Dr Karl Spracklen, a senior lecturer at Leeds Metropolitan University, is an authority on race and social identity in sport. He believes that racial discrimination, formalised into a deliberate, if unspoken, policy by a tiny handful of clubs, certainly exists in golf, but that does not make the sport any better or worse than the society it is part of:

'The fact is most sports in this country are white and

middle class because that's the background they came from . . . they represent a demographic from the late nineteenth and early twentieth centuries. The challenge, obviously, is to get enough people from ethnic minorities to want to change that, but that is not going to be easy. I mean, let's face it – why should a black, working-class person put themselves through the hassle of going to a private club and trying to integrate with middle-class white guys talking about four-by-fours and conservatories?'

Hayward believes the problem is more cultural than purely racial: 'If you are retired Major General Fortescue and you see a black man in the clubhouse with dreadlocks and wearing a baseball cap on backwards, you might react badly, not because of his race, but simply because it is not what you have been used to seeing in the club – it is the complete opposite of anything that you can readily accept.'

The conundrum for golf is how to tackle such genuine feelings of alienation when they apply as much to the ethnic minorities themselves as to retired major generals. Every one of the guys I spoke to at Wyboston Lakes enthused about the opportunity Unitee Golf gave them to relax, enjoy playing the game and socialising with people 'just like me'. The middle-class white men who founded the first golf clubs over a hundred years ago would no doubt have said exactly the same.

7

If John Henry Taylor played his golf in this day and age we'd be sick of the sight of him. As a five-times winner of the British Open – and an Englishman to boot – newspapers and television in this country would have made him into a sporting superhero. Every commercial break on Sky Sports would have 'JH' endorsing balls and clubs in his Grumbleweeds West Country accent, he'd never be off that cart thing Steve Rider sits in all day when the BBC have scraped enough together to buy the rights to a golf tournament, billboards across the land would be plastered with his face – the firm jaw, the flat cap, the most famous 'tache in sport since David Seaman – and golf clubs would fight like cats in a sack to have any association with Britain's genuine world-class golfer.

But JH Taylor played his golf a hundred years ago and he counted himself lucky if golf clubs gave him a hut to get changed in out of the rain. Of course, he shared this shabby treatment with every other professional golfer – a species viewed by the gentleman amateur as at best a single rung up the evolutionary ladder from invertebrates and caddies – and yet Taylor, at least by Edwardian standards, *was* a sporting superhero. Part of the 'Great Triumvirate', along with James Braid and Harry Vardon, he dominated golf at the turn of the nineteenth and twentieth centuries, winning not only those five Open titles, but also the French and German Opens, the British Matchplay and, in one of his few trips to the United States, finishing runner-up to Vardon in the 1900 US Open. He was the first player to play all four rounds of a major championship under eighty (at the 1900 Open at St Andrews) and was a superb bad weather player, already a stroke or two up on his opponents as soon as the rain fell or the wind blew.

More than for his achievements in major competition, however, he would have been a marketing man's dream because of his classic rags-to-riches background. Born into poverty in rural North Devon, his situation was made worse by the death of his father while he was still an infant. The young Taylor was forced to start his working life at the age of eleven and took a string of jobs, including mason's labourer, gardener's assistant, caddie and then greenkeeper at the local Royal North Devon Club at Westward Ho! To make up for his lost schooling, he educated himself by reading the likes of Dickens and Boswell, and succeeded well enough to be able to write his autobiography in later life without need of a ghostwriter. A short, stocky man, Taylor was refused entry to the Army on the grounds of poor eyesight and flat feet. That was the Army's loss – Taylor was so accurate off the tee he asked for marker posts to be taken down because he was fed up hitting them and flying off into the rough, while those flat feet took him over hundreds of thousands of miles of fairway around the country with nary a twinge.

And so, perhaps, the story of a golfing great could have ended – poor boy made good, terrific player, Open champion, retires to write his memoirs. But JH Taylor was more than just a great player. Without Taylor, the game as it is taught, played and organised today would not exist.

Not content with having pulled himself up by his boot straps, Taylor worked tirelessly off the course to improve the lot of his fellow professionals and was the driving force behind the founding of the Professional Golfers' Association (PGA) in 1901. Conceived from the outset as a trade union for the underpaid itinerants who played for paltry sums in competitions from Caithness to Cornwall, the PGA quickly became embroiled in a series of disputes with the R&A over such matters as playing conditions and prize money. Needless to say, it was not immediately effective, but over the years, as its voice grew stronger and the game inched itself reluctantly into the twentieth century, the PGA became a major force in golf administration. By 1925 it had even managed to breach that bastion of amateur resistance, the clubhouse, and competitors in the Open that year at Prestwick were actually given access to a locker room!

The PGA became the model for its American counterpart and set about organising a training and instruction programme for the hundreds of new professionals taking up the game and looking for club work and tournament play across the Atlantic. Taylor, who took the game and its disciplines very seriously – 'To try to play golf really well is far from being a joke, and light heartedness of endeavour is a sure sign of eventual failure,' he once wrote – became one of the first instructors of what is essentially the modern golf swing. As Dr Guy Yocom comments in *Golf Digest*: 'Golf instruction hadn't evolved very far at the turn of the century, but Taylor had a prescient understanding of how the club should be swung. His observation, *"The knees should be bent, the head kept at the same level throughout the playing stroke,"* is as valid in the era of graphite shafts as it was in the age of hickory.'

In short, the man could probably pit his credentials against any in the entire history of the sport and still come out near the top. But though a major champion, self-made man, seminal teacher and founding father of the modern age of golf, it is not for any of these that I am interested in John Henry Taylor.

Almost fifty years after golf began to be played in England by Englishmen, there were still no public courses. The initial hostility to the game on common land mentioned earlier persisted for decades and applied across the country. Farmers in Lincoln were so incensed at golfers taking up grazing land that they regularly destroyed tournaments by driving their cattle through the middle of matches. On London's various commons, early attempts at staging regular golf matches proved so problematic and unpopular with other users of the land that golfers resorted to wearing red coats (a tradition carried on at a few London clubs to this day) and had to be preceded by a 'forecaddie' carrying a flag to warn of the danger.

Complications arose in London with the Enclosure Act of 1845, which removed many acres of common land from public use and put them in the hands of private landowners, and the subsequent Metropolitan Commons Act of 1866, which stopped all further enclosures, but gave rights of access for recreation to all members of the public. The net result by the end of the century was that common land in the city available for golf was severely restricted – and those few acres that remained were the subject of bitter conflict between golfers, cricketers, footballers, picnickers and those who just wanted a walk in the park without having to weave their way round wicker baskets or dodge flying balls of varying shapes and sizes.

Of course, the principal reason for the game's unpopularity among the great unwashed was that it was already pretty much class-specific. For example, in Mitcham, at the time still a village on the outskirts of the city, the Prince's Golf Club was founded in 1890 simply because the wealthy chair of the Mitcham Common Conservators, one Henry Deeley, happened to be an enthusiastic golfer who, like many of his class, had discovered the game during his regular holidays in Scotland. Along with his A-list chums, including the Secretary of State for Ireland and future Prime Minister, Arthur James Balfour, the Earl of Chesterfield and a host of other leading citizens, Deeley turned Mitcham into the most fashionable golfing location in the Southeast. Before long, a ladies' club had been established and, thanks to a convenient train link to Victoria, the common became the favoured haunt of Mayfair and Belgravia socialites. In typical style, these gorgeous creatures of high society deigned to allow the drab natives to play golf (on their own land) at certain, strictly curtailed, times of the day. Only legal action on behalf of the villagers some twenty years later secured public playing rights.

It is hard to imagine how Balfour, who had to be accompanied everywhere by armed detectives, even on to the links, managed to find time for golf. When he wasn't suppressing Irish rebels, laying the foundations of a Zionist homeland in Palestine or being First Lord of the Admiralty (surely a full enough CV for any man?), he was sitting staring out of windows and scribbling his latest thoughts on the human condition, being something of a dabbler in philosophy. Yet not only did he play golf at every opportunity, he bored the pants off anyone within earshot with his enthusiasm for the game. Thanks largely to him, golf became the favoured sport for members of both houses at Westminster and soon London commons from Tooting and Blackheath to Mitcham, Wimbledon and Clapham became positively infested with parliamentarians, all hacking about the place when they should have been running the country.

But despite the lack of land and the self-conscious pretension, golf's popularity gradually spread across the social spectrum. The advent of the guttie ball at the turn of the century, making the game much more affordable, was undoubtedly a major factor, as was the deliberate adoption of the sport by the middle classes. But too often, it seems to me, historians give little or no credit to the game itself. Surely it must have been the merits of golf as a pastime – the simple pleasure in playing the game – that not only enticed Balfour and his noble peers on to the links, but could outweigh expense, inverted snobbery, not to mention sheer inconvenience, and persuade more and more ordinary working men and women to take up the sport at the dawn of the twentieth century.

The fact is that by the outbreak of the First World War, golf was arguably the fastest growing sport in the country. Those scenes of golfers crowding on to the public links of Edinburgh and East Lothian more than a generation before were now being re-enacted on dozens of heaths and commons across England. The response to this demand was piecemeal and inadequate. Non-members were allowed on to private golf courses on very few occasions, usually as a guest and only, of course, if they didn't offend the members with their language, dress or insurrectionist notions of universal suffrage. The Corporation of London took over the running of the Royal Epping Forest Club at Chingford in 1908 and provided reasonably affordable golf for all and sundry, while Bournemouth, Brighton and Eastbourne boasted their own 'municipal' courses. These, as mentioned earlier, however, did nothing to satisfy demand for low-cost golf, as they were priced for, and marketed exclusively at, a high-class holiday clientele.

But in 1909, the London County Council opened a golf course built on a wooded stretch of land near Chigwell Row to the northeast of the city. Hainault Forest, as it was named, can claim to be the first purpose-built public golf course in England aimed at the 'ordinary' golfer of modest means. Although some way out of the city and inaccessible in the days before adequate public transport, and although, at one shilling per round, still relatively expensive, Hainault Forest became an immediate success, with queues at the first tee almost every day. It wasn't long before the man who had designed its eighteen holes was resolving to repeat the exercise elsewhere in the city and indeed champion public golf across England.

JH Taylor was fired up with what he called 'the cause' of bringing golf to the masses, but his plans, as with much else in the country, had to wait while the Great War exacted its awful toll. When it was over and the country had recovered sufficiently to turn its mind once more to such frivolities as sport, Taylor took up where he'd left off and set his sights first on Richmond Park.

He began by writing a letter proposing a nine-hole course in the park and sent it to the *Daily Mail* (bizarrely, Lord Northcliffe, its barking mad proprietor, was all for public golf). The responses ranged from unqualified support to accusations of 'vandalism', but Taylor was encouraged enough to gather together a committee to take the project on. With his old friend Lord Riddell and four others on board, the next step was to seek an interview with His Majesty's Office of Works, under whose jurisdiction the park was administered.

They called at the office of the Earl Crawford and Balcarres, First Commissioner of Works, early in 1922. Taylor describes the encounter in his autobiography, *Golf: My Life's Work* (1943): 'The reception, although cordial, was not encouraging . . . At the mention of Richmond Park [Lord Riddell] was instantly pulled up by Lord Crawford who explained that a public golf course in Richmond Park was out of the question. It was a royal park, it was maintained for rest and recreation for the general public and such a dangerous game as golf could not be allowed as it might endanger life and limb. Indeed, continued Lord Crawford, they were prohibited from granting it by the statutory powers which were irrevocable.'

Only the suggestion that a small piece of land just outside the perimeter of the park proper might be used prevented the whole enterprise being declared dead in the water there and then. Lord Crawford, although he clearly thought the idea barmy (at one point he asked Taylor where he thought the players would come from, to which Taylor tartly replied, 'London has a population of seven million') reluctantly agreed not to stand in their way. The idea that the Government would actually help was, of course, out of the question. 'Please understand that not one penny will be given by the Treasury to help the scheme,' the minister said.

Once Taylor came up with a layout – now for a full eighteen holes – the Office of Works gave its consent and, financed entirely by £4,000 raised by the committee, the course was built within months. In June 1922 the Prince of Wales, the future abdicator, hit the first ball off the first tee and Richmond Park Public Golf Course was up and running. Needless to say it was a roaring success and golfers in their hundreds, from all over the city, converged on the park, queuing from early morning and causing all kinds of congestion in the surrounding roads. Although Labour had won power by the time the committee went back to HM Office of Works to ask permission to build another eighteen holes, it was even more reluctant to help a scheme that didn't fit with its idea of serving the interests of 'all the people'. Golf, for many members of the early Labour Party, was still viewed as a sport for the idle rich. Eventually, however, the extension was granted – at a much increased rent – and the new course was built. In 1925 it was opened, this time by a drive from the Duke of York, the future King George VI. Taylor, ever the keen observer of golfing technique, amusingly notes in his autobiography that George had a much better swing than his elder brother.

Before long, the courses were coining it – easily making the rent and ploughing extra revenue back into their upkeep. It took just one year for the Office of Works to do a complete volte-face on the question of public golf. In 1926, it wrote to the committee telling them it was invoking the small print in its terms of agreement and was taking over the management of the courses (and the profits) forthwith.

But Taylor was already moving on. Together with his long-time friend and business partner Fred Hawtree (a professional golf course architect who actually provided most of the technical know-how for Hainault Forest and all that followed), he founded a company that went on to design and build more than fifty courses over the next thirty years – a large number of which were public. While it would be ludicrous to say public golf in England would not have happened without the drive and influence of JH Taylor, it is no exaggeration to say that he and Hawtree were pathfinders for the 'cause'. At a time when the rest of English golf was still obsessed with membership criteria and designs for club ties, they gladly accepted work from progressive local authorities and laid out municipal links from Croydon to Manchester. More importantly, perhaps, in 1927 they established the National Association of Public Golf Courses (NAPGC), a body that sought to bridge the gap between private and public golf. The NAPGC, officially recognised by the R&A and the EGU, is still going strong today, representing more than 200 public courses and organising national medal and matchplay events.

Reflecting on his illustrious golfing career, Taylor, who lived to the ripe old age of ninety-two, often said he was especially proud of his role in helping to bring golf within the reach of men and women of modest means. In particular, he identified the building of Richmond Park's first few golf holes in the face of establishment hostility as one of his greatest achievements. Hawtree and he may have built Hainault Forest before the First World War, and one or two other private courses may have already been taken over by local authorities, but it was the high profile of Richmond Park – the right project in the right place at the right time – that proved to be the groundbreaker for public golf in England.

Five-thirty in the morning is a truly awful time of the day. If an alarm clock that goes off at, say, 7.30a.m. can be described as a soft but firm cough from a gentleman's gentleman as he lays the boiled egg and tea on the bedside table, then the one that rings two hours earlier is a dawn raid by the bailiffs with an armed police escort and battering ram. I am standing in David and Louise's kitchen fifteen minutes later like a baby untimely torn from the womb, my clothes hopefully on the right way round and failing to understand that the toaster only works if it's actually switched on.

The thing about Richmond Park is that ever since those first nine holes opened in 1922, it has never ceased to be one of the most played golf courses in Britain. At the height of its popularity in the 1960s and 1970s, players queued outside the gates from the early hours of the morning, sometimes through the night, just to get a morning tee-off. That level of activity has eased somewhat in recent years, but the golfer who hasn't booked a weekend tee time (like muggins here) still needs to get there before the park gates open just before 7a.m. if he is to have any chance of getting a game.

My efforts to get fed and out of the house without waking the family are threatened when I stand on a golf ball in the living room and lurch heavily into a wall. I remember now that drunken putting lesson for two-year-old Joe last night and his parents' feeble attempts at sharing the kid's obvious enthusiasm for knocking lumps out of their furniture and my pride at his prowess with the ol' flat stick.

'When are you leaving?' they asked.

Just after 6a.m., as it turned out. Plenty of time, I say to myself, since according to my trusty *A-Z* Richmond Park is but a page and half from Battersea. With hardly anything on the roads at that time, the discourtesy car and I sail through Wandsworth and Putney and in no time I see the vast expanse of the park off the starboard bow. Unfortunately, the only entrance to the park from this end, Robin Hood's Gate, is on the other side of a dual carriageway and is not just closed but barricaded with concrete bollards. No problem. I'll just hang a right at the first opportunity and go round until I find a way in. And were Richmond any normal park I would have gained entry within minutes. But this park is roughly the size of Dumfries and Galloway, and quarter of an hour later I am still quartering back and forth through endless suburbia desperately looking for a gate, glancing ever more frequently at my watch and envisaging the lengthening queue at the first tee.

Just as I'm sure I'm about to hit Hertfordshire I turn up somewhere called Star and Garter Hill and there on the right is a large gate into the park. It is still closed, but obviously not for long, because there is a small line of cars and their owners are sitting on bumpers and in opened doors pulling on golf shoes. I have to say it is not the golfing fraternity I had envisaged; I count two Mercs, a BMW and a Range Rover. The guys I get chatting to are frightfully well spoken and have clearly all bought their clothes from Middle-class Weekends 'R' Us – bright yellow corduroy, pink polo shirts (collar turned up) and navy jumpers with a hole here and a frayed cuff there. I get chatting to one of their number and he invites me to join up and make a four-ball. The gates soon open and we jump into our cars and drive through what really does look more like a large country estate than a park, before eventually reaching the golf courses.

There are two eighteen-hole courses now, the Duke's and the Prince's, made up of various bits of the original Taylor layout. Sadly, the old clubhouse burned to the ground earlier in the year and all that remains is a rather battered old pro shop and a Portakabin in which, I later learn, the course's various clubs now meet. Inside the shop the three friends I am with meet up with a fourth and I am bombed out of the four-ball. But just as I'm paying my £22 green fee a woman I less than gallantly estimate to be in her mid-fifties invites me to join her and her friend for their regular Saturday morning round. Melanie introduces herself and Carolyn and we walk to the first tee of the Duke's Course where we meet up with another early bird, a tall, elegant chap by the name of Rajeev. And then we were four.

It is another overcast day that threatens rain, but even this early in the morning it is muggy and slightly uncomfortable. Like most parts of the park, the few acres the courses are laid out on are pretty well wooded with large mature oaks and chestnuts. It all looks reasonably flat and pleasant. In fact, if it weren't for the ever-present hum of traffic and the Roehampton flats on the horizon, you could easily think yourself in deepest rural Englandshire.

The first is a dogleg left and Rajeev and I spank a couple of good ones down to the corner before Melanie and Carolyn tee up and find the right semi-rough with their drives. It is a curious reversal of the normal chivalric convention that, no matter who has the honour, men usually tee off first in a mixed match. This, of course, is to save the time it would take for the ladies to hit and then walk back behind the men's tee for safety while they drive. I just mention this in case the combination of commenting on a woman's age and barging on to the tee first might give the impression I am some variety of cad. The ladies (and I shall refer to them as such throughout) struggle to extricate themselves from the rough and only reach the green after having taken something like half a dozen shots each. Rajeev and I share honours with steady par fours.

Walking after our drives at the second, Melanie and Carolyn – whom I am beginning to suspect from their slightly plummy accents are not a pair of lorry drivers – explain that they play at Richmond because there isn't a club in the area that would allow women to play at this time on a weekend.

'We both work full-time, but a lot of private clubs round here still don't seem to think such a thing is possible,' says Melanie.

There is no malice or note of grievance in her voice. I suspect she is well past complaining and just accepts it as an unfortunate fact of life.

Carolyn says, 'I suppose we're just waiting for retirement before we think about joining a club, maybe take some lessons and get better at this game.'

'I don't think I'm ready for a club yet,' says Melanie. 'Sitting around all day, taking it easy. No, not just yet.'

And with that she gives her ball another mighty smite with a fairway wood and it takes another determined hop, like a frog on a mission, towards the green. Melanie, Carolyn tells me in an offstage whisper, has no fewer than five woods in her bag.

'She can't hit an iron to save herself, the poor dear,' she says. 'Eventually she accepted the fact and now she even carries a nine-wood. But she can hit these better than anyone else I know.'

And better than most I've ever seen with a fairway wood – not including a certain nine-wood wielding black policeman, of course. Neither Melanie nor Carolyn, it would be fair to say, are in possession of the fullest, most athletic swing in golf, but like many who play regularly and cheerfully admit they've never had a lesson in their life, they have wrung the most out of what technique they have; perfected the imperfect.

Rajeev, on the other hand, has clearly been under the

tutor's gaze and has a long, powerful stroke with every-thing moving in the right direction at the right time. Old JH, I suspect, would have been impressed. He tells me he is a ten-handicapper who is playing more like an eighteen these days, but he's playing very steady golf over the opening holes and I take this to be the usual golfer's pre-emptive modesty. You never start a game by saying how well you've been playing recently, because you know that nothing is more likely to tempt fate; what the golfing gods have given, they are more likely to take away if you start getting cocky.

He bogies the short par three third, but then we all drop at least one shot here, because (for some reason we only discover this after we've all played our shots) the tee is actually pointing at least twenty feet to the left of the target. It is one of those plateau tees and the whole thing, not just the movable markers, is off line. Somebody, as they say in these parts, is havin' a larf.

The hiccup at the third, in fact, is my only blemish in the opening holes and I am going along quite steadily at one over par for four holes. I've got the half set on my back again and it's all quite easy going and enjoyable. Then we reach the par five fifth. Out of the blue I top my drive and barely make it on to the fairway. As I'm limbering up with a three-wood for my second, Carolyn warns me there is a ditch that runs across the fairway. Tish tosh, my ball will still be rising when it passes that, I say, and motion for her to stand back and prepare to be impressed.

'What did you get there?' asks Melanie innocently on the next tee.

'Eight,' I say through gritted teeth.

This, I think, convinces the ladies I am really a duffer after all and for the next few holes they take me under their wing, offering swing tips, yardages and warnings about hazards only a pitching wedge away. They also clearly believe my ball has been letting me down and they start shouting at it like it was a Labrador. 'Go on, now. Go on! That's a boy. Now sta-y . . . stay! Well done.'

It's all very sweet, but faintly embarrassing and I look at Rajeev striding majestically about the place and yearn to be playing with the big boys again.

From time to time we've heard the odd shout from the four-ball of young guys behind us. They look a bit rough, I have to say, and Melanie and Carolyn admit they played with a couple of them the other week and were not overly impressed with their decorum. On the seventh tee, Melanie slices her drive into the rough.

'Oh, sugar!' she exclaims.

'Aw, fuckin' hell,' bawls one of the lads from the sixth green just behind us.

Not at Melanie, we are relieved to see, but at his own stupidity for topping a chip through the green. He is painfully thin and dressed in quite pricey looking golf gear, but there is a dangerous, loose-limbed swagger about him, like Charles Howell III's evil twin. 'That's him,' mutters Carolyn, as we walk down the fairway. 'We played with him and his friend. I have to say he was most uncouth.'

Melanie joins us. 'Yes, I suppose that's one of the downsides of playing public golf courses like this. You meet all sorts and usually they're fine, but every now and then . . .' She turns and frowns at the four-ball behind, who are by now having a sword fight with their putters.

On the par four eighth I finally manage to restore my fragile male ego by almost driving the green. The ladies seem to take this as a sign that their work is done and leave me to my own devices after that. Still, I only manage a par and bogey the par three ninth to complete the front nine in forty-two – seven over par.

Melanie, I've discovered, runs her own accountancy firm and Carolyn, who backpacked from Australia forty years ago and never went back, used to be in television and theatre and now has a marketing consultancy. I sidle over to Rajeev on the next tee in the hope of discovering some earthy, working class justification for JH Taylor's efforts to bring golf to the lowly paid.

'I own a pharmaceutical company,' he tells me. 'I've five manufacturing plants in India.'

The company, in fact, is one of the biggest in the Indian sub-continent and makes medicines and preparations under licence for GlaxoSmithKline and others. Rajeev himself travels abroad almost two weeks out of every four.

'That's why I like playing here,' he says. 'I never know when I will have time for a game and this place allows me to play at the drop of a hat.'

Well, what did I expect? Our friends in the group behind are proof that, thankfully, the genuine scruff can still get a game here, but the golfing map of London has changed dramatically since the course was opened eighty years ago. There are low-cost options, municipal or pay-and-play, for the golfer all over the city now and gone are the days when working men travelled across London for the chance of a game. Richmond Park today is therefore more of a truly local course. And where do the locals live? Richmond, Wimbledon, Kingston upon Thames, Kew – not exactly a wretched wilderness of urban deprivation.

Once or twice I get the chance to bring up the subject of Taylor and the courses' origins, but it is Richmond Park's future, rather than its past, that most concerns my playing partners. As a royal park, it is technically Her Maj's property and is still run on her behalf by an arm of central government, currently the Department of Culture, Media and Sport. That has, in turn, franchised the management of the courses, but the contract is up for renewal and plans to completely revamp the whole golfing operation, change the layouts, make a new entrance and build a golf academy have been knocking about for years. The uncertainty has led, say regulars, to a lack of investment in course maintenance and a general 'end of term' feel about the place. My companions this morning are scathing.

'It's all so unnecessary,' says Melanie. 'Why can't they just leave it as it is? They're just trying to compete with all these new places.'

'Yes, and then they'll charge more and the original idea of Richmond Park being a public course that doesn't cost the earth will be lost,' says Carolyn.

My start to the back nine is not encouraging. A pulled drive into some trees leaves me with what I think is a clear shot back on to the fairway of the tenth. Lurking unseen just below the surface of the tall grass right in front of my ball, however, is an old tree stump. My follow-through is therefore brought to a jarring halt almost before it has begun, my arms are in danger of becoming detached at the elbow and I swear I can feel the slipstream of the ball as it whizzes past my right cheek.

Miraculously, I break neither bones nor nine-iron, but I'm sufficiently shaken to screw up the rest of the hole and I record a triple bogey seven. Melanie is still dinking her way round the course serenely, Rajeev is only occasionally suffering from a loose shot here and there, but Carolyn has really come on to a game. Although on the face of it her swing is little different from her friend's, Carolyn is naturally the more sporty of the two. Once into the groove, her loopy, up and down kind of action fairly imparts a decent charge to the back of the ball and she starts recording as many pars as either Rajeev or myself. One less than perfect strike on the eleventh, however, still manages to hop over that ditch that transects the entire course and trundle down near the green.

'Uh, oh. Never mind – a BABU will do,' she says.

'BABU?' asks Rajeev.

'Yes – Bloody Awful But Useful.'

Rajeev himself hits two magnificent shots on to this par four and is standing over his four-foot putt for birdie when suddenly we are transported to a disco somewhere in Mumbai. Bhangra music fills the air and I'm just thinking how cool it is to have your own incidental music for shooting birdies when Rajeev shoves the putt right and walks testily towards his bag and pulls out his mobile phone. The ladies and I exchange glances as if to say, 'I wouldn't like to be on the other side of *that* call.'

At the next my troubles resume with a pulled drive on to a steep bank, a second that flies straight into a bush narrowly missing a large wood pigeon – the nearest I'm to get to a birdie all day (honk, honk) – a drop out and an indifferent fourth *and* fifth. The only reason I didn't get a triple bogey was that my sixth, a putt from way off the green, motored forty feet before putting a dent in the pin and dropping into the cup.

Things up ahead begin to slow down and, as the fates usually ensure on these occasions, this is accompanied by a rumble of distant thunder and the first spits and spots of some big raindrops from the huge grey clouds that have bubbled up above. We've reached a busy wooded interchange on the course where our tee, the fourteenth, is next to the thirteenth green, twelfth and fourth tees, and the third green – and all of them close to a caravan selling hot filled rolls and drinks. With the end of the round in sight, none of us is inclined to have a break for victuals, even though we have to wait a few minutes on the tee. Meanwhile, it's like half-time at a football match with groups of guys milling about the place munching on bacon rolls and slurping tea from paper cups. The group on the twelfth tee features one bloke who clearly doesn't let little things like a round of golf get in the way of a hearty breakfast – he has a tray piled high with rolls and a large tea balanced on his bag while he sticks the bacon roll he's currently working on in his mouth and lets loose with what I have to admit is an impressive drive.

Our delay is explained by a player from the group immediately ahead, who tells us that the three-ball two groups ahead of them have been slow all the way round. When they were pulled up about it, they promptly started taking even more time over their shots and dawdling on the green.

'I have to say that could be one advantage of playing at a club,' says Melanie. 'It's fine meeting different people, but you do sometimes run into some idiots.'

'Yes, but wouldn't you always end up playing with the same crew – and probably all of them women?' asks Carolyn. 'I can think of nothing more hideous than a four-ball of women. Particularly the sort of women who do nothing all day but golf and shop. Ladies who lunch – eeuch!'

Rajeev is telling me how he likes to squeeze in a round of golf even when he is visiting his factory in Bangalore (he keeps a set of clubs over there), when suddenly it is our turn on the tee. Caught unawares and now struggling to pull on my waterproof top, I hastily tee up and hook a three-iron left of the green. The shot I am then faced with is an exact replica of the one I had a few days ago on the ninth at Portobello – a lob over a bunker on to a narrow strip of green. And the result is exactly the same – I dunch it straight into the sand and eventually take a five.

There are slight delays on all the tees from here in. On the seventeenth I get a chance to tell Rajeev about my meeting with the guys from Unitee Golf. He says he believes more and more Indians and Asians are taking up the game in Britain, because they are getting wealthier. (Not the kind of insight that does much for my romantic notions of a democratic and cheap sport.) The Indian immigrants to Britain were mostly labourers and manual workers, he says. It has therefore taken them a couple of generations to make money, set up businesses and give themselves enough free time to play sports like golf. In the States, where his son works, the immigration was mostly doctors, engineers and such like, and a lot more of them play golf. 'My son is a five handicap, but then he started playing when he was twelve. I started when I was forty-two,' he says.

Has Rajeev, I ask, ever encountered any discrimination, even abuse, at a club or on the course?

'I have been in this country for eleven years and I can honestly say that I've never had any kind of discrimination. I believe if you get something said to you then you're at fault because you invited it – you must have behaved in a way that made you deserve it. If you go to live in a country you should accept their way of life, their culture.'

It is certainly an interesting perspective and one I'm sure a few of the guys I met the other day would take issue with, but just as I'm about to press the matter further there is the most ear-piercing screech from the trees directly above us. To my surprise, I am the only one who is jumping about the place with his hair standing on end.

'Oh, that's just the parakeets,' says Melanie with a casual wave of her hand. 'They nest in this part of the course.'

The birds, so the local story goes, escaped from an aviary many years ago and decided to take up residence in this corner of the park. So much to their liking is it that they successfully nest and breed here, pushing some of the other native birds out of the area. Although I can't see them, just the odd rustling among the branches, it makes for a tropical end to the round – warm rain and a jungle soundtrack.

We all score well on the seventeenth, a short par four, but suffer a catalogue of mishaps on the last. Melanie and Carolyn seem to be running out of juice and succeed only in scuffing their balls along the ground, while Rajeev just reaches the top of his backswing when someone in the group behind does something so notable it triggers an explosion of swearing that rings round the course. He slices badly. My tee shot, on the other hand, is a thing of such sublime loveliness I fear the English language is just not equipped to cover it. A three-wood to a tight green on a 247-yard par three fails to do justice to it in much the same way that 'Gemmill beats three players and scores' fails to capture the thrilling, almost balletic beauty of Archie's goal against Holland in Argentina '78. It is a stroke of power and athleticism. My swing is full and smooth, and I am in complete control as the dead centre of the sweet spot hits the ball and sends it in a soaring trajectory to land with just the right amount of fade and check to bounce right around a guarding front bunker and roll down the narrow neck of the green towards the pin. I am in the textbook follow-through position and just know that years of playing have, at this precise moment in time, kicked in to make me now and forever Man and Swing in Perfect Harmony. Then I three putt for bogey.

8

Ever fantasised about setting a weary foot inside the door of a staging post in the old Wild West after several dusty days in the saddle? The kind of place where a pot of stew and beans is always on the hob, there's coffee in the pot and plenty of hot water and towels for the woman in the stagecoach who's decided nine months pregnant is the perfect condition to be in for travelling from Carson City to Tombstone? Well, I have. Unfortunately, I find that I am not only allergic to horses but not in the right space/time continuum. The best I can do, therefore, is the Travelodge at junction eleven on the M4. It lacks any of the above, or sawdust on the floor and imminent attack by the Sioux, but it does have a blunt frontiers-woman in charge and a room with as many frills as a bunkhouse for leather-arsed cowboys.

'Can I have a room please?' I'd asked at the desk. No one has ever counted the seconds in an awkward silence, because you never know you are going to have one and therefore don't start counting at the beginning, but this was way beyond anything I'd ever experienced before – and it came with a glare of almost open hostility.

'Did you . . . have you called?' she growled eventually.

'Well, I spoke to a guy in the Travelodge back up the road and he said you had a room.'

'Do we?'

'Apparently, yes. Perhaps you could check?'

'Aw, shit.'

'I'm sorry?'

'Someone's been buggering about with this computer again . . . Right. So-o . . . it's a *room* you want?'

Travelodges are glorified dormitories – they don't do anything *but* rooms. What did she think I was going to ask for – club class to Dubai? Anything by Motorhead?

Ten minutes of single-finger typing all my details and almost coming to blows over the fact that Edinburgh is a city and doesn't have a county attached finally procured me a beige room with brick-hard furniture, cold and cold running water and a bar of soap from a doll's house. Still, it was satisfying to finally get inside one of these places, given my abortive attempts in Essex.

I am travelling vaguely westwards and have an idea of where I am heading for, but not in any great hurry. A very long lunch and reminisce with an old chum after my round at Richmond Park meant Reading was about as far as I could get today. I wonder if there's a public golf course round here I could play tomorrow . . . ?

The dermatologically-challenged youngster in the service station's Little Chef flounders for a while, caught out by a question not related to deep-fried potato options in the all-day breakfast.

'We-ell . . . there is one not far from here, but it's a bit . . . you know?'

He is as incisive and informative as he was half an hour ago when I asked him if they had any coleslaw I could have with my steak. (It already comes with it, you see, and he almost burst a blood vessel trying to figure out whether or not I was asking for an extra portion.)

'It's a bit what – rough, crap, expensive . . . what?'

'Just, eh, short. It's only nine holes.'

That's fine, I can do short. In fact nine holes in the morning, leaving me time to get another few miles under my belt before the day is out, would be perfect. The effort of remembering the name of the course and directions makes him break out in a sweat, but he finally manages to write it all down on a scrap of paper for me.

'Great, thank you. Do you think I could have some cream with my cheesecake?'

The look says, 'Coleslaw, golf courses, cream – what are you, the customer from hell?'

Hurst Golf Course is run by Wokingham District Council and is wedged into an awkward little corner of the M4 and A329(M) on the outskirts of a village by the same name. At first sight I can't imagine why my waiter would have been so disparaging – there's plenty of mature woodland, a nice enough clubhouse and a boating lake right next door.

I had expected the usual Sunday morning crush on the first tee, but, despite the overnight rain having eased and the sun once again threatening to put in an appearance, the place is almost deserted – unless you count several billion flies. Between the car park and the door of the clubhouse I get set upon by the vanguard of what I am about to discover is a winged plague of Biblical proportions.

Inside, I find myself in a single room that is clubhouse reception, tea room, restaurant, bar and pro shop all rolled into one. As the latest depressing pictures from the Middle East blast out from a twenty-four-hour news channel on a flat-screen TV that takes up an entire wall, I ask the chap behind the counter if I can hook up with anyone going out for a round in the next half hour or so. He scans the book in front of him.

'No.'

'Why not?'

'There's no one going out at the minute.'

'Alright. I'll just play nine holes on my own.'

He sucks what is left of his teeth.

'We don't allow singles on a Sunday. They tend to slow things down a bit.'

Apart from two golfers heading up the first fairway there is absolutely no one else in sight. After a bit of extravagant over-acting on my part – looking for golfers on the ceiling, under the cold filled rolls tray, that sort of thing – he relents and agrees to take my money and let me play. I hand over £8.50 for nine holes, but I've got the full set of clubs with me and ask how much it is to hire a trolley.

'Do you have a credit card?'

'What, for a trolley?'

'Uh-huh. You need to leave your credit card here as a deposit. We've just got these trolleys in new and we get a lot of thieves here.'

None taken.

I hand over the plastic and receive a disappointingly ordinary looking handle in return which, once outside, fits on to a disappointingly ordinary looking – but shiny – trolley.

It is to be the first round I've played on the trip without a partner – well, for the moment at least. The two-ball up ahead have reached the green and, once I catch up with them, one of three things could happen. Preferred option one is that they invite me to join their game. Not so great, but acceptable would be option two – that they simply let me through. The third possibility, of course, is that they do neither and just keep me waiting and seething over every shot. But let's not even think about that – be positive.

I am determined not to be in too much of a hurry anyway. My last two rounds have confirmed my 'here today, gone tomorrow' form; a very satisfying seven over par seventy-seven after a five-hour round in a high wind at Wyboston Lakes, followed, after a few non-golfing days with David and Louise (that clearly did me no favours at all), by shooting eighty-five for a thirteen over par score in much more clement, albeit wetter, conditions at Richmond Park. I've noticed that an old failing of mine – pulling short irons way left of the target – has returned to plague my game and I am committed to ironing it out.

To make solo golf rounds interesting, however, takes more than a kink in your swing to work on and on these occasions I usually compete against an imaginary opponent who is to play exactly to my handicap as determined by the course's stroke index. I learned recently that this habit actually has an historical resonance, echoing as it does the phantom golfer first used by clubs in the 1890s to determine the scratch score for their courses. Yarmouth Golf Club jokingly named this flawless performer 'the Bogey Man' after a popular music-hall character of the time and the name spread across the country. When it reached a club in Gosport, however, the members decided to make 'Mr Bogey' an honorary member. Gosport, with a large military contingent, had the quaint habit of giving every member an *ex officio* military title, and so 'Colonel Bogey' was born. As course conditions, together with the standard of clubs and balls, improved over the years and players simply got better at the game, the 'ideal' bogey score was beaten so often that on most holes one less than it – par – became the new acceptable standard. Yet it was not the end for Colonel Bogey, who went on to transcend golf and become the personification of British military pluck and discipline, a stiff upper-lipped hero who even had a march named after him.

I'm sure Donald Rumsfeld craves an equally iconic place in military history, but for the moment he will just have to settle for providing my opposition at Hurst. The first is a very short par four up a hill from the clubhouse with some trees, a path and then the boating lake on the right. I am concerned about finding the greenside bunkers with my driver, so take a three-wood and play for position just below the raised green. Marching up the fairway I become aware, through the cloud of flies, that the course is absolutely covered in goose droppings – huge dollops of green, thankfully odourless, excrement. I scan the back of the scorecard but, amid all the usual clarifications about lateral hazards, immovable obstructions and the like, there is no mention of a local rule covering goose jobbies. Well, I for one will be kicking my ball into clean grass – without penalty – should I land in the shit.

A deft dink with the gap wedge and a couple of putts later I am walking to the second tee with a solid par under my belt – and all square with Rumsfeld. The flies, little black things smaller than the common variety but bigger than midges, are more dense here close to the water. I hope Donald isn't looking for much conversation because I plan to keep my mouth firmly shut for the duration. To my amazement, I notice a couple of joggers pounding down the lakeside path. Unless they are breathing through gritted teeth, by the time they get home they won't be needing any breakfast.

I've taken care over every shot on the first hole, and didn't even tee off until the group ahead had reached the second tee, but here I stand leaning on my driver, while one of the pair up front prepares for his next effort from the fairway barely 150 yards away. Obviously fresh from his latest lesson, the guy walks deliberately round from the back of his ball to the side, then stands with the club held pointing straight up like he's holding a banner saying, 'I Don't Know What I'm Doing'. He is staring at his grip and, even from this distance, I can see him frantically meshing and un-meshing his fingers. Finally satisfied he has them in a secure enough knot, he slowly lowers the club, at the same time bending stiffly at the waist like he's just been introduced to the Japanese ambassador. With the club now on the ground, he flexes his knees into the classic 'sitting on a high bar stool' position and makes a few little bounces up and down while glancing towards the target. At last he settles, stays dead still for an age, then unleashes a perfect *practice swing!* When it comes to the real thing ten minutes later, the Leadbetter action has been replaced by a convulsive lunge at the ball, which shows its contempt by shanking off towards the footpath. I find a few square feet of shit-free grass and sit down.

Since it never does the cause of the frustrated golfer any harm to keep those in front reminded of your presence, I am on my feet again and making sure I am ready to drive the moment I think they are out of range – the idea being to have my ball roll up a few yards on their heels as they head for the green. My calculations, however, do not take into account one further characteristic of Hurst, another delightful feature to rank alongside the green droppings and the flies – the fairways are as soft and giving to the club as the M4. Despite a deal of rain over the past couple of days, the turf is dry and only a fraction of an inch thick before it gives way to chalky bedrock. The first bounce of my ball, therefore, reaches almost as high as the initial drive and it continues to bound down the fairway heading inexorably towards my two-ball tormentors up ahead.

'Fore!'

How embarrassing having to shout that when you've just hit a perfect drive. Luckily I did, however, because one of them turned round just in time to take his backside out of the target line.

'Sorry!'

From their body language I think I've just blown any chances of them letting me through. Single players on golf courses are like refugees; they have absolutely no rights. They are there under sufferance (particularly, it seems, at this place on a Sunday) and must make way for all matches catching up from behind, while having no automatic priority over slow groups ahead. You are a sad Johnny No-Friends and will be punished accordingly.

Still, I *am* pleased with the drive that leaves me only a wedge to the green. Or, as in this case, the big bunker on the left. That pull is back again and, since I have plenty of time, I decide to chuck some balls down on the same spot and see if I can correct it. The only one of three extra balls that doesn't follow the first into the sand is a shank, which actually makes the green thanks to a lucky bounce off a tree. Only when I get to the bunker do I realise I have not marked any of the balls, they are all Titleist 3s and I have no idea which one was the original.

The start to the third hole passes across the back of the second green and the two-ball ahead are walking by just as I am standing staring at three balls in the bunker, trying to decide which one has the best lie. Their hubbub of conversation dies as they draw near and they stare resolutely ahead. I try a range of little sighs, tsks and ha's to try to get them to look in my direction, so I can pull off an apology for nearly injuring them with my ball, a comical 'Look what a mess I've got myself into' and a request to be let through all in one disarming, winning smile. But the bastards won't look.

To make matters worse, my bunker shot is over-hit and I take two putts to get down for a bogey five – while Rumsfeld has hit the green in regulation and his par is enough to take a one-stroke lead. The silver lining is that I think the message has gotten through to the two-ball ahead and I detect a definite quickening of the pace over the next few holes. The feature of the third hole is a blind tee-shot with a marker post which, should you send one right over it on line will put you, not in position *a*, but in a large bunker slap-bang in the middle of the fairway. Thankfully, I was only heading for *b*-minus and miss it on the right.

My confidence that things will continue to speed up are shaken by a sign at the fourth tee that says, 'Your round should not have taken more than forty minutes to this point. AVOID SLOW PLAY.' I must be honest and say I have taken less than forty minutes to get here, but although the exhortation is one I can sign up to, the timing isn't. To say forty minutes is OK for three holes of golf means Hurst believes a snappy eighteen holes should take bang on four hours – at least half an hour more than it should in my book. Still, the pair up front are keeping up the pace now and at the next I manage to get a shot back and level the match with Rumsfeld, who, I decide, hits five very poor shots and only manages a bogey because his last, a bladed bunker shot, would have landed in the lake had it not hit the pin on the way by and dropped in the cup. He really is rubbish.

Walking down the fifth fairway, I think I've found the spawning ground for Berkshire's entire population of flies. Emerging in their multitude from the grass, they scramble and fly just off the ground ahead of every step I take. It is like those films taken from the air, looking down on tens of thousands of flamingos on a lake, watching them spread out like a giant bow wave as they take off ahead of the helicopter.

Although I nearly hole a bunker shot on this hole, sadly it is my second (having landed in it straight from another bunker on the other side of the green) and Rumsfeld's par is again good enough to take a one-shot lead. The sixth is actually a very attractive par five dogleg right past a delightful pond with weeping willows, lily pads and moorhens pecking along its banks. The green is tucked away in the corner of some trees, with a gravel path leading back out to the seventh tee. My second shot, a five-wood with absolutely nowhere near enough fade on it, lands squarely on this path. By the time I reach it, the two guys in front are walking towards me.

'Not my best effort,' I say with a smile like I was auditioning for the Osmonds.

The younger of the two, the one with the ten-step setup and swing, blanks me completely, but the older one at least smiles back. Progress!

They crunch on up the path and round the corner, thereby missing the best shot either of them are likely to see this or any other day – a full-blooded gap wedge nipped perfectly off the path, high over a tree fifty yards in front to land, spin and stop six feet from the pin. I am astonished at my own genius and start looking around desperately to see if any one else saw it, so I can milk the moment of as much glory as possible. But only Rumsfeld and the flies have witnessed the shot of my trip so far. A quite awful attempt at the birdie takes the shine off the hole, but Donald's three-putted for bogey six so I still get the match back to all square.

I dawdle to the seventh tee, keen not to get up behind the pair in front again, but the young guy has barely made it on to the fairway by the time I reach the tee. I can tell he is keen to keep plugging away, but the older bloke walks over and has a word. Finally, there is a resigned shrug, a huffy glance over the shoulder and I am waved through. I smack a reasonable enough drive up the left and then start that half-walk, half-jog thing golfers do when they are playing through. From selfish, inconsiderate gits to paragons of Corinthian spirit standing loftily on the sporting moral high ground, the slow players in front are instantly transformed when they wave you through. Now you are the one who is all flustered and apologetic, and rarely on these occasions do I play the hole without fluffing at least one shot.

'No hurry,' says the older of the two as I trot past. 'You're obviously making a better job of this than we are.'

His companion, who has busied himself with trying to remember steps five to eight in his backswing, looks up from his studies at that point and scowls.

'Thanks. Still, it's a nice morning for it,' I gasp, not breaking my stride. 'Sorry about the drive at the second, by the way.'

'What? Oh, don't worry – it missed me.'

He seems a nice chap, but I am already pulling ahead in a desperate effort to finish off the hole and get out of their way, so further conversation is out of the question.

It is the third time this morning that I have landed in green goose goo, but I kick it out and into a decent enough lie in the semi-rough. I calculate in the blink of an eye that I am a solid six-iron from the green. Or, in this case – *yet again* – the bloody bunker to the left. Out of breath and sweating by the time I reach the sand, the next three shots are executed almost without thinking and I leave the green with a bogey and one adrift of Rumsfeld once more.

An excellent, low-punched, three-iron recovery from trees on the left at the next saves par and puts me all square once more with nine-handicap Donald. I need a birdie at the par three ninth to finish ahead of him, but one last disastrous pull with a seven-iron later and that is looking like a tall order. The resulting chip and run through the green does its best to deliver, but shoots by the pin and nestles in the fringe beyond. However, just as Rumsfeld is preparing for his infamous bare-bottomed victory dance, I chip in for par and a half in the match.

Thankfully, Hurst is conscious that its course doubles as a large public convenience for wildfowl – although in two hours out there I never saw a single goose – and provides one of those pressurised air cleaning machines for taking the muck off your shoes. You'll obviously want to clean up the trolley as well, before figuring your credit card is a small price to pay and roaring off with it in the boot of your car.

The man of the moment is now past the hearty back-slapping, 'You're a diamond geezer' phase of the evening and is beginning to get a little maudlin.

'Oi loves you,' he says to his pal thickly. 'C'mere.'

And he gives the guy a bear hug that almost cracks his ribs.

'Steady on,' says the other.

'It's just a cuddle, loik. There's nuthin' wrong with tha-at,' says Geezer. 'Oi'm not a queer, y'know.'

Which may be the case, but I still wonder about the wisdom of even bringing up the possibility on this, his last night before being sent to prison.

That, I am convinced, is the tableaux that is playing out before me this evening in the White Horse, Tiverton – soon-to-be-convicted man enjoys last night of freedom before getting sent down for crimes and misdemeanours. He's been the centre of attention all evening. The barmaid, everyone in the little upstairs room with the pool table, a group of large middle-aged women and half a dozen guys down in this, the main bar, have all been offering words of encouragement and support. He, in turn, has been doing the rounds, getting free drinks and projecting such forced breezy confidence it is painful to watch.

I am sitting in the corner with a pint of Tawny, reading the paper. At first I thought a copy of the *North Devon Journal* would have me fitting right in, but I've just noticed that pride of place above the mantelpiece has gone to a framed completed jigsaw and I'm beginning to suspect that any kind of reading might be viewed as just the sort of la-de-da intellectualism they kill people for round here.

To be honest, the front page story about Bideford's plans to save a condemned block of toilets and turn them into a new bandstand is failing to hold my attention. I am much more interested in the pub's living soap opera; in particular, the behaviour of the two guys nearest me at the bar. Ostensibly part of the whole 'Farewell, See You In Four Years – Maybe Two With Good Behaviour' party, they have been singularly lacking in the festive spirit. 'Shifty' might be a word to describe them. 'Guilty' would be another one. Drinking their pints at a rate of knots, they've hardly exchanged a word and yet the only time they have not been looking at each other has been when they've been either glancing nervously across at the main man or out into the street.

I hear a car pull up outside and they both quickly drain their glasses. There is a dreadfully acted fond farewell to Geezer from both and they are out the door before you can say 'narks'. No sooner is the door closed behind them when another of the party spits spectacularly on the floor they've just crossed. There are knowing looks all round, one guy immediately says something short and to the point into his mobile phone and puts it back in his pocket. I am suddenly very uncomfortable indeed. Not wanting to be caught either reading big words without moving my lips or looking at anyone in the pub, I stare fixedly at my pint and start working myself up for a fast exit, when the spitter staggers over to my table, crashes into it and nearly sends my drink flying.

I'll tell you what is more intimidating than tattoos on an angry drunk – home-made tattoos. The arms he plants knuckle-down on the table are covered in crude scribblings and hieroglyphics which, for all I can tell, speak of his undying love for his combine harvester. I look up at a quite astonishingly ugly face that is having a great deal of difficulty containing copious amounts of sweat, snot and saliva.

''Ave you got a loight?' he drips.

I almost giggle in relief, before apologising that I don't.

He shuts his eyes and nods once very deliberately before pushing off with his knuckles and veering over to the other side of the room.

By now, the condemned man is hugging every woman in the bar, paying particular attention to the only one not built like a prop-forward.

'Leave it out,' shouts someone, 'or I'll tell your old lady.'

At that Geezer turns and drapes an arm round his accuser. There are tears in his eyes.

'Oi loves moi woife,' he says with intensity. 'Ev'ry noit oi covers her in kisses . . . Oi does!'

The women sigh, the men jeer – and I get up to leave. As I'm nearing the door, Geezer catches my eye and mouths, 'Thanks for coming'. Suddenly I find myself hoping my theory is well wide of the mark and he is in reality bound for nowhere more perilous than a two-week residential course on tractor maintenance in Taunton.

Over a luminous chicken curry in the Saffron Indian Restaurant up the road, I pull out my dog-eared copy of Cousins' *Golf in Britain* and re-read his considered opinion on artisan golf clubs. 'The private club golfer is usually one who has never known the artisan world and has no wish to enter it. Not from any snobbish feelings of superiority, but because he is geared to the private world and accustomed to finding his fun and his friends there. The artisan is content with his world for similar reasons,' he writes. As I've discovered with the lads at Backworth and the black golfers at Wyboston Lakes, there is a lot to be said for the relaxation and enjoyment to be had in playing this game in the company of those you are familiar and comfortable with. But it was not for the chance to play golf with your social peers that the artisan movement was founded – and it is not the reason it continues to this day.

In simple terms, an artisan club is one attached to a parent club and made up of those unable, for reasons of breeding, class or finance, to gain membership of the latter. Through a carefully worked out and rigorously adhered to agreement, the members of the artisan club pay a reduced fee and often undertake certain green-keeping tasks in return for golf on the course at restricted hours (usually early in the morning and late at night). In the years before public golf became widely available in England it was the only way those outside the gentleman and professional classes could hope to get a game. This applied particularly in rural areas where feudal attitudes prevailed, even after the first, urban-based municipal courses were built.

Crucial, obviously, to the smooth working of this system is the strict demarcation of those who are and are not eligible for membership of the artisan club. Definitions vary across the country, but generally speaking anyone who is a manual worker (plumber, builder, fisherman etc.) can join an artisan club – and yes, the distinctions still apply today. Should you be lucky or hard-working enough to gain promotion from the shop floor to management, albeit on the lowly paid bottom rung, you will be forced to forfeit your artisan membership. In these more 'enlightened' times, you will almost always be able to join the parent club – at the full fee, of course – but in years past the newly created blue-collar worker could find himself overqualified for the artisans, yet still not socially acceptable enough for the members in the main clubhouse.

Obviously stories abound concerning the attempts by

ineligible golfers to join or remain in artisan clubs, either to avoid paying the full whack at the parent club or just to keep playing the game at all. A favourite is that of the member of a Hertfordshire artisan club whose employment was listed as 'meat cutter'. A survey of the club's membership for the parent club's records soon focused on the suspiciously well-spoken butcher . . . who turned out to be a surgeon at a London hospital.

Cousins is adamant the first real artisan club in England was the Cantelupe, founded in 1897 and based at Forest Row in Sussex, while the rest of the golfing world generally accepts that Northam Working Men's Club at Westward Ho!, founded in 1888, has the stronger claim. Whatever the differences in the small print of their respective constitutions, the two were essentially the same species of golf club and heralded the start of an artisan movement that spread across the country. (It has to be noted here that a form of artisan club already existed in Scotland, but these were quite different animals. At a time when most, if not all, golf clubs north of the Border were non-course owning and played on the common links, many of them drew their membership specifically from artisans in the area. They were independent of any other club and, in truth, had more in common with the likes of the Honourable Company of Edinburgh Golfers than with these new, dependent clubs in England.)

As a manifestation of the *noblesse oblige* Victorian/-Edwardian attitude to the lower orders, artisan sections would be hard to beat; the private club assuaged its collective feelings of guilt (remember this was still the age of 'rational recreation' and the belief that if you weren't going to pay the proles a decent wage you should at least let them exercise every now and then in fresh air) *and* earned more money from fees and got work done on the course for nothing. Result!

It was often easy to tell if a club had an artisan section. Apart from the main clubhouse, professional and starter's hut, and perhaps a shed for the greenkeeper, there would be a basic, ramshackle shelter off in some corner – the artisans' 'clubhouse'. I've been to several courses with artisan clubs over the years and, in truth, the accommodation nowadays is little better, mostly consisting of converted garages, Portakabins, tiny huts – the artisans can count themselves lucky if they have a window let alone electricity.

While Cousins and most sporting historians that preceded him tended to forgive the clubs their patronising opportunism on the grounds that at least they provided working-class golf where previously there had been none, later studies into the sport's social history have been less charitable. John Lowerson, in particular, laments the lost opportunity for the artisan movement to pioneer wider participation in golf simply because it 'found it difficult to break out of the patterns of deference built into its origins' (1989). He quotes the 1921 Artisan Golfers' Association (AGA) estimate that if every private golf club had an artisan club attached, there would be something like 200,000 more working-class golfers in the country.

Many clubs, however, did not allow artisan sections to be formed, often, it has to be said, because the members themselves could not countenance the inherent snobberies involved, but usually because their finances were healthy enough and they saw no reason to share their few acres of upper-middle-class paradise with 'staff'. Healthy relationships between senior clubs and their artisans undoubtedly existed in a spirit of mutual tolerance and benefit, but all too often artisans were treated like servants.

In his book *Sport and the English Middle Classes* (1993), Lowerson highlights the 1910 match between Cantelupe and Walton Heath's artisans at Ashdown Forest. Unusually, this was covered by *The Times*, but quite obviously as a piece of colour writing rather than honest sports reporting. Lowerson concludes that so patronising was the account – including referring to the players by their first names (an Edwardian convention reserved for house boys and dogs) – that it was obviously never expected that any of the participants would ever read it.

As a member of an artisan club you would be expected to enter the course by a particular gate at certain hours, doff your cap, speak when you were spoken to, play at the crack of dawn or not at all, beg for the merest creature comfort in your hut, take time out from your precious few hours away from the factory or the workshop to mow their fairways and repair their divots and never, under any circumstances, set foot inside their sacred clubhouse. Such restrictions were accepted by the pre-socialist worker, conditioned, as he was, as much by the social rigidities of the age as his 'superiors'.

Remarkably, however, some artisans were still embracing their role as second-class citizens more than eighty years after the movement began. For example, in 1973, when Labour members of Watford Council tried to foment class warfare over the fact that the West Herts Golf Club had barred working class golfers from entering its clubhouse, the then honorary secretary of the AGA dismissed their efforts as unwarranted and unwanted. 'It is merely a question of *natural selection* [my italics],' said William Farley. 'The artisan members at Watford and at more than 180 other clubs are happier with things as they are.'

Questionable though the origins of the artisan movement

may be, a distinction does need to be made between the forelock-tugging attitude of their predecessors and the modern AGA (co-founded by JH Taylor and Fred Hawtree). The artisans of today see themselves as the custodians of a tradition of accessible, working-class golf that pre-dates any other south of the Border. No one I've spoken to at the AGA would view their role as subservient, far less one that is the result of 'natural selection'. They also, quite rightly, point out that the average member of an artisan golf club plays golf on a better class of course (often championship standard) than others of their income bracket forced on to municipal links.

Yet the eighty-odd artisan clubs that have made it into the twenty-first century know that their jackets are on a shaky nail. There are hundreds of public, municipal, pay-and-play golf courses nowadays, say the full fee-paying members of parent golf clubs. Hell, there isn't even any waiting list here and we don't care any more whether you wash cars for a living or buy a new car when your old one gets dirty. Why should you get what is effectively subsidised golf? In the absence of a good enough answer, they have closed their artisan clubs down in increasing numbers; ten have been disbanded in the last five years. Those that survive are being asked, not unreasonably, to contribute a larger proportion of the full membership fee and are having to re-define their roles within the parent club structure. Is there room for the artisan movement in this day and age when cheap golf is readily available, when clubs are desperate for members and deference to one's betters has given way to 'kiss my arse'? Perhaps a trip back to where it all began will help me find out.

9

I must confess to a degree of conservatism when it comes to one characteristic of club golf. Never having developed a taste for shell suits or the sight of overweight men in football shorts, I can see the merit in dress codes. While I object to having to put on best bib and tucker for the privilege of giving a club my hard earned £2.60 for a plate of soup and a cheese roll, I do think a prohibition on beachwear and Manchester Utd shirts in the clubhouse is perfectly reasonable. Do we object to wearing the trendy designer shirt we bought that day for a night out clubbing? Would we dream of wearing the colours of our deadly rivals for an afternoon on the football terraces? Dressing appropriately is surely an important element in enjoying the whole sporting/leisure experience.

As with many things connected to the game, however, the whole dress code issue tends to be the subject of grotesque caricature, thanks to the behaviour of a minority of anachronistic old clubs. Not being the sort who ever took to ties (I find it hard, in fact, not to look at a tie and think what a silly, redundant little vestige of a once-functional item it is – like my appendix), I tend to get hot under the collar when forced to wear one. Since I don't choke myself to go to work, I see no reason to do so when I'm supposed to be relaxing at a golf club. But, like most golfers, I've had my fair share of run-ins with those who you feel would forgive a career of murder, mayhem and child molestation so long as one sported a clean cuff and a firm knot. (I recall turning up for a game with a friend at Pollok Golf Club in Glasgow and being told by a member that my jacket had to be on – not slung over my shoulder – and my tie straightened under a buttoned-up collar. And I was still in the car park!)

Of course, rules about jackets and ties were drawn up by those for whom such apparel is the cornerstone of outfits for any and all occasions, save perhaps going to bed. There survives a large minority of mostly middle-aged and elderly men for whom the mere fact that it is Saturday is no reason to let one's standards slip, invite chaos and anarchy and forego the double Windsor. Politicians, mostly of the Conservative persuasion, are among their number and what fish out of water they look whenever they appear on the news with their 'I'm in the country now' tweed jackets and ties. Like pasty-faced Goths in lovely summer weather, Tory MPs and weekends just don't seem to go together.

It wasn't that long ago that golf was actually played in a shirt and tie and many clubs are still administered by those for whom the advent of the polo shirt was a calamity to rank alongside the admission of women and the end of national service.

A glance at the notice above the entrance to the wood-panelled locker room at the Royal North Devon Golf Club leads me to suspect I am in such an institution now.

Dress, it says in bold lettering, should be 'clean, tidy and inoffensive to others who may be more formally dressed'.

Looked at one way, it could merely be an expression of the perfectly laudable ban on Essex leisurewear, but it's a tad too pedantic for my liking, not to mention vague – I could be wearing my only decent suit and tie and still manage to offend a passing member in his bow tie and cummerbund. Not far from this notice is the rogue's gallery of past club captains and a regiment of whiskered old lords, vice admirals and lieutenant colonels they look, too. The steel trap that is my mechanism for forming balanced opinion, based on an exhaustive analysis of all the available information, is about to snap shut when a guy in a Hawaiian shirt walks past and gives me a cheery wave.

'Can oi 'elp you?' he asks as an afterthought. I tell him I'm looking for Martin Turner, the president of the artisan section, and he directs me to the Northam Golf Club's hut on the other side of the car park from the main clubhouse.

'No, they're not a stuffy lot at all,' says Martin, who is there to greet me. 'In fact, we have a very good relationship with them. And so we should – their secretary used to be ours.'

We stand in the doorway to Northam's 'clubhouse', a converted shed that once housed mowers and other machinery for the course. Martin would love to take me inside and show me their trophies, pictures and other memorabilia, but the shed has no windows and he's just discovered the electricity supply has gone on the blink. So we lean on the wall and he continues to explain how closely the two clubs work with each other.

'Apart from when Royal North Devon are holding their

own competitions, we don't have any restrictions on when we can play or access the clubhouse,' he says. 'We all know each other and we all get on. They're no different to us really.'

Why, therefore, would anyone in their right mind want to pay the full fee (currently just over £400) and join Royal North Devon rather than pay what I assume is buttons by comparison and join the artisans of Northam?

'A-ah,' says Martin and I get the awful feeling something complicated is on its way. 'In 1999, we signed this agreement that gradually increases the size of our fees and the amount that we hand over to Royal North Devon for the use of the course. When I joined in 1989, the annual fee was £5. Now it's £200.'

He goes on to 'explain' the sliding scale of percentage fee hikes over a ten-year period, some of which remains for Northam to use in running its own affairs, but an ever-increasing proportion of which goes directly to the parent club, the idea being that at the end of that term in 2009 there is greater parity between the two. I'm prepared to take all this as read, but Martin has a higher opinion of my journalistic rigour than I do and insists on familiarising me with a table showing incremental changes year-on-year, the agreed formula at the beginning and how it can be deployed, as if by magic, to confirm relative fee rates at any given time in the ten-year period.

'It's quite simple,' he says at last, incorrectly assuming he had established this fact. Whatever the details, it is obvious there is a constructive relationship between the two and that, for the moment at least, the threat of closure does not hang over Northam.

'We are the oldest artisan club in the country and both clubs here are very proud of that,' says Martin.

It is a glorious day at Westward Ho!, but the sunlight is not penetrating the stygian gloom of Northam's hut, so we adjourn for a cup of coffee in Royal North Devon's lounge. This, I am delighted to see, has been turned into something of a shrine to JH Taylor, the local lad made good and a former member, of course, of what was formally known as Northam Working Men's Club. There are old photographs and paintings, and letters to and from Taylor, including a snippet of correspondence between him and Rudyard Kipling.

Presently we are joined by Paul, a tall fellow who simply frowns slightly, smiles and says, 'Fine, thanks,' when I ask him how the boiler and shower are doing.

'Got it all sorted?' I enquire.

'Er, yes,' he replies.

I have to say I would have thought he'd have been a little bit more diffident, but he seems a nice big affable chap and it's hard to hold a grudge. So I let it go. After all, I'm sure there was nothing he could've done about it.

Our tee-off time is fast approaching, so we make our way back out to the car park to get kitted up and it is here, a few minutes later, that I am introduced to a young guy in a bright yellow t-shirt.

'This is Pixie, he'll be making up the four-ball,' says Martin.

'Look, I'm really sorry,' says Pixie, shaking me by the hand. 'My mobile was switched off all day and I had no idea until I got home last night.'

For a moment all four of us stand in a circle staring at each other . . . the sky, our feet, scratching our heads – four monkeys trying to figure out the meaning of life, the universe and everything.

'A-ah,' says Martin eventually. '*He's* Paul.' And he points at Pixie.

'So you're Pixie,' I say to Paul.

'No. He is.'

'Then who was fixing the burst shower and the dodgy boiler?'

'I was,' says Pixie.

'Was it yours?' I ask Paul.

'No,' says Paul with a sigh. 'Mine's fine.'

I stare at him for a while with my mouth open ready to say something intelligent that will make sense of all this. But nothing comes to mind.

'So you're not a plumber?'

'I'm a postman,' says Paul.

'With a perfectly fine shower and boiler?'

'That's it,' he says, relieved to have finally gotten this across.

It is Pixie who, as Paul, is the secretary of Northam Golf Club – and a plumber. Pixie who arranged to meet me here yesterday, who didn't show up, didn't answer any calls to his mobile, condemned me to a day of cream teas and chicken-in-a-basket at Westward Ho!, finally phoned last night as I was hunting for a hotel in Barnstaple and explained that he had been called away to fix a boiler and shower. But not Paul's.

'Why is he called Pixie?' I ask Martin as we make our way to the first tee.

'Dunno. Never asked.'

So I do.

'When I left school I was four foot seven and skinny,' says Pixie.

'A-ah,' says Martin yet again.

Pixie, who has obviously bulked up more than a little

since school, takes our four balls and drops them on the ground to determine the teams for the day (the two that land closest together play together) and this results in Martin and me taking on the other two in what I am beginning to realise is a fairly serious game of four-ball better-ball. The intricacies of differential membership fee gearing and who is, and is not, a plumber having convinced me I have the mental acuity of a buttered scone, I leave the working out of relative handicaps to the other three. Fully five minutes later it turns out that my team-mate, Martin 'The Bandit' Turner, with a handicap somewhere in the low twenties, gets more than half a dozen strokes on Paul and Pixie, and this suits me just fine.

Between my earlier dips into the history of golf in Britain and recent introduction to the life of JH Taylor, I feel there has been a certain destiny about coming here to the Royal North Devon, which, you may remember, was arguably the first course in England to be built specifically for Englishmen to play (albeit by the ubiquitous Old Tom Morris from St Andrews). The course stretches over a piece of low-lying land known as the Burrows, a panorama of which can be seen from the clubhouse and the slope down to the first tee. It is an oddly-shaped spit of land that pokes out from under the cliffs of Northam and Westward Ho! and is dotted with rocky outcrops and marsh. This is classic links land and in 1864 it would've provided Old Tom with a very familiar canvas. Like most courses of that vintage, it has been tweaked and lengthened over the years and is now a roughly 6,500-yard par seventy-two.

The first hole is a reasonably straightforward par five apart from the drive, which must negotiate a burn and small expanse of reedy bog thirty yards or so in front of the tee. Martin has the honour and finds the fairway with an easy swing that makes me suspect our opponents may have grounds for their complaint about his handicap. My effort is a little pushed, but otherwise safe enough. Paul and Pixie, on the other hand, having predicted all sorts of disaster for our tee shots, then proceed to top both their own drives into the bog. One up after one.

As I'm climbing back over the tape fence that protects the first green, having secured a steady opening par, I find myself in a minefield of droppings. I ask if sheep are allowed to graze all over the course.

'Not just sheep – horses, too,' says Paul.

'And they're not only allowed to graze on the course, they live here all the year round,' says Pixie. 'It's part of the original agreement with the townsfolk when the course was built. In fact, no one's got more rights on the course than they do.'

Doesn't that make for a bit of a mess? I ask.

I get some knowing looks back, but none of the three seem prepared to speak their mind. I get the impression this is a sore point, but obviously one golfers hereabouts have had to live with for almost 150 years with no hope of the situation ever changing. What it means is that for the second round in a row I am playing golf in a large toilet. Thankfully, in this case there is a local rule.

'If it's scattered, loik,' says Pixie, 'you have to play the ball where it lies, but if it's piled up and fresh you can move it.'

Lovely.

Walking the opening few holes it is clear this is a golf course not only blighted by several hundred livestock, but rabbits as well; scrapings and the eponymous burrows are all over the place. Between piles of dung and the holes ready to twist the ankle of the unwary, golf at Royal North Devon is obviously a game to be played with your head down at all times. Yet it is not, by any means, an unpleasant place to stroll around. If you do dare to raise your eye for a second there are wheatears fluttering overhead, hovering like little kestrels, and carpets of gorgeous, soft purple Devon violets stretching out across the sand dunes.

'It's the badgers that get me,' says Paul suddenly and with some passion. 'The bastards are digging up the eleventh and the tenth fairways—'

'And the twelfth,' says Martin.

'—and the twelfth, but there's nothing we can do, see. The bastards have got protection, haven't they?'

As it happens, I'm rather fond of badgers. More than once I've reported on the little chaps' efforts to escape the clutches of morons with fighting dogs, but I suspect a plea in mitigation might not go down too well in the present company.

'Bastards,' I agree.

Martin and I win the second hole thanks to a solid par from your correspondent, but we lose the third after Pixie finally gets into a rhythm and fires a lovely mid-iron straight at the flag for a birdie. There's a bit of a wait on the fourth tee and I ask about public golf in Devon.

'Ain't none,' says Paul. 'Least ways, none up round these parts.'

Are there any municipal courses, I wonder?

'Nope.'

The guys have heard there might be a pay-and-play

course down on the south coast somewhere, but they're not sure where and they wouldn't travel that far for a round anyway.

'If you want to play golf in Devon,' says Martin, 'basically you've got to join a club. That's why the artisan clubs are so important.'

'But there're less and less of them, ain't there,' says Paul. 'There used to be seven artisan clubs in Devon. Now there're only three.'

'It's not fair, is it?' says Martin. 'There are still people round here who can't afford to join the big clubs. It'll just mean fewer people playing the game.'

Pixie, we have finally established, is a plumber and Paul a postman. Martin is a ship's carpenter who, along with 500 other local men and women, is looking for work, having recently lost his job, when the local shipyard at Appledore went into receivership. If he got a job in management . . .

'I wouldn't be working with my hands anymore and I'd have to leave Northam Golf Club. Simple as that,' he says.

'Oh yeah, we'd make sure of that,' says Pixie with a laugh. 'Should've kicked you out years ago anyway cos you're a bandit.'

Strangely, a two-ball on the fourth tee makes way for us. They are quite insistent and have that look of near novices to the game who could do without any kind of audience for their swings. They also look as if they are more than a little daunted by what is in store, and with good reason, for what is in store is what used to be the largest bunker in Britain. Cape Bunker is an absolute monster that stretches the entire width of the fairway – a good thirty or forty yards – and has a face of railway sleepers I estimate to be no less than twenty feet high at one corner. The only reason it is no longer the biggest bunker in Britain is because some years ago the club built a narrow strip of turf through the middle and now it is technically two bunkers.

Paul, who was most scathing about this decision to pander to golfing cowards while on the tee, is inevitably the only one of us to land in it. Pixie clears it with a mighty drive, while Martin and I take irons and play well short of its gaping maw. It is not his first effort that gets Paul out, and between that and having to walk some considerable distance to find a rake and then smooth out the lengthy route he had to take into and out of the thing, I can tell he is a little less proud of the course's most famous obstacle than he was on the tee. But he manages a crooked smile that broadens to a huge grin when he finds that his playing partner has damn-near driven the green. All square.

This stretch of holes runs along the northern edge of the Burrows, a perimeter marked by a high bank, on the other side of which lies a huge expanse of grey stone beach, known as the pebble ridge, that falls away sharply to the sea. During my enforced dawdling in Westward Ho! yesterday I'd come across several references to 'pot walloping' and gathered that, whatever it was, it happened out here during one particular weekend in May.

'It's chucking stones,' Pixie tells me. 'Everyone goes down on to the beach and throws stones that have been pulled down off the banking by the sea back up on to the ridge.'

'It's a good laugh,' says Paul. 'They make a day out of it and there's competitions and all sorts.'

Don't you just love the English? Repairing sea defences, rolling cheese down a hill, supporting Tim Henman at Wimbledon – they can make an event out of anything.

The awkward par three fifth is halved with bogeys all round, but another stroke for Martin at the dogleg sixth puts our noses in front once again. I am surveying my target line down the seventh when Pixie sidles up and warns me to be careful about the bunkers. But which ones?

'They're just about driving distance, a little left of centre there. You can't see them,' he says with a twinkle in his eye.

I look to my partner for some local knowledge I can rely on.

'You're fine,' says Martin. 'Don't listen to him.'

'Hah! Nice try,' I say to Pixie and fire a veritable howitzer down the middle of the fairway.

'Uh-oh, looks a bit sandy to me,' says Pixie, even as the ball is still rising.

'Yep,' agrees Paul, studying the flight path with a grin. 'We-ell . . .' It lands and starts bouncing down the fairway. 'Yep . . . nope . . . oh, ah . . . oh yes. Sand.'

From where I am standing, a perfect tee-shot has just been abducted by aliens. One moment it was rolling nicely into position *a*, the next it has disappeared.

'Told you,' says Pixie, with undisguised glee, while Martin is suddenly determined to get something out of the deepest pocket in his golf bag and is too busy to talk.

When we reach the spot, two of the smallest but deepest bunkers on the course are sitting side by side, and my ball is in the front one. From the lie of the land it is obvious that a 'perfect' drive hit bang on line will be gathered up by the slopes all around and fed into one or other of them. It is the first bunker I've been in, but will not be the last. Royal North Devon has no fewer than 174 bunkers. Add in all the reeds and rushes, the craggy mounds, horse dung, rabbit holes and badger roadworks and you can imagine that driving accuracy is at a premium. Thankfully the golfing gods are in a fair-minded mood today and ensure that some woeful chipping and putting by both Pixie and Paul mean Martin and I still manage to win the hole and go two up. In fact, I must be Mortal of the Month up there, because at the very next hole, having been the only one to miss this 184-yard par three from the tee, the gods allow my bump-and-run recovery to hit the pin and drop for a birdie. Three up.

For a few holes I've been noticing deep horseshoe prints in the turf and now here, on the ninth tee, I can see a herd of ponies slap-bang in the middle of the fairway.

'Don't worry – they'll get out of the way,' says Martin.

Naturally, I don't believe him, but Pixie gives me a reassuring nod so I hit off anyway. Sure enough, by the time I reach my ball the ponies have eased out of my way and left me, for all I know quite consciously, a clear line to the green. This being a par five, it is only as I'm standing over my third shot that I realise something odd about the target. Are there two flags on that green? Indeed, there are. Nobody can come up with an explanation for this, but we all agree to play for the one in the middle of the green. My gods are still on the case, because Pixie then fires in a half wedge that bites a little too soon and finishes four inches from the wrong hole. Martin is getting another stroke and my three-putting is not enough to stop us going four up.

'C'mon partner,' says Paul. 'We're getting fucking slaughtered here.'

And so they are. The next two holes also go our way after, I have to say in all modesty, some nerveless putting on my part. I can't hit a green in regulation to save myself, but when I eventually get there I'm finding the pace and consistency of the putting surfaces very much to my liking. By now Paul can see the writing on the wall and is joking about jumping ship and joining Martin and me – despite the fact that it is his own wayward driving that has been mostly to blame for their sorry performance. We've lost count of the number of drives sliced or topped into the rushes and gorse – but his provisionals have all been belters.

'I know. If it was the second ball that counted, I'd be a scratch player,' he says.

Strolling down the twelfth fairway after yet another perfectly placed provisional, Paul joins Martin and Pixie in explaining some of the obligations the Northam members have at Royal North Devon.

'There's divoting,' he says. 'A couple of times a year, we all goes out in the evening with buckets of seeded soil to repair the divots, see.'

'And beer – we've got the beers as well,' says Martin.

'Oh, we has a lovely time of it alright,' agrees Pixie.

But what about the snob factor? How do they feel having to do this when the members of Royal North Devon are all sitting up in the clubhouse sipping gin and watching them?

'It's not like that at all round here,' says Paul, strongly. 'We don't feel inferior to them, do we?' His friends agree wholeheartedly.

'Golf isn't a snobby game here,' Paul continues. 'Everyone knows what we're like – we like a drink and a laugh. You go to some clubs and they can be a bit off, but those are the ones that don't need the money we gives them through the bar.'

'As for the others,' says Martin to general amused agreement, 'well I reckon we've just brought them down to our level.'

Given the fact that Royal North Devon knows it has an historical artisan section, that the legacy of JH Taylor is inextricably linked to both institutions, and that members and office bearers of one club often 'graduate' to the other, it is little wonder there is a close and happy relationship between the two. But, as I've mentioned before, that is not the case with all artisan clubs and their senior counterparts.

Once upon a time they were the favourite sons of the golfing world, seen by many as the saving grace of a game gone sour on privilege and prejudice. Even in 1952, as the second great wave of municipal golf course development was sweeping the country, Lord Brabazon of Tara (a pioneer airman in his day, as well as the man credited with using the first golf trolley in Britain) could write in *A History of Golf in Britain* that the artisan movement 'will restore golf to its pristine glory in this country, so that everybody takes an interest in it, and I believe that some of our great players will rise from the artisan ranks'.

Starting with Abe Mitchell of Cantelupe who turned professional and became a successful Ryder Cup player, not to mention JH Taylor himself, the artisans did produce some great golfers, but the advance of public golf and the decreasing wealth of many private clubs over the last sixty years has left them behind the times. Today they are a beleaguered lot and some recent jibes in the golfing press have only served to heighten their sensitivity. So much so that artisan golfers I had spoken to at other clubs did so only strictly off the record. A complaint from one I talked to in the London area is typical of many: 'We know that the main club are just looking for an excuse to close us down . . . They want to make us an "offer" of full membership with a slight discount, but it's a joke. They just want more money so they can do up their clubhouse.'

It is obvious from the example of Royal North Devon and Northam that, with a little common sense and under-standing on both sides, it is possible for artisan clubs to continue – and in places like Devon, where there appears to be little else in the way of low-cost golf on offer, it is vital that they do. But let's be honest – the proliferation of public pay-and-play golf in most parts of the country means the old rationalisation for artisan sections no longer applies.

Artisan clubs that are limited to men (and it is usually strictly men only) who fulfil some hundred-year-old defi-nition of honest, hard-working yeomanry *are* an anachro-nism. The root cause of the problem is not artisan clubs *per se*, it is golf clubs' legendary conservatism and inertia. Membership provision needs to be adaptable to take account of changing social and work patterns. The idea that in the age of short-term contracts, shift work, long commutes, working from home and flexi-time a guy can only get into a club based on whether or not his hands are dirty at the end of the day is preposterous and insulting. Let's bring the poor sods in from the shed and stick the mowers back in. Allow clubs within clubs to exist for those with different needs and incomes and call them artisan sections if you wish, but treat them as equals and don't make them cut the grass for the privilege of sharing the bar and locker room.

A private train of thought, there. My playing partners today are obviously perfectly happy with things as they are in Westward Ho! and I'm not about to sow the seeds of sedition here on the twelfth fairway. Not when I am poised to deliver the *coup de grace* with ruthless efficiency and what has become my usual dollop of good fortune.

A thinned three-wood second shot to this long par four manages to avoid every bunker and sneak on to the front edge of the green. Two putts later it is all over – Pixie and Paul have been beaten seven and six. Gone for a dog's licence, as they used to say in old money, and Martin is clearly relishing the bragging rights he will have for the next few days.

This is usually my cue to play appallingly for the remaining holes. Sure enough – and much to our erstwhile opponents' annoyance – I start hooking and dunching all over the place, find at least four more bunkers, the ditch at the seventeenth and contrive to drop five strokes in six holes. In my defence I can say that what started out as a roasting day with sun block on my nose has ended in freezing rain with my waterproofs keeping the back seat of the car nice and dry. Where that squall came from I have no idea, but Westward Ho! is not exactly a sheltered spot and locals often pay more attention to the forecast for County Cork than they do for the rest of England.

Given the plumbing emergency that resulted in an extra day in Devon, I am keen to hit the road as soon as possible after our round. As it happens, the troublesome boiler has still not been fitted and Pixie has promised to return this evening to finish the job. Paul's missus turns up to 'escort' him home and Martin has got the wiring in the hut to try and fix. There are handshakes all round in the car park and we all head off on our separate ways.

Suddenly, I am tired of English market towns. From Stamford to Colchester, Tiverton to Barnstaple, I've wandered the same streets of Mothercares and WH Smiths, ye olde black and gold bollards and hanging baskets of geraniums and trailing lobelia. Outside the same White Hart and Rose & Crown pubs the same taut young men and their ample girlfriends have stared at mobile phones, texting (probably each other) as I've walked past in search of something other than curry or pizza to eat. My few days in London already seem like an eternity ago and I crave the bright lights. I want to feel the buzz of a big city again. I want razzmatazz, sophistication. I want danger, excitement and urban cool. I want Birmingham.

'Yoroit? . . . Grite!'

Ron gives me a big grin and the thumbs up as I tuck into 'Cajun chicken' and chips in the restaurant of the Kensington Guest House in Selly Park. See what I mean – less than an hour after arriving in a city and already I'm on a learning curve. I had not previously appreciated that boiled carrots were a mainstay of New Orleans cuisine.

Ron runs one of the few remaining independent hotels in the area – 'Everyone else has shut. Either they were too expensive or they just weren't good enough' – and has an impressive collection of signed photographs from TV celebrities on the wall of the reception area.

'Pebble Mill's just up the road,' he'd told me with impressive nonchalance as I was signing in. 'We like to think we provide the right standard of accommodation for people in the entertainment industry.'

From rural mundanity to metropolitan glamour in a single bound!

I finish my meal and wander into the lounge for a nightcap and perhaps a spot of urbane badinage with my fellow guests. Stuart is from Hull and is in town on a scaffolding course. He is drinking Stella Artois out of a can.

'How many blacks do you have in Scotland?' he asks. Probably not as many as there are round here, I say.

'Well, there's probably as many whites here as there are blacks where you come from. I can't get used to all the black faces. I'm not a racialist mind, but I just feel intimidated by them all—'

I excuse myself and go to get a refill.

At the bar I discover that I am drinking wine out of a box – and it's finished. I have some difficulty in ordering a whisky without ice before Richard sits down at the next bar stool and introduces himself. He is a local guy, delivers sports cars for a living and is drinking lager and blackcurrant.

'The Ferrari 550 – that's my favourite,' he says.

I say I'm not sure what it looks like and he responds by showing me a photograph of one he delivered earlier – proof, at last, that all those billions spent on third generation mobile phones were not wasted.

'Ooh, I've eaten so much I could burst,' says a clearly tipsy woman in a tracksuit who's just weaved into the room. And to prove her point, she lifts her top to show everyone her belly and much else besides.

'I mean, I like garlic but that curry was strong. Woof!'

She is in her early forties, looks like Ruud Van Nistelrooy and is, according to an offstage whisper from Stuart, 'gagging for it'.

'I learned something great today – who wants to volunteer?'

If the lack of a headlong rush disappoints her, she hides it well and provides further information. She is on a week-long nursing course and is keen to practise a new manoeuvre for getting heart attack victims out of a chair. The clear implication is that it would not be public spirited of us all to deny a vital NHS operative the chance to practise life-saving techniques. But we do anyway.

To her credit she does not give up and at last Richard reluctantly puts down his Day-Glo red pint and accepts the offer of one of the lounge easy chairs. As quick as you like, his arms are crossed, an elbow is tugged and he is lying on the floor, his head nestled in the bosom of the squiffy nurse – which, you feel, is exactly what she was planning all along.

Stuart and his pals down their cans of lager – 'Stella Act-a-Twat, I calls it' – and head thither for some night club action in swinging Selly Park, while a couple of Baltic-sounding guys in the corner order more beers and stare fixedly at some programme on the TV that appears to be about two families who swap babies, open up a bed and breakfast in Tuscany, then choose one of their number to represent Britain at the next Eurovision Song Contest.

Van Nistelrooy, meanwhile, is trying get the bar interested in a debate on plastic surgery – a thin excuse for her to repeatedly grab her breasts and proclaim them 100 per cent home-made. Eventually the lager and blackcurrant robs Richard of the last of his resistance, not to mention judgement and discretion, and he follows nursey up the stairs.

'Come on love – I don't charge much,' she says over her shoulder.

10

Instant though the successes of Hainault Forest and Richmond Park in London were, the spread of municipal golf across the rest of the country was not something that could've been confused with wildfire. Some cities, notably Nottingham, Bristol, Manchester, Leeds and Sheffield, did dabble with public courses – either 'municipalising' private ones gone bust or building their own. But between 1920 and 1930, only twenty-eight municipal courses were built in the whole of the United Kingdom – and almost half of those were in Scotland, which already had thirty-two of them up and running before the First World War. During the same decade, private courses were being opened at an average rate of around twenty every year.

The reasons were partly financial; although land prices were falling, cities were expanding at a fair lick and suitable land on the outskirts was often difficult to snatch away from the speculators and private housing developers. And, of course, there was the small matter of the Depression. Plans for public golf courses, however, also ran up against objections from ratepayers who disliked the idea of spending their money on what was still largely held to be a rich man's game. Participation was not yet so widespread that it could be seen, even by the paternalists, as an improving leisure activity. The fact that this was probably down to the lack of facilities doesn't seem to have dawned on them.

The examples of Braid Hills in Edinburgh, which took in almost £1,200 in 1909 from more 181,548 paying customers, and the public course in Sheffield, which attracted 10,000 players in its first three weeks, were often quoted by supporters, but these riches failed to persuade cautious councillors up and down the country that available land should be laid out as a golf course rather than a public park.

Another problem was that, even when municipal courses were built, they often priced out the low paid, just as effectively as Bournemouth had in the 1890s with its 'public' course for toffy tourists. In Scotland, that alleged bastion of accessible public golf, city corporations laying out the new wave of purpose-built courses were not above a little exploitation themselves. The Hazlehead course in Aberdeen, for example, was built in 1927 through the labour of unemployed men who were not taken off the dole, just given a little extra bonus for their efforts. The self-styled 'people's golf course' then charged a green fee that was widely attacked in the city as too expensive for the low paid – and certainly too much for those who had just burst a gut building the thing.

Birmingham City Council actually inherited a ready-made golf course at Warley when it refused to renew the lease held by Edgbaston Golf Club in 1906. As local historian John Moreton details in his chronicles of golf in the West Midlands, the council permitted the club to remain there until it moved to a new site in the city four years later, at which point it came under pressure to run the original course as a municipal. But despite pleas from the golf correspondent of the *Birmingham Post*, in particular, councillors demurred and when war broke out in 1914 part of the course was ploughed for agriculture. By 1921, however, attitudes towards golf had mellowed sufficiently for the council to pay for a remodelling of Warley and in May of that year the city's first municipal course was opened. Two years later it was making a profit for the council of £1,275 and a year after that it was reported as being seriously overcrowded.

There's nothing more zealous than a convert, as they say, and with Warley raking it in, Birmingham suddenly became very enthusiastic about the whole municipal golf thing. Over the course of the next ten years it opened four new public golf courses around the city – three of them designed and built by our old friends JH Taylor and Fred Hawtree. The first of those, Lickey Hills, was made possible by a donation of the land and £2,500 towards the costs from local businessmen, philanthropists and all-round good eggs (creme, presumably), Edward and George Cadbury.

Birmingham City now has eight municipal courses under its management and I am in town to play whichever one can fit me in at short notice. I am delighted to say that my playing partner will be the aforementioned Mr Moreton. As luck has it, his house is not that far from my hotel nor from the course we've decided to try and get our round in this afternoon.

It has been necessary on occasions to tell people on this trip that I am not, by trade or inclination, an historian. (Which is not to say you can have anything other than complete faith in whatever historical details appear in this book – I've always been very careful to steal them from people who know what they're talking about.) Should anyone remain in some doubt as to what a real historian looks like, I would bring them round to meet John Moreton. A tall, bespectacled former school master, he greets me at his front door with a warm, yet slightly distracted, smile. It turns out that he is in that classic state of disarray only the truly bookish seem to get themselves into; halfway through proof-reading a history of a local club that he'd been sent and trying to organise a match for the junior golfers he coaches, he realised his washing needed to be hung up and was in the middle of dithering between all three jobs when I turned up and demanded tea and conversation. At last he decides to sit me down in his front room with a brew and piles of papers and newspaper cuttings I might find useful, so he can at least attend to his smalls.

Between towers of classical and jazz CDs, I can see that John has amassed an impressive collection of golf books. Just how impressive I don't really find out until I go through to his study a little later, where frankly every book that has ever been written about the sport must be on the shelves. There are hundreds of them – from *Big Boys' Bumper Books of Golfing Trivia* from the 1950s to the most recent biographies of Tiger Woods, from Bernard Darwin, the first great golf journalist, to Peter Alliss – they are all there. Then there are the stacks of club histories, the reams of county match results, the memorabilia and bric-a-brac and old golf clubs, many of them hickory, propped up in corners and hung on the walls.

'I don't like to throw things out,' he says, in case I hadn't noticed. 'You never know when something will become useful. I just wish I always knew where to find it when it is.'

After an agreeable lunch at his club, Moseley, during which I have to be strong and decline the offer of a round at what looks like a lovely – but not public – golf course, we set off for Harborne Church Farm. Formerly a dairy farm, this site at Vicarage Road has been a golf course since 1883. The original fifteen-hole private course, however, was divided in two in the mid-1920s, when the council ran Northfield Road through the middle of it. The private members of Harborne Golf Club bought extra land on one side of the road and established their own eighteen-hole course, while the council squeezed a nine-hole municipal course into the bit that was left on the other side of the road and opened it in 1926. A mere 2,441 yards long from first tee to ninth green, it remains one of the tightest courses in the country.

In the café-cum-clubhouse we meet up with Paul, the resident professional and an old acquaintance of John's. Spookily, Paul is married to the granddaughter of Bert Rudge, the first ever professional at Harborne Church Farm. Before we tee off, he kindly lets us thumb through a collection of old photographs of players on the course and beaming winners holding their trophies, mainly from the 1930s and 1940s. The thing that strikes me immediately is how smartly dressed everyone is; it's all collars and ties for the men and best bonnets and smart skirts for the women. I am reminded of some pictures from the same era I have seen recently that were taken on the occasion of the annual matches between parent clubs and their artisan sections. While the artisans had all turned up in their Sunday best suits, the private members looked as if they were about to spend the afternoon digging up their gardens. I'm sure there's a penetrating sociological significance to that, but I'm whisked on to the first tee before I can come up with it.

It is a hot, sultry day and I've opted to leave half my clubs in the car and carry the rest. John has decided to give his hickories a run out and is carrying a handful of rusty spoons, mashie niblicks and the like in an old canvas bag that looks straight out of one of the photographs we'd just seen. A very reasonable £6 is all it costs us for nine holes.

John has the honour at the 282-yard par four opener and hooks one into the high conifers on the left, while I top a five-wood drive that, a little less aesthetically than I had wished, nevertheless achieves the aim of avoiding the large bunkers close to the green. As I'm walking after my ball, a group of young boys, who appear to be selling ice cream, approach from under some trees.

'Choc oice!' they intermittently shout. The Aston Villa-shirted youth in front draws near.

'Yoroit – have you seen a dog, mister?' he asks.

I tell him no, we've just started.

'Give's a shout if you do,' says another. 'You can't miss him – he's a Staff and he's called Choc oice.'

And with that they continue across the course whistling and shouting 'Choc oice!' at the top of their voices.

It is obvious that John is a golfer of many years' experience who, it appeared from our conversation at lunch, has played practically every course in the British Isles. But, having come to a kind of unspoken agreement that this afternoon's game would be completely uncompetitive, we never really got round to discussing handicaps. Watching him now flounder his way to an opening quadruple bogey eight at the first hole, I am guessing this is not the time to ask.

Coming off the first green (with a par) I get an idea of just how tight the golf course is. In one small clearing of the mature oaks and beech trees that help define the various holes, we have to walk past the fifth and seventh tees and the fourth green before reaching the second tee. I can see no signs to guide us and, it being some years since John last played here, he takes a while to get his bearings and steer us in the right direction. Our confusion is made worse by having to wait while a *five*-ball of more young lads hollers and hacks its way on to the fourth green from what looks like entirely the wrong fairway. Between them they are dragging only four golf bags – almost as big as themselves – and this is presumably how they conned their way on to the course. But I can see that one of their number is playing by simply taking an appropriate club from whichever pal with a bag happens to be nearest. John is obviously consumed by inner conflict over this. The committed coach of junior golf is delighted to see boys out on the course enjoying the game, but the old teacher is less than pleased at the flagrant abuse of the rules and etiquette. At last he contents himself with a shake of the head and an aside in my direction.

'Shouldn't be allowed, of course. But that lad there's got a decent swing, don't you think?'

The second hole, according to the stroke index, is the hardest on the course and it certainly demands some care over the drive, since you have two brooks that cross your path – one just below the tee and another roughly 200 yards away. From the elevated tee the fairway of this 348-yard par four dips down and then rises back up to a green guarded by bunkers left and right. Like the ninth at Portobello and the sixth at Hurst, it is an example of the kind of excellently designed, challenging golf hole even the most prosaic nine-hole municipal golf course can throw at you. The danger for the reasonably decent player (ahem, I thank you) playing so-called 'Mickey Mouse' golf courses, is that you do not take sufficient care and attention; that you get all complacent and cocksure and believe yourself to be capable of taming the course, yea verily without even breaking sweat. Older, wiser golfers are aware of this trap but, not having quite reached this level of golfing maturity myself, I take my driver with the intention of clearing both brooks with one mighty blow. As often happens, however, when I try to add a little pepper to my usual languid drive, it hooks horribly and I am in the trees left and only 150 yards from the tee. John's first effort barely makes it off the tee, but we decide a Mulligan is in order and his second is a nice placement just short of the second brook. By some miracle we find my ball in a clearing and I manage to hack out sideways, find the green with my third and then very nearly hole from twenty-five feet. But it lips out and I settle for a bogey to match John's.

Two groups ahead, a young beau is teaching his girlfriend how to play golf. His patience is admirable . . . and lengthy. While we are hanging about on the third tee, the single player behind us finishes the second and starts practising some pitching and chipping. John and I agree to invite him to join us.

Steve is a pocket battleship of a man. He is like a shorter version of Ray, the well-defined police superintendent at Wyboston Lakes, with a similar arm-and-shoulder swing that makes the bystander wince when it – occasionally – makes contact with the ball.

Are there many black guys in Birmingham who play golf?

'No, not really,' he laughs. 'All my mates think I'm crazy playing golf – they don't understand it. But you don't until you've tried. I just got hooked. I thought, I can do this.'

A bouncer – sorry, door supervisor – for a café/wine bar 'off Broad Street', Steve took up golf after mucking about with his girlfriend's dad's club in their back garden. He is, he says, an all-round sportsman who's tried his hand at most things and usually ends up being quite good at them. Golf, he admits, is presenting him with the kind of challenge he hasn't experienced in other sports, but he is determined to master it.

'I'm watching it now on TV and I've got a couple of books . . . I'll get there.'

We eventually get to hit our shots to this downhill par three and, while I find the green, John pushes his off to the right and Steve launches an enormous hook high into the trees separating this hole from the seventh fairway. We compare clubs and, as with Ray, it turns out Steve has hit two clubs less than me . . . and twice as far. It takes a while to find Steve's ball and even longer for him to get it back on to the green. Like most people just starting out in the game, Steve has put all his efforts into mastering the full-blooded batter with an iron or wood and has no idea how to play the short game. We perhaps did him no favours in interrupting his chipping practice a moment ago.

Still, there is no rush. Harborne Church Farm is busy this afternoon – everywhere you look there are two-, three-, four- (and five-) balls, with at least two groups on every hole. Attractive though the course itself is, you are never more than a few yards from the surrounding busy roads and between the roar of traffic and the frequent shouts of 'fore!' as untutored shots fly across wrong fairways and zip through greens at shin height, a round here is not a peaceful experience.

The greens are slow and bumpy and I three-putt for a bogey before we take on the par four fourth and more ditches to cross with the drive. This I manage with a little more aplomb than the last time, but both John and Steve top their tee-shots into the scrubby banks of the first ditch. John is happy to pick up and drop out for a stroke, but Steve, who has obviously just got to the chapter headed, 'Play your ball as it lies', is determined to hack his way out of trouble. This, of course, he is much better equipped to do than most, but by the time his ball pops back on to the fairway he has cleared most of the undergrowth from the banks of the stream and is panting like a race horse.

'Haven't lost a ball yet,' he says with a wide grin. Given his tenacity, I'm not sure if that's just today or ever.

As often happens on courses like this, the greens are not just slow but more than a little spiked up and cratered with a hundred pitch marks never repaired. These, then, are my excuses for three-putting three times in four holes, once – on the short par four sixth – after having driven the bloody green and having a decent chance for an eagle!

During the by now usual ten-minute wait on the seventh tee, Steve gives John and me an insight into the world of door supervising – a job he's been doing for ten years.

'It's really interesting – you get to meet all sorts of characters,' he says. 'You very rarely get any trouble. At least I don't. It's all about spotting the danger signs and taking steps to stop it happening before it does.'

What, by thumping them first?

'No, the opposite. We get to be nice and reasonable, because they know that behind it we can take care of ourselves, know what I mean.'

Apparently, the biggest problem for pubs and clubs is trying to keep underage drinkers out. Not long ago, the police in Birmingham launched a sting operation and, using a handful of under-sixteens they'd recruited for the job, tried to find out how many could get past the door.

'Most of the bars in Birmingham failed the test,' says Steve, 'but not mine.'

There is a shout from the trees off to the left.

'Hey! Wankers!'

And with that, the boys from the first hole, now with a large chocolate brown and white Staffordshire bull terrier in tow, all turn round, drop their trousers and give us an impressive synchronised moon.

'Away to the pub and behave yourselves!' I shout, which confuses them no end.

John, by now, has re-acquainted himself with the whippy nature of his hickory shafts and is improving steadily. He is also helped, I think, by having something more rewarding to concentrate on – helping Steve overcome some of his more obvious technical failings. On the evidence of these few holes, I suspect John is an excellent coach. While I would be itching to correct all fifty-three faults in Steve's setup and swing, John – once he'd determined that Steve was only too happy to listen to words of advice – keeps his pointers to the bare minimum and never strays anywhere near dampening Steve's enthusiasm, even when the latter breaks several rules in the book all at the same time.

Like at the eighth tee when, first of all, he asks me

what club I'd used on this par three (something he wouldn't be allowed to do in competition), then picks up a fallen leaf, chooses the line for his shot and places the leaf on that line a few feet in front of his ball. The sound of John and me sucking in our breath at that one forces him to look up, but we signal him to just carry on – it can wait. In any case, it certainly works for him, because he hits a fantastic shot with a five-wood slap-bang in the middle of the green 200 yards away. Sadly, he then three-putts for bogey, while John and I, who'd both missed long, chip up and single putt for par. So *that's* how you play these greens.

I'm standing on the ninth tee three over par and feeling pleased with my efforts. At 392 yards, this is easily the longest hole on the course and my drive, I determine, has found the perfect position just at the apex of what is a dogleg right. But I'm wrong. I'm actually in a ditch under a tree and it takes two hacks to get me clear. The shot that does extricate me, though, is a bit of a slice and, only after I've played my fourth effort, still short of the green, do I realise that, although I'd made sure the fifth/fourteenth green was clear, I'd been holding up a group on the sixth/fifteenth tee.

Standing somewhat out of breath near the ninth/-eighteenth green, I pull out the scorecard and realise I have been out of bounds for most of the hole. As one might expect for a golf course as cramped as this, the local rules section governing out of bounds is extensive. For example, on the hole I've just played, a ball is out of bounds if it '... *comes to rest in or to the right of the ditch on the sixth or fifteenth fairway, on the fifth or fourteenth green, in or to the right of the cutting on the ridge behind the fifth or fourteenth green, in or beyond the ditch to the left of the ninth or eighteenth fairway after the brook, on the practice putting green or on or beyond the paths dividing the course from the clubhouse'.* Take my word for it, that doesn't leave much to play on.

The final green has changed little in the last seventy years and the scene of John, Steve and me sinking our last putts and congratulating each other on our play could easily have come straight out of those grainy old photographs. We've all had our adventures out there, but I think there is some encouragement for each of us in how we played over the piece. As a last contribution to Steve's on-going golfing education, John picks up one of the free copies of the R&A Rules Book in the clubhouse and suggests he flick through it every now and then.

I leave Harborne Church Farm with visions of a crombie-coated bouncer with the ear-piece, shades and leather gloves, reading his wee blue book and telling people in the queue to shut up while he tries to get his head round the rule on fixed sprinkler heads.

I was pleased to learn from John that Harborne Church Farm actually has a bit of history to it. The second municipal course opened in Birmingham, it was the first that the council allowed to be used for play on a Sunday. That may not sound terribly radical nowadays, but Birmingham in the 1920s was a hotbed of nonconformist Christianity, with a particularly powerful lobby of religious groups led by a Free Church Council. This body could whip up a city-wide petition against the latest sign of moral decay faster than the *Daily Mail* can start an immigration scare.

Having taken my leave of Ron and the refined charms of the Kensington Guest House, I decide to stop off on my way out of Birmingham at the Central Library to check the newspaper archives for any reports on the controversy. To be honest, it doesn't take much to get me to indulge in one of my favourite methods of whiling away a spare hour or two. Simply put, old newspapers are a hoot. For example, I am trawling through microfiche of the *Birmingham Gazette* from 1926 – the time when the whole Sunday play issue reached a climax – and come to the edition for Monday 22 March.

'Why Countess Fled' is the headline above this 'news' item, which I quote in full: '"I have made only one visit to a beauty parlour," said Priscilla Countess Annesley in London yesterday. "And then was told that they could do nothing with me unless they skinned me."'

Edwardian deference to the aristocracy was clearly not as prevalent as we've been led to believe. On the same day, with the front page full of Germany's efforts to join the League of Nations, the editor, perhaps not accidentally, found space for a report on the 'Cult of the Nude' in that country. The police in Berlin, apparently, were finding themselves powerless to stop the spread of 'athleticism' in theatres and bathing pools.

Even before delving into the reports on the contention over Sunday golf, it is clear that the nation positively hummed with ethical discourse. Two days after Germany's problems with 'athleticism' were revealed (if you'll pardon the pun), the Bishop of Swansea lambasted the salacious press, saying: 'The supply of news of sexual items and divorces is creating a demand . . . and the supply should be stopped.'

The next day, reports from a meeting of the

Birmingham and Edgbaston Debating Society revealed that F Hickinbottom, ex-president of the Birmingham Chamber of Commerce, supported the 'increased liberty permitted to the rising generation', in particular the modern practice of explaining to girls and boys the 'natural functions and beauties of life'. Countering, Mr Siward James perhaps strayed off the moralistic message a touch when he confessed that 'the girl of today was extraordinarily attractive', though he did recover in time to 'condemn her for smoking cigarettes and drinking cocktails'.

As for the plans by the city's parks committee to allow Harborne Church Farm to open on a Sunday, well this really did provoke a storm of protest. More than 27,000 people from 207 churches and chapels across the city signed petitions against the move. (The accusation from some councillors that hundreds of letters of protest had in fact been written by schoolchildren instructed to do so by their teachers and parents was never convincingly refuted.)

For days before the crucial decision was due to take place, the letters page of the *Gazette* smouldered and smoked with fire and brimstone. What use was a low handicap for securing everlasting life? asked more than one offended church-goer.

'Those who desire Sunday golf evidently don't care about the growth and divine riches of the soul,' wrote an objector who signed himself 'Seer'. 'They are only concerned with their physical pleasures. They are like children who cling to toys when they should be acquiring knowledge. How will a man stand in the day of trouble, or in the hour of death, if he has not built up a lively faith to support him, but has only a record at golf to boast of?'

Some objected to the increased labour and traffic Sunday play would bring, others saw allowing Sunday golf as but one small step away from introducing 'the Continental Sunday'. Not, as it turns out, a sneaking partiality for croissants rather than ham and eggs, but actually a veiled reference to Catholicism. (?!)

Particularly worked up, however, were those who saw golf on the Sabbath as the thin end of a wedge that would be driven home by those who sought to undermine the very existence of a God-fearing England. Turning Sunday into a day of sport rather than worship 'would be a national disaster, and result eventually in a marked modification of the English character', wrote one HJ Rushton. 'For any section of the public . . . to act so banefully as to affect national interests and national character is, in my opinion, a form of selfishness which is as deplorable as it is unwarrantable, and is a base betrayal of a high trust.'

Gosh! And all this because the council wanted the low paid to be able to play a round of golf on a Sunday – a facility no one was denying the middle-class members of the city's private clubs. Indeed, during Harborne Church Farm's earlier existence as a course run by a private syndicate, there had been no attempts to stop Sunday play.

The motion in favour of allowing the course to open on Sundays was passed by forty-seven votes to forty on 30 March. A close enough call, but how much chance the objectors actually had of blocking the move I'm not so sure – not when the Lord Mayor himself had come out strongly in support of it. Speaking to the press some days before the vote, Alderman Percival Bower attacked those who would prevent Sunday golf as the same nuts who had written to him recently demanding that shop lights be switched off on a Sunday because it encouraged young people to 'perambulate the streets at night'.

'I don't know whether the source from which this criticism emanates feels that the souls of people who play on private grounds do not require the same attention as the souls of those who play on public grounds,' he commented. 'I do not know the reason for what I regard – and I say it with a full sense of responsibility – as interference by busybodies.'

In a reasoned editorial after the dust had settled, the *Gazette* pointed out that one of the principles of nonconformity was freedom. The council, in its opinion, had correctly decided for freedom in the face of calls for unwarranted restriction. It quoted councillor Morland: 'In matters which are not hurtful or annoying to others, a man's own conscience should be his guide.'

The precedent, of course, had been set. In the following years the issue of Sunday play raised its head at other municipal courses – the new one built at Cocksmoors Woods and the existing one at Warley. More deeply held religious misgivings – or 'pious humbug', according to one councillor – were expressed by the churches and their supporters, but the battle had been lost.

As I drive out of Birmingham, my head is spinning with images of moral crusades, Bibles being thumped, hell and damnation. It might not be quite Sodom and Gomorrah, but there is no question Birmingham today is not somewhere the strict Sabbatarians of eighty years ago would want to live – not only is there wall-to-wall sport, but a fair amount of athleticism as well. And if Mr Siward James objected to girls who smoke cigarettes and drink cocktails, what on earth would he have made of nurse Van Nistelrooy and her booze-fuelled libido?

Who knows, maybe these years will become infamous as the time when Britain began its slide into decadence and debauchery, when a Godless population put physical gratification above all other considerations and abandoned any search for spiritual growth and enlightenment. And if, in the future, we do ever pull ourselves up from that cesspool of depravity, perhaps we will see not only the error of our ways, but exactly where it all started to go wrong for this once great nation . . . the first tee at Harborne Church Farm, where a plaque will read: 'This was the Thin End of the Wedge.'

II

'What *is* that smell?'

Maybe he thinks it's a rhetorical question, because Michael doesn't answer. I'm on the second tee, going round the points of the compass with my nose in the air, trying to pin it down, but Michael is ignoring me.

'Right. That was a net four each there so I still get to go first.'

A four my backside. He took three just to get off the bloody tee, another five at least to reach the green, then gave himself a three foot 'gimme' after two putts. *And* I'm giving him a stroke at every hole.

Michael tees up his ball and takes his driver. The practice swing is just as alarming as before; all the way round on the backswing until the head of the club is almost touching his left leg, then back up, over the top and down with increasing venom to fizz through the bottom of the arc, probably nowhere near where he imagines the ball would be, and then through to an almost balletic finish with his hands high and the clubhead now inches from his right leg. By my estimate, that clubhead has done 630 degrees in just one swing.

Sure enough, his first effort misses the ball by almost

a foot and the follow-through is greatly curtailed, but he steps back quickly and says, 'That was a practice. Right, here goes.'

It's not the sort of behaviour you would expect from a friend during the fluffiest bounce game, let alone a stranger you've just met who has insisted you play for the drinks afterwards. However, I content myself with nodding an 'of course, carry on,' while trying to keep my face straight. Michael is only thirteen and I am trying desperately not to behave like the competitive dad from *The Fast Show*. The drinks in question, by the way, are cans of Coke from the pro shop.

We'd met on the first tee, here at St Michaels municipal golf course, Widnes. As often happens, the pro, or whoever it was who'd taken my £7.80 for eighteen holes, paid no attention at all to the fact that there was a lad on the tee and told me I could go any time I liked. If they are not being treated with domineering disdain, junior players at public or private courses are usually simply ignored; adults look right through them or over their heads like they don't even exist.

When I got outside the clubhouse (with grilled windows and so much barbed wire it looks more like a police station on the Falls Road), Michael, a skinny four and a half footer resplendent in regulation Liverpool FC home top, immediately knew his place and prepared to go back for some more putting practice. But I waved him on. I'm not sure how much this unnerved him or how bad his efforts would have been anyway, but he hit two fresh air shots before making enough contact to send his ball scuttling down the fairway.

Disappointed that no one else was going to be joining me for a round and dreading the prospect of following this youngster for the next few hours, I invited myself along in a two-ball – an offer Michael only warily accepted. By the time we finished the first, however, he relaxed enough to announce (he tends to announce rather than ask) that we are in a match and will be playing for those Cokes afterwards.

His second swing on the second tee does the business and a nice big loopy drive flies up towards the top of the slight rise in this par five.

'That'll werk,' he says with satisfaction.

Still feeling slightly nauseous from the all-pervading stink, I slice badly into trees on the right.

'Ha! You'll never find it in there, mate.'

Not the conventional response to a partner's misfortune, but Michael shoulders his bag and sets off for the trees to at least join in the hopeless task. I don't get far after my ball before the handle comes off the trolley for the fourth time already, sending my bag and clubs once more in a nose-dive into the turf. I would be genuinely surprised if a thirteen-year-old scally from Widnes did not already possess a working knowledge of indecorous language, but I still feel restrained from swearing warmly as I gather up the clubs, load them on the bag, put the bag back on the trolley and try to find a new way of fitting the handle that might keep it on.

My mood is not helped when five minutes of hunting in the undergrowth of hawthorn bushes, bramble and beer cans proves Michael right and fails to turn up my ball. I drop one in the semi-rough and take a shot penalty. (Of course, I should've gone back to the tee, but that is a rule more honoured in the breach than in the observance – certainly in unofficial golf matches.) In any case, the fact that Michael is clearly only going to count the shots that he likes hardly puts him in a position to complain.

I have to single putt the second green to match Michael's 'five', then watch him take another fresh air 'practice' swing before connecting with his next on the third tee on his way to a four-net-three and a win. I am remembering John Moreton's leniency with youthful exuberance and am determined not to complain about such trifles as accurate scoring.

Yet, as we progress through St Michaels' dull opening holes with its namesake continuing to wring every advantage he can from his own unique interpretation of the rules, the source of that feeling of déjà vu I've been having finally dawns on me. Years ago I'd read a short story about just such a round. It was John Updike's *Intercession*, first published in the *New Yorker* in 1958, and it tells the story of a Connecticut man, Paul, taking a skive from his work one day and nipping out for a round on a sun-baked public course. But his plans for a leisurely afternoon trying to master a game he'd only just begun playing are wrecked by repeatedly crossing paths with a braggart of a kid, who keeps challenging him to beat this drive or that putt, all the while turning a blind eye to his own duff shots:

'Paul laughed; such frank competition tickled him. This age was so grainy, so coarse.'

To be fair, Michael is nowhere near as objectionable as Updike's young character, but I am sharing Paul's amusement at once again being involved in the kind of no-holds-barred, in-your-face competition I haven't been in since I was at school. This is where you don't commiserate with your opponent when he misses a putt but laugh in his face and say your one-armed, blind and bedridden grandmother could do better; where you don't acknowledge your own best shots with a grim little smile and a mouthed 'thanks' but punch a Tiger Woods uppercut in the air and shout 'Beat that short-arse!' across the fairway. In fact, once I get into the swing of it, Michael seems to enjoy himself a lot more; the nervous scowl is replaced with a cocky grin and he starts stringing together some decent shots. Clearly more comfortable in this kind of game, he also stops minding his Ps and Qs.

'That's fookin' shite,' is his considered opinion of my pulled tee-shot at the par five fourth hole.

'I'd like to see you do any better.'

'Easy,' he says with a smirk. 'Next hole. You'll see.'

This hole starts from a corner of the course defined by Dundalk Road and the busy A562, the main road into Liverpool from over the Runcorn Bridge. In fact, it was while driving along here yesterday on my way to my chum's house in Garston that I'd spotted the course and, on the spur of the moment and in the spirit of aimless adventure, decided this would be the venue for my next game. From here you get a view of some of St Michaels' neighbours in scenic Merseyside. There's the scrap metal dealership and several other small industrial units just across the road, the cranes from a container terminal at Ellesmere Port, the ICI Chemicals and Polymers plant, and, towering over everything else, the giant coolers of the Fiddlers Ferry Power Station. One of these *has* to be responsible for that smell.

The fourth is the second and last par five on the course and runs 510 yards, with the A562 screened by some weedy looking trees down its left flank. Michael has hit one first time, right down the middle, and I'm beginning to suspect that I might be in for a match here. My ball is in thick stuff on high banking to the left and it takes an age to find it. Even then, all I can do is hack out to the right side of the fairway, on the other side of the trees I'd lost my ball in on the second hole. When I get there, after stopping off twice to pick up my spilled clubs, I find another ball on the fairway next to mine. It can't be Michael's, because by now he is practically on the green (playing in turn is another convention he's yet to get the hang of), but there is a young guy searching about in the same trees I'd been in a little earlier. Just at that moment, he finds a ball . . . but it turns out to be the one I'd lost on that hole. This second one, meanwhile is indeed his.

I mention this because I'd been disproportionately saddened by the loss of that ball; it was, I'd realised, the first one I'd lost in the entire journey (if you don't count the one I left in the dog shit at Portobello). From under hedges at Backworth and across the vast plains of Earls Colne, from the reedy banks of Wyboston Lakes and the goose-fouled semi-rough at Hurst, from umpteen dodgy lies at Westward Ho! and plucked from out of bounds at Harborne Church Farm, I'd always managed to find my ball. Its rescuer on this occasion was perhaps not expecting a tearful thanks and a hug, but he got it anyway.

Michael wins again to go two up (he'd spent most of the hole miles away from me and I would've had little chance of counting his strokes even if there were any point in doing so). But I peg him back with a solid par three at the next – a feature of which is a large electricity pylon just left of your line to the green – because not even his creative accounting can accommodate six efforts to get out of a bunker.

To play the sixth you must walk through an underpass beneath the A562, which brings you out to another part of the course where the next nine holes run up and down between the dual carriageway and the factories and workshops on Ditton Road. It's a lot more noisy – and smelly.

'Seriously, Michael. What *is* that bloody smell?' I ask.

'Oh, that. It's the broo-kh,' and he points to a cutting some yards off that reveals a stream emerging from the pipe it's been funnelled into under the road. What's in it, I wonder.

'Dunno. But you don't lick your ball after it's been in there,' says Michael in deadly earnest.

The noise is not just coming from the road and the surrounding industries. The sixth tee lies pretty close to what I later find out is the ninth green, upon which a four-ball of what looks like two teenage couples are horsing about. There are two older men leaning on their clubs on the fairway who would obviously like them to get on with it – and shut up. In fact, I wouldn't be surprised if the guys stacking iron girders with forklift trucks in the foundry yard over the fence didn't want them to shut up as well so they could get on with their work in peace. My God, what a racket! They are bawling and shouting at the top of their voices, or rather, the girls are. Not making a sexist point here at all – their boyfriends are larking about just as much – but it is the high-pitched screeching and squealing that is setting my teeth on edge and giving me a headache. Between that, the traffic and the smell, this is turning out to be a deeply unpleasant round of golf. Only the cheery indifference to it all of my playing partner is keeping my spirits up.

Eventually, Derek, whose surname appears to be

'Yookunt', stops grabbing Cassie as she's about to putt, while her friend, whose name hasn't been announced to the rest of Merseyside yet, is persuaded to pick up her ball after at least seven attempts to putt out.

In too much of a hurry to put as much distance as possible between us and the caterwauling, I hook my drive into the semi-rough. Michael, who is entirely unfazed by the commotion, takes his time and hits another beauty down the middle, if a little low.

'That'll werk,' he says for the umpteenth time.

A moment later and I am distraught. Not only can I not find my ball in ankle-height clover, but the teenage four-ball is advancing slowly up the tenth fairway, which runs parallel to this one. I drop another ball and hit a blind approach to the green over the summit of a hill, walk ten yards and come across my original ball. I may be about to lose another hole, but the ol' ball retaining record is still intact. Sure enough, Michael notches up another win to go back to two up, but I recover enough form to par and bogey the next two holes. All square.

We're on the ninth tee now, but the frightening four-ball have only just made the eleventh green, a hundred yards or so away.

'Darren! No-o!' screams Trisha (we were introduced halfway down the eighth). She then starts running round the green trying to avoid the bigger of the two lads – the one who is laughing like Sid James – as he tries to wrestle her to the ground. Amazingly, Derek pays absolutely no attention and calmly surveys his putt. As Trisha shrieks by him on her third circumnavigation of the green, he pops it in from all of twenty-five feet – a feat which earns him a long snog from Cassie.

Tearing myself away from the golfing soap opera, I hit

what I think is a nice safe three-wood down the fairway. Michael follows me with another topped drive that he greets with the same grim satisfaction that it will 'werk'. But while he is in position *a*, twenty yards short of the brook, I am nowhere to be seen.

My heart sinking with the fear that a ball is finally to be lost – and in a polluted burn – I get to the bank and look down. The milky white water is rolling its way seaward, the sulphurous stench is appalling, but my ball is perched up nicely on the bank in what is a reasonably playable lie. Nevertheless, it takes me two more shots to reach the green and, despite a twelve foot putt for par, Michael's stroke gives him the win.

'That'll learn ya – ya gorra play shorrof the brooo-kh. You'll know the next time, eh?'

The next time? Not if this and Muirfield were the last two golf courses in the world, but it's the latest evidence of Michael not quite grasping my visitor status. He spotted the accent alright, seemed mildly interested in where I was from, but has since consistently spoken to me as if I've just got here but will obviously be staying to take advantage of the area's many delights – some of which, like the church, the chippy and the stadium of Widnes Rugby League Football Club, he has been pointing out as we go along.

As for him, I get to find out precious little. He lives 'up the road', goes to a school 'up the road' and learned to play golf with his dad and uncle. He doesn't get to any Liverpool games because no one in his family has a season ticket and trying to get one on matchday is 'merder', but he thinks Man United, and everyone who supports them, like Billy and Daz (?) in his class, should be shot. Any more information than that he doesn't volunteer and I will not be wheedling it out of him. I am already beginning to feel slightly self-conscious about hooking up with a minor and any questioning just makes me feel more like the kind of guy kids like him should be warned about.

Going down the tenth, we pass within feet of the four-ball as they come back along the twelfth and there appears to be a lull in the histrionics – or maybe a collective huff. On closer inspection, it is actually a collective puff as they all pull on cigarettes and stroll down the fairway in a calm, almost serene, kind of way. Makes you wonder exactly what went on at the eleventh green after we'd left them.

Anyway, they've settled down enough to play some shots and make a little progress (they've let the two-ball through, but there are still two more groups between us and them). The girls, given some peace and time to think about their game, are clearly intent on doing the best they can, but the baseball bat grips and jerky swings suggest the only tuition they've had was probably from Derek and Darren. Still, that's the beauty of municipal courses – even complete beginners can come and have a hack.

Michael, who is now playing some genuinely nice shots, wins the tenth without even needing his stroke – my approach from the left was with at least two clubs too many and a bogey from way back of the green is the best I can do. He is back to two up and swaggering about the place like he owns it. Two holes later, he is three up after matching my par on the short eleventh (the hole with the great name, 'Diddley Dee') and then easily winning the next with who knows what. I certainly wasn't counting, since I spent most of the hole hacking through the trees down the left – twice all but losing my ball then spotting it at the last moment. My final recovery only reached a large bunker above the green, behind which is parked the 'Buttie Van' where sat several golfers enjoying a snack and a chance to watch me take two to get out of the sand and eventually rack up a quadruple bogey eight. Among those sitting on white plastic chairs munching on burgers is the teenage four-ball and I am delighted when Michael declines the offer of a break and we get to press on ahead of them.

The short par four thirteenth goes Michael's way, but from God knows where I play the fourteenth perfectly – a blind drive over a hill followed by no more than a wedge to the green and single putt for birdie and victory.

'You're dead lucky, you,' is Michael's gracious comment.

Back through the underpass, we stand on the fifteenth tee with Michael three up and four to play. To be fair to the wee man, he really knows how to buckle down and do what he has to to win. First, there is another low, but straight drive. 'That'll werk.' Then another topped, but straight approach to this short par four that scuttles between guarding bunkers on to the green. 'That'll werk.' And he crowns it all with the first lag putt he hasn't raced ten feet by all day, leaving it eighteen inches from the cup. His four is easily good enough to beat my bogey five (hooked approach into sand) and win the match. The sheer delight in his beaming face and fist-pumping little jig are worth losing just to see.

We're walking over to the sixteenth tee when the handle comes off again and my trolley takes yet another nose dive.

'Why don't you push it?' says Michael.

I am left standing there holding the handle, utterly

speechless. It is so obvious a solution I feel completely foolish for not having thought of it earlier. Equally obvious, however, is the fact that Michael has waited until the match is over before offering it. He'll go far, that boy.

The sixteenth green is down in a dip close to the stinking burn and there is a group of three fat young boys larking about with putters. The oldest can't be more than seven.

'Have you got any balls or tees, mister?'

I am by now obsessed with not losing a ball, so all I give them is a handful of tees. They clearly know better than to ask Michael, who is busy puffing out his chest and trying to look all adult and serious.

'Can I putt it for you, mister,' asks another after I chip on to the green. The match lost and being well on my way to a rubbish score, I let him have a go. He takes four efforts just to get it to stop within four yards of the hole.

'Thanks, mister. What did you get?'

'*You* got an eight – I'm taking a five.'

'Soo-perb!'

We leave them behind and head for the seventeenth, a semi-blind par three straight uphill. After teeing off, however, I look back from halfway up the hill and see the boys examining the tees I'd given them and practising shots without any golf balls. Ah, what the hell – I take two of the three balls I've been using for a fortnight and chip them back down on to the green to their great excitement. It's a more honourable retirement than flying out of bounds or plunging into the deadly brook.

I finish the round with a couple of bogeys while Michael

also seems to be tiring and has a relapse of air shots and shanks. We walk back into the fortified little clubhouse and I do the honours with a can of Coke for Michael.

While there, he nods a hello to a couple of blokes who then look enquiringly, and not entirely amiably, in my direction. I am suddenly uncomfortable again about being a stranger with a local boy in tow. We make our way down to the car park, sharing our drinks and chatting through some of the highlights – all Michael's – of the round we'd just played.

'You off home now?' I ask.

'Yeah, s'pose.'

'Do me a favour will you – make sure you go straight home, eh? Do not speak to any strange men, get in their cars or express an interest in any puppies they might have for sale.'

Michael smiles knowingly and says he will.

'OK. I'm going back up to the clubhouse for an alibi – sorry, some lunch.'

> *The game is ancient, manly, and employs*
> *In its departments women, men and boys.*
> *Men play the game, the boys the clubs convey,*
> *And lovely woman gives the prize away.*

It had struck me during the round at St Michaels that, apart from Carolyn and Melanie at Richmond Park, the screaming teenagers were just about the only women I had come across so far on this trip. Golf, of course, is just as infamous for its male chauvinism as for its snobbishness, but while I have been seeing the proletarian game that proves golf is not, in fact, monopolised by pampered private members, I cannot say I have encountered a sport that is equally enjoyed by both sexes.

Written almost 200 years ago, the little ditty above, reproduced by Geoffrey Cousins in *Golf in Britain*, just about sums up the attitude of men to women and golf in the nineteenth century. From the founding of the St Andrews Ladies' Putting Club in 1867 right through to the modern era of Annika Sorenstam and Michelle Wie, the women's game has come a long, long way. But we all know that to this day there are men, some of them in positions of power in the club-dominated administration of golf in Britain, who would still subscribe to the notion that women's role in the sport should be limited to serving soup and showing a bit of leg while handing over the summer foursomes cup.

To be strictly fair, the obstacles in the way of wider female participation in golf before the turn of the nineteenth and twentieth centuries were not limited to male intransigence. Prosaic as it may sound, women's fashions through most of the Victorian era effectively put the kibosh on any kind of strenuous exercise. Imagine having to walk out on to a golf course in three tonnes of crinoline, corseted underneath and lugging a bustle about on your backside, not to mention the ever-present bonnet, and you get an idea as to why women limited themselves to putting; it was simply impossible to raise the club above shoulder height.

Thereafter, it is true that strict ideas on female propriety continued to impose an impractical dress code on women golfers well into the twentieth century. In fact, it took until 1933 when Gloria Minoprio turned up for the British Ladies' Championship in slacks before a woman wore anything vaguely suited to the game. Even then golf was scandalised – and it wasn't just the men. The

Ladies Golf Union (LGU), supported by every other competitor, condemned this 'departure from the usual golfing costume'. It wasn't until after the Second World War that trousers became widely acceptable for women.

(The game's obsession with how women should be dressed has sadly stayed with us. Take the example of Judy Owen, a former training manager for the PGA, who was dismissed by her employers for refusing to wear a skirt into the office. In 1999 she had to take her case to an industrial tribunal, where she successfully won on the grounds of sexual discrimination. During the case, she said her manager at the PGA, one of the sport's most important administrative bodies, referred to women golfers as 'dykes and lesbians'.)

In 1893, when the newly formed LGU decided to hold its inaugural championship, it took place at Lytham – not St Andrews or some other venerable Scottish links – and most of the thirty-eight entrants were English. The extent to which golf in Scotland had or had not been a 'democratic' sport accessible to all classes before the late Victorian age may still be the subject of debate, but what is not in question is the fact that it was almost exclusively a male-dominated game – Musselburgh fishwives and Queen Mary notwithstanding. It was not until shortly before the turn of the century that the Ladies' Putting Club in St Andrews spawned proper golf clubs in the town aimed at organising matches on the Old Course, but by then ladies' clubs were already springing up in Westward Ho! and elsewhere in England. Unlike the situation in the men's game, the establishment and early growth of organised golf for women happened almost simultaneously north and south of the Border.

Before that championship in 1893, the LGU sought the

advice of some prominent male golfing administrators. The response of one of them is quoted by Cousins: 'Women never can unite to push any scheme to success. They are bound to fall out and quarrel. They will never go through a ladies' championship with credit or without tears. Constitutionally and physically women are unsuited to golf . . . temperamentally the strain will be too much for them.' True to form, old Geoffrey describes these sentiments as being offered with 'the best of motives' (?).

The LGU, of course, went from strength to strength and even in its early years showed an innovative streak by introducing a handicap system fully thirty-five years before the men's game did. Today, it administers the ladies' amateur game throughout Great Britain and Ireland and is made up of the four national organisations for England, Ireland, Wales and Scotland. Based in St Andrews, it has around 2,750 affiliated clubs, representing something like 220,000 lady members, although its secretary and chief executive officer is a bloke – Andy Salmon.

'Yes, I am a man running a ladies' golf organisation. But the chauvinism even I have come across is still quite shocking,' he told me. 'It's not blatant, but it's things like getting a set of minutes back from a meeting and the account of what a man said is full and accurate while the woman's point of view is either edited right down or ignored altogether.'

Salmon believes the lot of women in golf is getting better, although not as quickly as it should. The root of the problem is that the game is still largely in the hands of individual clubs – not even the R&A (itself an all-male club) can tell a club how to run its affairs – and an awful lot of clubs are still stuck in a social time warp.

'Every time I speak to a journalist I criticise clubs, but that's about the extent of what I can do,' he says. 'The structure of clubs and their competitions reflect what society was like when men went out to work and women stayed at home, but society has changed – most couples now have both partners working – and golf clubs need to start reflecting that.'

All-male clubs are, of course, the most obvious target for those taking up the cudgels on behalf of women in golf. But even in mixed clubs, we still await changes in the law (proposed amendments to the 1975 Sex Discrimination Act are going through Parliament at the time of writing) to ensure women are treated equally; have the option of paying the full membership fee in return for unrestricted access to the first tee; and are allowed, along with their guests, anywhere in the clubhouse (apart from the toilets). One encouraging sign came recently in a selected poll of Scottish golf clubs by the newspaper *Scottish Club Golfer*. Asked if there should be total equality of rights for men and women in golf clubs, 100 per cent of those who responded said 'yes'.

But what about on public golf courses? If women are still second-class citizens in many clubs, are they any better off on municipal and pay-and-play courses? The LGU, in common with every other official body, can only guess at the number of golfers who are not members of clubs, but who regularly play on public courses. The usual ball park figure employed is about two and a half million total for all golfers (men and women) in the UK – roughly twice the number who are members of clubs. Since, as the Golf Research Group reports, only 11 per cent of all club members are women (see below) and fewer women play municipal as opposed to private golf, we can see that it all adds up to a pathetically small number of women playing on public golf courses.

'Even those few non-members will be lost to the game if officialdom does not embrace them,' says Salmon. 'At the moment, the attitude is very much that if you are not a member of a club, we are not interested in you.'

Of course, it may be to the advantage of those women who do play on public golf courses that officialdom is not interested in them. It can be argued that public golf is the perfect arena for women to get started in the game because they're left in peace to turn up when they want, can wear what they want (certainly on some municipal courses) and can play to whatever standard they like without feeling the eyes of every male club member scrutinising their swing or the length of time they take to complete a round. That more of them don't do so takes us back to the whole issue of golf's image.

Vivien Saunders is a former British Women's Open Champion, a founder of the women's tour in Europe, owner of two golf resorts, the chair of the Association of Golf Course Owners and was awarded the OBE for services to women's golf. One might reasonably say she knows what she's talking about.

'This is a game that is in serious trouble,' she told me. 'Golf is just not attracting women – and women and juniors are the growth markets. In fact, the average age of women golfers in Britain is something like sixty-four and getting older. Where is the next generation coming from? There is a huge potential for golf out there – and it is young women – but golf is putting them off. It is just not welcoming.'

Saunders makes a compelling case. Women in general

do not naturally take to the game easily; so they prefer tuition and practice before simply joining friends and going for an experimental hack around the park – the way most men and boys got started. Yet the clubs that can offer such help only succeed in putting girls off with their stuffy attitudes, dress codes and male-oriented schedules.

Add to this the fact that golf is rarely, if ever, offered to girls at school or college, plus those features that blight the game for all players, such as the length of time it takes to play a round because no one is clamping down on slow play and the up front investment in shoes (an average of £50) that is needed just to be allowed on to a course, and you have a sport, says Saunders, that is almost entirely by-passing half the population.

'I go to Sweden and Spain a lot and the game is completely different in these countries . . . it is family-friendly – children are made welcome in clubs – and the dress codes are much more relaxed,' she says. 'You see young women wearing fashionable clothes – yes, including jeans and trainers – learning the game and enjoying themselves. To be honest, most male club members in this country would have apoplexy at the thought of their lounges filled with happy, casually dressed women and children having a good time.'

The Golf Research Group's analysis of golf club memberships seems to back this up. Its 2002 report on the finances of golf clubs in Britain concludes: 'Only 11 per cent of members are women, and six per cent are juniors, which in percentage terms are the lowest in Europe. Unlike many countries that perceive golf to be a family sport, in the UK it is still perceived to be a male oriented game.'

After speaking to Vivien Saunders, I checked out her website and I would recommend that anyone who mistakenly believes the bad old days of misogyny have disappeared does the same. With her permission I would like to relate just a few of the many hilarious yet depressing incidences of male chauvinism and discrimination suffered either by Saunders herself or those who have told her their experiences.

- While at Royal St George's in Kent in the 1980s in an utterly doomed attempt to be appointed their new club professional (despite having an MBA and PhD, being a national champion and coach to England, Ireland and Wales), Saunders was informed that Lord Lucan still had his name on a locker in the changing room. 'Without a resignation, he was still considered to be a member and more acceptable than any woman.'

- On a trip, a few years back, to the Notts Golf Club at Hollinwell for a match, one of the Cambridge University team (coached at the time by Saunders) took his mum with him to watch. Sadly, women were not allowed on the course on a Saturday (and are still not – I checked) nor indeed on the premises. Not being able to drive, she was left stuck in the car for the entire day. In fact, her son had to come back and drive her away from the club just so she could go to the toilet.

- At another all-male club, a woman made the mistake of entering the clubhouse after her husband had suffered a heart attack on the golf course. She later received a letter from the club secretary reminding her of the restrictions.

Of course, tweedy lady members can be just as guilty as their male counterparts in putting potential young women golfers off the whole idea. For a start, many of them guard their 'special' status within clubs jealously. They don't want full voting rights, access to the course on Saturdays or whatever – not if it means having to pay the full whack. And, being mostly the middle-aged or elderly wives of male members with no work to go to through the week, they insist on holding AGMs and other meetings on Tuesday afternoons and the like with no regard to their younger members or potential members who do a nine-to-five day.

Attitudes among lady members can also be every bit as strict and unyielding as those on the other side of the mixed lounge. Saunders told me of a woman in Cambridgeshire who won her local ladies' club's 'Granny Trophy' but was later disqualified because the committee discovered that her grandchild was illegitimate.

It all seems a far cry (!) from the shriekers of St Michaels in Widnes, but it seems they really are in a tiny minority of young women who have even set foot on a golf course. When you consider how critical image and perception are to your average youth, be they male or female, it is easy to see how golfing stereotypes – dominated by the clubs – become all-important . . .

'Right Kylie, you've got a choice. You can hang around Burger King in your latest gear with your pals, eating chips and talking on your mobile to other pals hanging around outside KFC – or, here's an idea, how about investing all your pocket money for the next year on a set of second-hand golf clubs, a pair of unflattering shoes and some pink diamond jumpers, and spending your weekends being laughed at by boys and told off every five minutes by crusty old gits in matching knitwear?

'. . . Thought so . . . Get me a Whopper with cheese will you?'

12

The fortunes of women in golf, it has to be said, did not
exercise us greatly in the Penny Lane Wine Bar. I know
we tossed the subject around for a while, but if we came
to any conclusion on the matter, I fear it shared the fate
of whatever few billion brain cells were dispatched that
night. It was one of those evenings when there occurs a
mystical conflation of hot topics, cold beer and three
idiots self-important and drunk enough to believe they
actually know what they're talking about. If I remember
correctly, sexual discrimination in golf clubs followed
shortly after the merits of teaching philosophy in schools
and just before Stephen Hawking's latest thoughts on
black holes. It is hard to be precise about the running
order, because this was a single conversation over several
hours, pints and chilli burritos across the road later that
began with quantum field theory and the nature of God
and ended with a critique of Liverpool's summer sign-
ings and whether or not they would be enough to ensure
at least a Champions League spot next season.

The other two idiots were my friend Boot, on whose
couch I was crashing for a couple of nights, and his chum
since boyhood, Clive. Boot works for the *Liverpool Echo*,

but his nickname owes less to his pals' clever allusion to Evelyn Waugh's reporter hero in *Scoop* than to their removal of the letter 'h' from the end of his surname. Clive works in a hospital doing something that I remember he told me years ago, but now forget – and he had absolutely no inclination to explain it again since he was on holiday. Clive never actually goes anywhere on holiday, he just drinks in different pubs for a fortnight. But he keeps his mobile switched on so we were able to summon him from whatever far-flung corner of Liverpool he'd been in that day.

I would not pretend that Boot's gaff is exactly luxurious, equipped as it is solely with the necessities for sleeping, watching TV and eating tuna sandwiches. But after the madness of the Kensington in Birmingham, a hotel in Barnstaple that believes you can never hear enough Richard Clayderman and an almost entirely sleepless stay in Tiverton thanks to plumbing that whistled and banged like an orange walk all night, I was glad of the chance to dump the bags for a day or two and enjoy some peace and quiet.

A day of failing (yet again) to discover the point of cricket on Boot's telly, while he worked a shift at the *Echo*, was followed by another night of liver abuse in several city centre bars. The next morning I reluctantly decided it was time once more to answer the call of the open road – the road, in fact, to Scotland. Not since my failed effort to play a round of golf then get from Tyneside to Essex in one day had I set myself such a daunting challenge – Liverpool to Inverness by nightfall.

My original plan had been to stop off in Glasgow, play a round at my old municipal, Alexandra Park, meet up with family and friends and make a quick dash along the M8 to make sure Marian wasn't enjoying herself too much in my absence, but my experiences in Birmingham and Widnes had more than slaked my thirst for inner city golf.

My memories of the game in Glasgow are crowded with muddy, unkempt fairways, abandoned kitchen appliances on the greens and what a friend of mine refers to as 'feral children' on the other side of the hills from blind drives, offering to sell you back your own ball. After the confines of Harborne Church Farm and the odorous mayhem of St Michaels, that is the last kind of golfing experience I needed. In fact, I decided that nothing south of the Highland line would do and that I would head straight for the most northerly municipal golf course in Britain.

According to my road atlas, Inverness is 386 miles from Liverpool and the journey should take *precisely* seven hours and twenty-eight minutes. An explanatory note admits this time does not allow for rest breaks – nor, presumably, for Toyota Starlets and any journey involving the M6. In other words, it is completely useless. Since I'd decided it might be a good idea to sleep off the drink from the night before, I didn't manage to get on the road until mid-morning. Nevertheless, I was determined to reach the capital of the Highlands in time for dinner. It being a Sunday, it only took me an hour to travel the thirty-six miles to Preston – something of a record, I'm sure, for the M6 – and thereafter it was plain sailing to the Lakes and on up to the Border.

I'd heard a hypnotist recently describing how he'd mastered the art of making time go slower or faster depending on whether he was doing something he enjoyed or was, for example, on a flight to Los Angeles.

I am sure I have somehow managed to do the same on this trip because I quickly slipped into 'discourtesy car time' and convinced myself that, even though my foot was permanently flooring the accelerator, I was in fact cruising. Devon had provided the car's first real test in terms of steep hills to negotiate and the technique I'd perfected there – leaning forward in the seat and shouting 'c'mon, c'mon!' – served me well again when I reached the A9 late in the afternoon and started the steady climb out of Perth, an incline that never really levels out until fifty-odd miles later at the high point of the Drumochter Pass. By the time I reached Inverness it was ten hours after I'd left Boot's house. I was knackered and hungry, but exhilarated not only at having travelled so far, but from that last hour of driving through gorgeous Speyside with the Monadhliath Mountains on one side and Cairngorms on the other – a journey that never fails to take my breath away. Industrial Widnes seemed a satis-fyingly long way away.

Something someone once told me about Torvean Golf Course running alongside the Caledonian Canal led me to guess that it was the wee red flag on my map to the south west of Inverness and so I headed for that end of town and came across the Loch Ness House Hotel in the fading light.

The room I was given in the annex was like an oven and reeked of the paint job it'd clearly just had – masking tape was stuck round the windows and door. Still, after a satisfying dinner of cullen skink and roast saddle of venison, albeit in one of those funereal restau-rants Highland hotels specialise in – all antlers and depressing fiddle music – I didn't care what state the room was in, nor whether it was the fumes, exhaustion or the three glasses of house red that had me flat out the moment the door closed behind me.

Between Harborne Church Farm in 1926 and St Michaels, which opened in 1977, lies I suppose what might be called the golden age of municipal development in Britain. Although Scotland's coastal towns and cities already had a fair number of council-run courses by the end of the First World War, only a handful of English municipal facilities pre-date Birmingham's drive to provide 'working man's golf' in the 1920s. And two years after St Michaels was opened in Widnes, Margaret Thatcher came to power and very soon thereafter the notion that a local authority would spend money on building a golf course and then subsidise it with rates to keep costs low became frankly laughable.

From 1920 to 1980, no fewer than 152 of Britain's total of 233 municipal golf courses were built, but the commonly held view that councils in the late 1940s and 1950s simply picked up from where they'd left off before the Second World War is wide of the mark. Post-war Britain under Attlee had much more important things to be getting on with than building golf courses. Besides which, as my parents' generation never tires of telling us, the country was broke and things that we take for granted, like fashionable clothes and bananas, could only be dreamed of.

It would not be until the days of rationing were over, until the welfare state had been firmly established and Britons actually had that thing called disposable income again that golf course development took off once more. By the end of the 1950s, 'we'd never had it so good' and a huge new population of white collar and skilled manual workers had money to spend. The golf fans among them – inspired by the newly glamorised sport of Hogan and Palmer – even found that a new source of cheap balls and clubs from the Far East meant the game was affordable as never before.

These were the factors that were to drive the astonishing boom in municipal course building that followed. It has been estimated that participation in golf doubled between 1954 and 1967. Even by the time Keele University carried out a survey of recreational demands in 1970, it found that of the sports people would most like to take up, given the opportunity, golf ranked first.

In the meantime, private clubs had found it particularly tough going immediately after the war. As David Hamilton points out in *Golf: Scotland's Game* (1998), economic downturns tend to hit private courses harder than those in the public sector. While municipal courses were shielded from the worst effects of slump or even depression by councils adjusting subsidies or offsetting losses elsewhere in their overall budgets, it is noticeable that in the 1930s and again in the 1950s, 1970s and 1990s, private clubs experienced collapses in income and responded, at least in part, by relaxing their entrance policies. Not surprisingly, the post-war years, certainly up to 1960, represent the slowest period for private course-building since before the 1880s.

Another misconception is that the boom in municipal course development that followed in the 1960s and 1970s was entirely about socialist ideals of bringing golf to the masses; that urban councils, fired up with the same democratic zeal as their predecessors in the 1920s and 1930s, were determined to deliver a kick in the privates, as it were, and return golf to 'the people'. In fact, a lot of new courses built by public money in this period – those laid out as part of Britain's new towns – were not aimed at the low paid at all. In a 1994 presentation to the splendidly named *Science and Golf II: Proceedings of the World Scientific Congress of Golf*, John Lowerson claimed that from Harlow and Milton Keynes to East Kilbride and Glenrothes, golf was used as a lure to bring in experienced businessmen. 'Because they were treated as industrial as well as residential magnets, there was a clear need to attract managers,' he said. 'Despite proclaimed ideals of social integration, the new towns of the 1950s and 1960s almost inevitably recreated many of the social divides of the older urban world.'

The persistence of golf's image as a game with a certain cachet, even as it was spreading to hitherto ungolfed corners of Britain and, indeed, British society, presented planners with a problem – and one that bore a striking resemblance to that which faced city councils forty and fifty years earlier. At a 1975 *Land for Leisure* conference held under the auspices of the Centre for Advanced Land Use Studies, one planning expert, RC Williams, said, 'I appreciate that there is a move within the sport for it to become attractive and available to a much wider section of the community . . . yet it remains a fact of life that the typical golfer comes from an atypical section of society . . . To a planning authority pressed to provide a wide range of leisure facilities and an even wider range of other services, golf becomes a legitimate, but land-extravagant and elitist sport which is expensive to provide and politically difficult to justify.'

It is easy to blame the established clubs and middle management golfers for this image, but, as local authorities laid out municipal courses by the dozen across

Britain, it became clear that the demand from the working classes they were struggling to meet was not for some utopian, egalitarian game – it was for exactly what the middle classes had been enjoying for years. At the *Land for Leisure* conference, Williams put it this way: 'Golf is popular partly because it has a well developed social life . . . of the 1,600 courses in the country at the moment, 90 per cent are private, and it has been difficult to persuade the new golfing public that further provision should not be in exactly the same way.' In other words, the newly wealthy blue and white collar workers with their plastic golf bags and cheap Japanese clubs did not just want to play golf – they wanted the private club attached, the nineteenth hole, the social events . . . the lot. This gets to the heart of the question about how different private member clubs and public courses – and those who play them – really are.

Long before the 1960s, private golf clubs had come to recognise what a boon municipal golf courses could be – they took the pressure off them to extend their membership *and* they provided an effective training ground for future members. It is still a convention today that the aspiring member of a private club uses the local public facilities to at least take the rough edges off his or her game before schmoozing a couple of members in the hope of getting a proposer and seconder. Moreover, there has always been a sizeable number of golfers who only frequent the municipal links because they can't get into any private club – not because they don't want to. Some of the people I've met so far on my travels – the guys at Musselburgh and Wyboston Lakes, for example – are quite content to play for the rest of their lives in the public sector, but for many others municipal golf is merely a stepping stone to the local private club. They may resent the 'nobs' and all their arcane, peculiar ways, but only because they are not among them. The notion that public/private golf equates to a clear cut 'us and them' situation is simplistic in the extreme.

In lieu of membership of the local private club (or 'getting in up the road' as it is commonly called), the new wave of golfers attracted to public courses wanted at least the trappings of club life. And so it was that most of the eighty-three municipal courses built in Britain between 1960 and 1980 – including Torvean, Inverness, in 1961 – either came complete with a members' club or formed one within months of opening. The finances may have been controlled by the local authority and, apart from not exceeding a maximum capacity, restrictions on membership were practically non-existent, but in all other regards they were clubs like any others; they held competitions and offered prizes, provided handicaps, held functions and paid for a load of V-neck jumpers with their badge on the front.

But not all of those clubs, I have just discovered, have been content to remain mere imitations of their privately-owned archetypes – all blazers and no budget. Having travelled hundreds of miles to play the most northerly municipal course in Britain, I now find that Torvean is actually run by its members' club.

'Och, aye, but it's still municipal,' says Willie Rusk, behind the desk in the pro shop. 'The club runs the place, but the council still owns the land. Don't worry, ye haven't wasted your time.'

In a rare example of councillors actually admitting their limitations, Highland Council decided a couple of years ago that it was the last body that should be running a golf club and gave the members a twenty-year lease on all its operations – with certain provisos, of course. Among them was that it should retain the unrestricted, low-cost nature of any municipal course.

A round at Torvean normally costs £20, but thanks to my navigation skills, first seen in North Tyneside, my round will cost precisely nothing. It is complimentary for guests at the Loch Ness House Hotel, which is located, I was pleased to discover over my kipper at a window seat this morning, right across the road from the golf course.

Willie says he will hook me up with one or two of the local old boys who play the course most mornings, but for the moment I am delighted to learn that he is the same Willie Rusk whom I'd read about in the papers some years ago; the man who built and ran a golf course on Eriskay. For the uninitiated, Eriskay is towards the southern tip of the Outer Hebrides, you know just east of Fiaray and Fuday . . . north of Gighay and Hellisay? That's it.

Willie was the Eriskay boatman who worked the sound between the island and South Uist before the causeway was built. Along with the parish priest and another pal, in 1995 he dreamed up and built one of the oddest golf courses in Britain – six holes carved out of rock and rough crofting land along the shoreline. It was not the biggest ('Och, it's quite a big course for its size,' one islander said at the time), but it still managed to include one of the most historic 'bunkers' in the country – the beach where Bonnie Prince Charlie first set foot on Scottish soil on 23 July 1745.

Sadly, the course was forced to close after only two

years when a local lobster fisherman built a four-bedroom house on the fifth green. Shortly afterwards, Willie moved to Inverness, but the competition that launched the course, The Eriskay Open, still survives and for the last four years has been played here at Torvean, where fields of more than 200, many of them from the island, are regularly attracted.

'It's gotten so big I've had to split it into two and introduce a seniors event. It's probably the biggest event in the north now,' says Willie. 'I only won it the once – when it was still on Eriskay. I was alright over six holes, but not so good when it went up to eighteen.'

We've been chatting for about half an hour when two elderly gents come into the shop and say they are happy to give me a game. Willie does the introductions.

'Chris, this is Willie. Willie, Chris,' says Willie as we shake hands. 'And over here is Willie – Chris, Willie. Willie, Chris.'

I'm always nervous about introductions because I have a dreadful memory for names. I hope I don't screw up this morning.

It is an absolutely stunning day. While Birmingham had been sultry and Widnes mild enough in a dull, blustery kind of way, today the entire Highlands is bathed in glorious sunshine with not a cloud in the sky. Any recent tourists to the area will, of course, think I'm lying through my teeth – but it's true, honest. There is dew still on the lush fairways as we make our way to the first tee. The air is warm but fresh and not so much as a zephyr is troubling the rowans growing heavy with fruit between the fairways. I am standing on the first tee, sucking in the sweet scents of new-mown grass and wild flowers in the hedgerows, surveying the twin hills that dominate the scene – Torvean itself and Tomnahurich – and giving serious thought to a quick verse of *These are my Mountains,* when I hear 'thwack' at my back and turn to see that one of the Willies has already teed off. This is old man's golf. No point in mucking about stretching or limbering up – you might do yourself an injury.

The opener is an easy little par three. The two Willies are either side of the green with longish irons, while my rushed seven-iron nevertheless finds the middle of the putting surface.

'Oh, that's a lovely swing right enough,' says the one that looks like a slimmed down Ernest Hemingway.

'Aye,' says the other. 'A nine handicap, y'say? You'll be teaching us a thing or two, eh?'

Minutes later they have both chipped on and single putted with carefree ease for pars, while I three-putt for bogey. Not a word is spoken, but I catch them giving each other a conspiratorial little smile and a giggle as we make the long walk to the second tee.

Only a few yards from this tee, through some trees, tourists are piling on to the *Jacobite Queen,* a cruise boat that very soon will make her way down a five-mile stretch of the Caledonian Canal, which begins by running alongside the second hole, and eventually out on to Loch Ness. From their vantage point on the upper deck, a small knot of passengers has a perfect view of our tee shots and I am delighted to say mine is the only one on the fairway. The Willies take two or three more shots to reach the green of this 346-yard par four, which is tucked away in a dark, wooded corner under Torvean Hill, but again I have hit a nice iron on. I'm a good thirty feet away, however, and give the first putt a fair belt.

'Will we tell him this is a fast green?' asks one Willie

of the other, a split second after my ball starts rolling.

'Oh, I'm sure he'll work it out,' says his pal, as it gathers an alarming pace, accelerates past the hole and is only prevented from rolling off the edge by some thick fringe. Another three putts, another bogey.

Having brought me and my nine handicap down a peg or two, the old boys seem to call a truce on the next tee and explain a few things about the course; how none of the holes are really as easy as they look and that, in case I hadn't noticed, the greens are a bit fast. Both men are seventy-three, but one takes great pleasure in helping the other on to tees and asking after his health.

'He's always doing that because he's the youngest,' says the Hemingway lookalike in good-natured exasperation, 'but he's only got two weeks on me.'

Conversation down the third turns to the news that Aberdeen Football Club have appointed a new manager. Surely, however, you chaps support Inverness Caledonian Thistle? Two cheerful old faces turn suddenly grim. Both, it seems, were Inverness Thistle fans before the still controversial merger with city rivals, Caledonian, in 1994. But while there was plenty of Caley blue in the new strip, there wasn't much Thistle red. A request from the supporters of the old Thistle club for more red was met, rather unsympathetically, by painting the toilets at the Telford Street stadium.

'That's it. You're getting no more money from me, I said. And ever since, I've been an Aberdeen fan,' says older Willie.

I resolve to ask my partners their surnames or nicknames so I can stop addressing questions to 'Willie' and have both of them turn and say 'Whit?' at the same time, but just as we reach the third green, the younger Willie is told by a group on the second tee that his friend, who's been recovering from a serious illness, is in the clubhouse and looking to play a few holes. He makes his apologies and heads back to see his pal.

It sets the remaining Willie off on a long list of ailments among the more elderly members. There are blocked arteries, triple by-passes, hip replacements . . . and all of them still out here at least once a week for a game. Willie himself has asthma and 'Arthur Itis' and has to take a bewildering array of pills every day.

'If you hear a rattle, Chris, don't worry – that'll be me.'

Over the next few holes I learn more about my playing partner. Willie Royan was once a printer on the *Inverness Courier*, did his national service, then started work as a lorry driver. In more than forty years he drove everything from malt whisky to herring all over the Highlands and beyond. Latterly he'd worked as watchman at the Inverness depot.

'I didn't want the job. The boss made this big speech to me about what a wonderful opportunity it was to be at home more and cut down the travel, blah, blah. And I just sat there and listened and then said, "Stuff it up yer arse," and left the office. But he was a sly bastard and when I got home I found out he'd already told my wife. That was it. I had no chance.'

The fierce pride of a man who liked to earn his pay the hard way still shines in his eyes, but all this was many years ago and he can tell the story now with a certain humorous detachment. Today, he is content to enjoy his retirement and the time it gives him to spend with his three children and six grandchildren.

I'd steadied the ship a little with a couple of pars before

I stood on the fifth tee. Little do I know it, however, but I am about to play the toughest hole of the entire trip.

'Where's the flag?'

'Y'see thon hill . . . and the hill behind that? It's just under the trees at the top of the second hill.'

At more than 560 yards, this par five is one of the longest golf holes in the Highlands. It is generally uphill, but breaks the monotony with an even steeper hill of rough that juts out in a spur from the foot of Torvean about halfway along. Beyond this is a deep gouge in the fairway, from the bottom of which it is a blind shot to the green just over the second summit. I have an absolute nightmare. I seem to remember being in the thick, wet semi-rough for the entire hole, stupidly not listening to the voice in my head screaming at me to put the five-wood away and just hack out sideways. The eight I eventually get given by Willie is generous in the extreme, but we're not playing any kind of match, so who's counting?

After this, I count a bogey at the next as a definite improvement before we double back on ourselves and climb some steps to the tee of the par three seventh. A lovely mid-iron from Willie (he was once a thirteen handicap but has been going backwards for years and now plays off twenty) lands smack on the green and he bends down stiffly for his tee. I step over to help, but he gets there ahead of me.

'Ach, don't worry, Chris. I can still pick up my own tee.' He stares into the middle distance for a second. 'In fact, I can still have sex if I try hard enough.'

Right, OK. Moving swiftly on, I hit a nice seven-iron on to the green below . . . and off again. Once down at the green I chip it back on well enough, but the pace of the greens kills me again and I three-putt for the third time in seven holes. Willie hits a deft lag from twenty feet and walks off with another par.

'Not bad for an old bodach, eh?'

[bodach, -aich, *s.m.* Old *or* churlish man. (*Dwelly's Illustrated Gaelic to English Dictionary*)]

Once past the eighth hole, which navigates round a wooded pond that used to be much bigger and was used as a skating rink in winter when Willie was a boy, the course crosses the A82 south out of Inverness towards Fort Augustus and Fort William beyond. Roads, in fact, are a sore point with the golfers of Torvean.

Originally a nine-hole course when it was opened in 1961, it was expanded to eighteen in 1998, but that meant straddling the T-junction of the A82 and a new road heading north up to Leachkin. The current layout, therefore, is in three bits. But worse is on the horizon, because plans have been approved by Highland Council for a city by-pass (or, as they prefer to call it, a 'southern distributor road'). The final phase of this will cut right across at least the first eight holes of Torvean, the only outstanding point being how it will cross the canal – by tunnel or bridge.

Willie, in common with anyone else I have ever heard talking about planners anywhere in the country, believes them to be a parcel of rogues, fools and gangsters, but he seems resigned to the fate of the club and, though he might not admit it, rather interested in the plans to redesign the course so that it is on one piece of land without the need to criss-cross busy roads.

Standing on the ninth tee, we have a perfect view of the hills north of Inverness and the spread of housing estates up their flanks.

'It's the fastest growing town in Europe,' says Willie.

He looks suffused with civic pride and I haven't the heart to tell him that two weeks ago someone told me exactly the same thing about Braintree. But I think someone should be told – not unless Euro-boomtowns are going to go the way of boxing, with several 'champions' all boasting that their title is the only one that counts.

Willie rattles off another par while I bogey once more before we turn east to play the tenth, also known as Tomnahurich, after the wooded hill on the other side of the canal that now seems to loom directly over the hole before us. Both it and Torvean are not big hills at all, but they stand out prominently in the otherwise flat floodplain of the River Ness. For desperate academic reasons too painful to recount here, I once had to study geology for a year and ever since I've had a tendency to pronounce with certainty about mountains and the like when in fact I haven't a clue what I'm talking about. So, if I say the two hills look like ridges of sand and gravel dumped by the glacier that I think carved out Loch Ness, you can be reasonably sure they are nothing of the sort. In any case, it turns out there's a lot more to Tomnahurich than periglacial deposits – or whatever.

'That's Fairy Hill,' says Willie. 'There's all sorts of stories about that place.'

Indeed there are. You can take your pick from Fionn, the Gaelic adventurer king, who somehow managed to escape from a spell cast by the Irish king by training his dog to walk two of every species of animal round the hill. Obviously. Or the fairy queen, who held her court there and paid two wandering fiddlers to entertain her guests for an evening. After eating her food and wine, however, they fell under her power and, unbeknownst to them, stayed there belting out tunes for 200 years. Then there is the thirteenth century seer, Thomas Rhymer, who rests in the cemetery there, allegedly with all his men and their white horses ready to rise again and save Scotland in her hour of need. But the most famous tale relates to the Brahan Seer, a sixteenth or seventeenth century Highland prophet who said, among other things, 'Strange as it may seem to you this day, a time will come when full-rigged ships will be seen sailing eastward and westward by the back of Tomnahurich.' Hundreds of years later Thomas Telford built the Caledonian Canal and, even as I am standing on the tenth tee, a fully rigged yacht is gliding past the hill, seemingly floating through the trees.

Willie is something of an authority on local history and takes my mind off a steady run of bogeys and double bogeys at the start of the back nine with tales of Clan Chattan, the Frasers, McLennans and McIntoshes, and back as far as the dark age foundations of Inverness itself. When not dispensing titbits of local history, I notice that Willie misses no opportunity to curse at any crows that come anywhere near us. And, I have to admit, there are quite a few flying around.

'Evil birds,' he says. 'They attack anything and everything they see and they're merciless. I'd kill the buggers if I had the chance.'

My own father has a similar attitude to magpies which, he is convinced, are single-handedly responsible for the lack of songbirds in his garden. Personally, I've always rather admired the intelligence and low cunning of crows and ravens, but after the twelfth hole I may be about to change my mind. As I walk down the fairway after just about the best drive I've hit all day, I see a crow fly down and land by the ball. He starts to roll it about then, as I get closer, he picks it up in his beak, flies off to the thick rough, drops it and – this is the weird bit – picks up a thatch of grass cuttings and covers it up!

'Told ye. They're buggers,' says Willie.

I confess to not knowing the rules governing such actions by the local fauna, but I'm damned if I'm going to play the ball as it now lies. With the crow cawing away with his pals on the branches of a nearby tree, I pick it up, put it back roughly where it was on the fairway and prepare to play on. Even as I am thinking about a club, I notice the crow flies back down, this time with a companion, and starts to pick up clods of grass looking for the ball.

'I'm telling you, it was a Titleist Pro VIx – brand new . . . I put it right here.'

'Aye right, so ye did. It'll be a Top Flight as usual.'

The twelfth yields another bogey. Although we're not playing a match, by my count, Willie, the arthritic, seventy-three-year-old twenty-handicapper, is six shots better off than me and would be four holes up without getting any strokes! I'm hitting the ball reasonably well, but my old failing of not being able to judge distances – particularly on this flat stretch of the back nine – is really causing me problems. The holes look easy enough, but the greens are very small and are surrounded by thick semi-rough and bunkers with sand like custard. But it is still a glorious day and I have rarely enjoyed a round of truly awful golf quite as much. By mid-morning the sun has seen off the dew and it is getting seriously warm.

'Ach, it's a good day to be above ground,' says Willie and I couldn't agree more.

Not even such splendid conditions, however, will

persuade my normal game to put in an appearance. After losing a ball by taking exactly the line off the fourteenth tee Willie told me not to, and then hitting a lovely three-iron into the par three fifteenth that just crawled off the back . . . and into an impossible lie in a ditch, we cross the second road to play the remaining three holes. I am twenty over par. The sixteenth, however, is to be the scene of my inevitable encounter with the Second Law of Lousy Golf (see Sean's miracle recovery from the trees on the seventeenth at the Essex). This is where I play to the best of my ability, re-ignite my passion for the stupid bloody game and resolve not to chuck it in after all.

A monster 471-yard par four from the back tees (stroke index one), it demands a drive to the top of a hill with water on the left and a large tree and the road to the right. Nothing less than a three-wood from there will be able to find the green, which sits tight by the water and has an approach to the right further guarded by bunkers. I execute the drive well enough and now stand over the second shot. If I were protecting any kind of score I simply wouldn't be thinking about it, but for about an hour now I've been saying 'Aw, what the hell,' before every shot. After a sweet strike with the three-wood, my ball soars high and true. I'm not convinced it is enough to clear the pond until it lands on the putting surface as softly, to use Lee Trevino's famous quote, 'as a butterfly with sore feet'. I don't make the birdie, but the par is enough to convince me I can still play the game. Perhaps even more gratifying is the genuine admiration and congratulation from Willie, who must have been wondering what kind of deluded fool he was playing with until now.

The last two holes, the eighteenth being a particularly

nasty slog up another hill, produce the standard bogeys for me and something of a weary collapse in double bogeys for Willie. With the hot sun now beating down on us, we are glad to be able to cross the road and head back to the clubhouse.

Torvean was built by the then Inverness Town Council because the area at the time only had one private course, the Inverness Golf Club, which had one of the oddest restrictions for visitors I've ever heard of: if you lived within a radius of ten miles you were simply not allowed anywhere near the place unless accompanied by a member. Visitor tee-times were being reserved, it seems, for tourists.

While walking off the course, Willie says he thinks that between the Inverness Golf Club, Torvean and a recently built course at Castle Heather, all golfers in the area are now pretty well served.

'I wouldn't say there's such a difference between all the courses now. People round here don't really think in terms of public and private golf. Take this club. Time was when it was a course for what I'd call the working man, but now we've got lawyers and all sorts playing here.' He grins. 'It's gone right downhill.'

A cool drink and a pleasant lunch with a few of his cronies in the bar and I take my leave of Willie and Torvean Golf Club. It is time to point the discourtesy car southwards again and head for home, but I'll be making one last stop along the way – one last look at a piece of public golfing turf . . . that just happens to feature the most famous golf course in the world.

13

Samuel Johnson couldn't tire of London without tiring of life, but could a golfer grow weary of St Andrews? Is it possible to tire of the famous links without tiring of golf itself – or, to borrow from Boswell once more, is there in St Andrews 'all that life can afford'?

For anyone even mildly interested in the game it's hard to avoid St Andrews. It now has its own event on the European Tour every year and seems to host the Open far more often than any other course. It is home to the R&A and, in the Old Course, must have one of the most photographed few acres on the planet. More than for any other sport I can think of, golf has this one town, one site that is venerated above all others, that has become, in fact, synonymous with the game itself.

I don't profess to be an expert on the place. I didn't study there and have never lived in the town, but I *am* a regular visitor. With my dearest golfing chum, Donald, who did go to St Andrews University and has never lost his affection for the 'old grey toon', I suppose I come up to play on one of the four main links courses maybe half a dozen times a year. I don't, therefore, get all misty-eyed whenever I see its distinctive profile come into view as I drive in on the A91, and I probably take the superb condition of the courses and the friendly staff for granted, but every now and then I am reminded of just what a special place St Andrews occupies in the hearts of golfers everywhere.

Like when I drive to the St Andrews Links Clubhouse down Granny Clark's Wynd, which just happens to cut right across the first and eighteenth fairways of the Old Course. The look on the faces of the American four-ball on the first tee in front of the R&A clubhouse is always highly entertaining. They've just spent thousands of dollars and travelled halfway round the world to play probably the only game they ever will on the hallowed turf, golf's Mecca, and here's some bozo driving his car right across the goddam fairway! Only a restraining hand and quiet word from the caddie stops them from storming back to the starter and demanding I be reported to the FBI. But you can still see their puzzlement – because they have just been told I am perfectly entitled to drive on a public right of way across public land.

Before even setting out on my travels I'd fretted over my casual use of the word 'public' to cover the proletarian game I was seeking to discover. Predictably, I've hacked around a fair number of municipal courses, such as those at Portobello or St Michaels, but the golf that anyone can play for a relatively modest outlay in bats and fees can also be had in private clubs (Backworth), new proprietary pay-and-play complexes (the Essex and Wyboston Lakes) or, for the locals at least, through artisan clubs (Northam Golf Club). Some of the venues I've been to are not public at all, yet the Old Course at St Andrews is. All you need is a handicap of at most twenty-four for men and thirty-six for ladies (a fair enough stipulation to keep things moving along on a course that has, after all, 42,000 rounds played on it every year). Oh, and the small matter of £110.

You see the problem; public golf course, land owned by the local authority, no unreasonable tee-time restrictions, no discrimination . . . but it costs a fortune. There are plenty of such public golf courses in Scotland – Carnoustie is another that immediately comes to mind; venerable links that were established on public land, but have evolved into 'classics' that now attract golfers from all over the world. Only a high green fee and/or a ballot system for tee times is able to control their use.

In mitigation, it should be pointed out that all residents of these Scottish coastal towns, descendants, many of them, of those who first played on the links, are not disadvantaged by this and retain unique rights to cheap golf on the famous courses. It may not be much comfort to the visitor who's just had to hand over a sizeable wedge for one round of golf, but I do think the local discounts are an important example of how the tradition of accessible, 'public' golf still thrives in Scotland. Others include the high number of municipal courses (seventy-one by the year 2000), the fact that (at the time of writing) 67 per cent of all courses in Scotland charge under £20 for a round (the lowest average rate in the UK) and the sheer volume of golf available to her citizens. At one for every 10,000, Scotland has easily the highest ratio of golf courses per head of population of any country in the world. In the golf-mad USA, for example, it is one course for every 17,000, and in England, just one for every 26,000.

Leaving aside that endless argument about how 'classless' the game is in its homeland (answer: it isn't), it is undeniable that more of the hoi polloi play golf in Scotland than elsewhere in the UK simply because there is a greater opportunity for them to do so. It is true that in some places, such as the Borders, most of the Highlands and the Western Isles, there is no *municipal* golf, but these rural parts are well served with plenty of low-cost, holiday courses, many of which have local discount schemes. In England and Wales, however, no fewer than fifteen counties, comprising who knows how many city and district councils under whose remit golf falls, have no municipal provision at all. North Yorkshire, Lincolnshire, Norfolk and Suffolk, Oxfordshire, Cornwall, Devon and most of south and mid-Wales – all of these and more besides with not a single municipal golf course among them.

If someone has carried out a comprehensive study and analysis of the patterns of municipal provision in Britain, then I'm afraid I haven't come across it. I did speak to a number of councils to ask why they had no municipal courses, but the answers were all variations on a theme of lack of demand. Perhaps golf, like both codes of rugby, is not only seen as class-specific, but also particular to certain regions; rugby league isn't big in Surrey – maybe golf isn't big in Glamorgan.

But times have moved on. If the word 'public' doesn't exactly define the golf market I've been looking at, then neither does 'municipal' – if it ever did. As I touched on during the visit to my old stamping ground in Essex, the last great wave of golf course development in Britain came in the late 1980s and early 1990s. Thanks to daft notions like 'best practice' and 'cost benefit analysis' – introduced by Thatcher's government and still stalking the land to this day – there was little scope for local authorities to continue building loss-making golf courses. Yet golf courses were needed . . . in their hundreds.

That was certainly the overwhelming consensus of the

Sports Council, the Golf Development Council, umpteen research bodies, sports quangos and just about every planning authority in the country who, since the mid-1970s, had all been warning about the desperate under-supply of specifically public golf courses. The last word – as so often happens in golf – went to the R&A which, in 1989, produced *The Demand for Golf*, a document that pulled no punches in identifying golf course development as a planning and leisure imperative for the next ten years. No fewer than 691 new courses would be needed urgently to satisfy demand, it said.

Stepping into the breach came private landowners, farmers (like Eric Hobbs at Earls Colne) and eventually the new chains of proprietary, pay-and-play golf courses. They were helped by low agricultural land prices, new planning guidelines and banks falling over themselves to lend. Between brand new eighteen-hole golf courses and existing nine-hole courses adding another nine, the total of eighteen-hole equivalent golf courses built between 1990 and 2002 was a staggering 727. In a little over ten years, commercial pay-and-play complexes changed the face of golf in Britain and today account for more than one in three of all the courses in the country.

I suppose that really concludes my wandering through the history of how public golf has developed over the centuries. From a completely free and unorganised ball and stick game on rough, untamed common land it has evolved into a fully catered, one-stop leisure experience on vast acreages of new grass and staked trees. Having charted this progress, however, can I say that the great divide between the haves and have nots I mentioned at the outset still exists in golf?

Well, yes. The new-look venues may present a more egalitarian face to the world, but occasionally on this trip I've played a game few members at Muirfield or Wentworth would recognise and fewer still attempt without security and a tetanus shot. Golf remains a game that encompasses everything from grim trudges through the muddy shadows of chemical plants and council housing schemes to the post-prandial strolls of Scottish law lords across sunlit championship links.

Why the game developed such a split personality I think is easy to answer; it was inevitable. More than any other popular, mass-participation sport, golf requires land – an average of 200 acres for an eighteen-hole course. It followed that, when golf grew too big for the common links on which it was born, those who could afford to buy land effectively took charge of the sport and made it into something in their own image. Purpose-built public provision has been playing catch-up ever since, but even after the boom in pay-and-play mentioned above, 55 per cent of all courses in Britain today are owned by private clubs.

Does this justify membership golf all but monopolising the sport's image? I don't think so; fewer acres they may have on which to enjoy their sport, but there are 2.4 million public, green-fee golfers and they outnumber private members by two to one. Perhaps the club golfer has become the sport's stereotype because golfers at the public end of the market cannot so easily be pigeon-holed. In just eleven rounds of golf, I've played with trawlermen and accountants, the owners of international pharmaceutical companies and plumbers, police superintendents and schoolboys. Such a cosmopolitan mix defies easy socio-economic description as much as it does tired jokes about pink gin and pretentious halfwits. For every one of these players there will be reasons for not being the member of a private club. It may not be through choice, although hopefully in this day and age there will be few cases of simply not being wealthy enough, or having the wrong postcode, but public golf has its own attractions. It is cheap, as accessible as most municipal parks and rarely has any of the uptight attitude to rules and regulations found in most clubs.

Despite grumbles I've heard about everything from green-fee prices to the state of the toilets, it would be fair to say the lot of the golfer on public courses is an improving one – certainly the quality of the courses themselves has never been higher. This makes the fact that non-member golfers are playing fewer rounds of golf even more worrying. The latest figures available show that the average number of actual rounds played each year on public courses fell by a quarter between 1985 and 2001. The causes could be anything from a string of dodgy summers and less golf on terrestrial television to spark interest in the game, to the fact that most youngsters nowadays shun sport in favour of growing fat arses and large prehensile thumbs in front of computer games. But whatever is responsible, it spells immediate disaster for the public courses that are losing revenue, and long term trouble for everyone else – public golf, after all, is the seed-bed for the entire sport in Britain. As Vivien Saunders said, the average age of women golfers is sixty-four, but it is not much better for the game as a whole. A recent seminar held by the English Golf Union was told that the average golfer in Britain is male (obvi-ously) and in his mid-forties. Hardly the profile of a thriving game with a secure future.

Promoting golf, selling it to the masses, is of course the responsibility of those businesses and organisations who run the game in Britain and make a profit from it. Unfortunately, there are rather a lot of them and they seldom seem capable of speaking with one voice. Richard Caborn, the Minister for Sport, was famously asked if the government could not put more money into developing golf. I'd love to, was the gist of his reply, but I have no idea who to give it to.

The R&A is everyone's favourite target when looking for someone to pin the blame on for golf's ills, but, as Andy Salmon of the Ladies Golf Union said, even the R&A can't tell clubs how to run their affairs. And they certainly don't lord it over the PGA or the LGU or the NAPGC or the BIGGA or the AGCS . . . or any of the seventeen governing bodies covering all aspects of golf administration in Great Britain. Many of these, in fact, were established precisely to provide a check on any ambitions the R&A might have had for wielding over-weening power. This myriad of special interests, however, has done little to encourage joined-up thinking on the game's future – and worse, has often allowed important issues affecting the game and the millions who play it to become little more than ammunition for petty turf wars.

As I've journeyed around the country, I've heard private clubs complain about municipal courses deliberately undercutting their prices; municipal clubs complain that, particularly in open competitions, private clubs discrimi-nate against their players; and pay-and-play courses complain that they are being financially disadvantaged by not getting any of the tax breaks afforded to private clubs.

Stephen Blake, European managing director of the Golf Research Group, told me, 'The game is fragmented from top to bottom; individual clubs and other courses are marketing themselves locally – often in competition with each other – instead of co-ordinating for their mutual benefit, while at a national level the governing bodies are all fighting their own corners.'

It should be pointed out that British golf is aware of

the problem and a few tentative moves involving SportEngland and the Scottish Executive on either side of the Border have been made to at least agree on what needs to be done to attract more people on to the fairways. They may work, but the blurbs I've read so far are absolutely awash with 'visions', 'critical benchmarking data' and 'stakeholders'. I fear the worst.

The administration of golf in Britain certainly bears more than a passing resemblance to some of the more surreal regimes in *Gulliver's Travels*. But though I've grown frustrated by countless tales of blazered fools who could fall out over how to eat a boiled egg (and in which part of the clubhouse you would be allowed to do so), I have to say that throughout my own travels my love for the game itself, and sense of kinship with all who play it, has remained undiminished.

Two writers on golf have featured heavily in what I like to call my research and have cropped up more than most in these pages. Their work was little more than a decade apart, but their contrasting attitudes to the game, epitomised here in two final quotes, encapsulate my own confused and contradictory emotions as I near journey's end:

The very spread of [golf] has done much to reinforce a fundamental sense of social division . . . It has emphasised gender divisions and inequalities. It has pandered to a suburban romanticism about controlled nature and it has encouraged the segregation of land use. Bumbling amateurishness rather than ruthless competition seems to have characterised many of its management's attitudes and it has fostered deference to traditions of dubious antiquity.

John Lowerson (1989)

The average player, intent on pursuing the little white ball over the springy turf in the open air, has neither the time nor the inclination to worry about the politics of the game. He is content with golf as it is.

Geoffrey Cousins (1975)

Looking out over the back of the R&A clubhouse and the Old Course and West Sands beyond, I could be pondering all this, stroking my chin and wondering, 'Whither golf?' – but I'm just not in a reflective mood. I'm still feeling too smug about my supreme 'beach towel moment' from the previous evening. You see, my uninterrupted view of the famous bits of St Andrews comes courtesy of a suite of rooms at the Scores Hotel – a *suite*. Parking the car in the one remaining free parking bay opposite, I'd nipped past an elegantly dressed woman at the doorway who was examining the hotel's photographs of rooms, typical meals and the like. On asking for a single room I was told the hotel was almost full and they only had this suite left. I managed to look disappointed yet interested at the same time. The receptionist hesitated for a moment, then said, 'OK, I can give it to you for just over the price of a single room.'

Literally three seconds later, the elegant lady appeared at my elbow and enquired of the other receptionist, 'I vos vondering if you haf ein sveet of rooms a-wailable?'

Pom-pomming *The Dambusters* theme under my breath, I took the key and bounded up the stairs to these quite magnificent rooms – a telly in each, huge double bed and a bath you could row across.

Now, stuffed with my last fry-up breakfast (and do you know, they never got better than the one at the Cherry Tree in Whitley Bay), I am reluctant to leave, but it is another gloriously sunny day and I have an appointment to play the only full-sized public course in St Andrews that doesn't cost the visitor a seriously private championship course price to play. To do so, I have to drive a little way out of town to the Eden Clubhouse next to the links driving range and practice ground.

This smart new development serves the Eden course (opened in 1914), the nine-hole Balgove, suitable for children and beginners, and the Strathtyrum, the one I shall be playing this morning. Like the Balgove, it was opened in 1993 and, although a full eighteen holes, it is still pretty short and is aimed at high handicappers. In any other part of the country, it would be ludicrously over-priced at £20 for a round, but in St Andrews it is a tenner less than the next one up (the Eden), £35 less than the cost of playing the New Course and, of course, less than a fifth of what it would cost to play the Old Course. Like all the courses in St Andrews, it is operated by the Links Trust, a non profit-making charity that ploughs all fees back into the upkeep and development of golf in the town.

I'm getting in a little putting practice when Jim Bowie walks up and introduces himself by holding out a handful of golf balls.

'Eh, no thanks. I'm alright for balls.'

'You sure? Plenty more where they came from,' he says.

I'd arranged to play with Jim through the Links Trust for a couple of reasons. Firstly, I did not want to risk being on my own and having to play a re-match against Donald Rumsfeld for my final round. I also quite fancied the idea of playing with a local rather than, as could easily have happened, a twenty-seven-handicapper from Baton Rouge who's been playing quite salad recently and is just thrilled at being here in Scatland, the home of galf.

'Oh, I'm not a local,' says Jim, as we walk to the first tee. 'I've only lived here for thirty years.'

And he's not joking. The St Andreans are as friendly and welcoming a lot as you'd want to meet – but they have very clear ideas on who's who, and from where. Originally from Clydebank, Jim is a trim and fit-looking sixty-five-year-old, a retired education adviser for the now defunct Tayside Regional Council. Apart from playing golf, he helps fill his days with giving the odd walking tour of the Old Course to visitors. But it's not the Old Course today, it's the Strathtyrum (named after the estate the land was purchased from) and Jim, a fellow nine-handicapper, has the honour.

He slices wildly off towards the eighteenth hole of the Eden Course, but greets the shot with a smile like he's just met an old friend.

'Aye, that always happens,' he says. 'It's usually twelve holes before I get warmed up.'

Luckily for him he's found a path between the gorse bushes and manages to find the correct fairway with his next shot, but the one after that is a bladed wedge that goes through the raised green of this par four at head height. My reasonable drive down the left has been followed by a fat nine-iron that comes up short and rolls back down the front apron of the green. The next chip, though I say it myself, is exquisite and stops inches from the cup. Jim has one attempt from the back then runs up the white flag. And so we are off.

There is a tempo to a good round of golf and the first hole always establishes it. While the Willies set too blistering a pace for me at Torvean, and Sean and Mike were all over the place at the Essex, this round, as Goldilocks might have said, looks like it will be just right. From these few exchanges, Jim and I have learned that we are golfers both of the old school: by all means have a chat between shots, but always as you are walking; give due care and attention to the shot, but don't dawdle; and, this being matchplay, don't hang about wasting everyone's time once the hole is lost. This will be a pace as swinging as anything Count Basie's rhythm section could lay down.

My drive at the second looks gorse-bound and, as we're walking over to investigate, Jim fills me in on some of the recent St Andrews gossip.

'The Hamilton Halls, I've heard, has been bought by an American and is going to get turned into timeshare flats,' he says. The Hamilton Halls is the distinctive red sandstone building to the right of the R&A clubhouse, formerly university residences.

'It's happening all over St Andrews. Wherever Americans spend money, American businessmen move in and reap the profits. And Americans spend an awful lot of money in St Andrews.'

Although Jim and I agree on the exact spot where my ball was last seen, we can't find it anywhere. The thing is, Jim had all but given up on the hole already, because he sliced again off the tee and this time couldn't find *his* ball. As at St Michaels, I drop one in the semi-rough, but my next shot finds a greenside bunker right up against the face.

'A half?' A half it is, with neither of us having hit a decent golf shot between us.

So how much is the local season ticket? I ask.

'£110,' says Jim with a grin. 'I always remember it because I know it costs us the same for a full year of golf on any golf course we like as it does a visitor for one round on the Old Course.'

Not that this keeps the locals entirely happy. Grumbles about how the Links Trust runs the courses persist – that it makes too much money and wastes it all on state-of-the-art lawnmowers and poncy catering in the clubhouses.

Jim obviously likes to shock people with tales of St Andrean parsimony. Here's another – Kingsbarns is one of a handful of modern golf courses built around the outskirts of the town in the last twenty years and it is arguably the best. A magnificent modern championship links course, it now features as part of the Dunhill Masters tournament along with the Old Course and Carnoustie. For ordinary mortals a round (this year) costs £135. For anyone from St Andrews, £12.

'But no one goes,' laughs Jim. '£12 for a round of golf? I'm not paying that, they all say. They're so used to paying for the season ticket and getting "free" golf for the whole year, they've gotten out of the habit of actually paying a green fee.'

We've halved the third in bogey fours and the next in bogey fives – sloppy play, but it's just such a lovely day to be out on these links that neither of us cares. The Strathtyrum runs between the Eden and Balgove courses, then out along the A91. If you were to strike out north and head for the shore you would walk across not only the Eden, but the Old, New and Jubilee courses before you'd reach the beach. The links at St Andrews are the largest public golf complex in the world.

'It's a terrific stretch of land for golf, there's no mistake in that,' says Jim. 'And if they kept going westwards they'd have enough room to build even more golf courses.'

In fact, a seventh public golf course for the town *is* being built by the Links Trust, but at the other end of town on old farmland. Needless to say, there's not a bunker or a parking bay that is not being scrutinised by a keen St Andrean eye.

'It's costing about £6 million and, of course, there are locals who think they should've spent the money reducing prices at the existing courses,' says Jim.

'Because obviously they are paying too much for their golf,' I say with some bitterness. Jim just laughs and says nothing. He has to live here.

The par five fifth yields a couple of steadying pars for us both, although Jim is still slicing badly and has hit some indifferent irons. Like most regular links golfers, however, his touch round the greens is superb and has kept him in the game.

'Do you ever do any caddying on the Old Course?' I ask.

'No, no. You need to be qualified to do that nowadays.' I look surprised. 'Oh, yes. There's a college here that teaches you how to be a caddie. The tourists want crusty old characters with Scottish accents and there are plenty of those in the town, of course, but they used to get drunk and, if they didn't like you, they would just bugger off halfway round the course.' Jim looks wistfully across towards the Old Course. 'Nowadays it's all students wearing tabards and minding their language. Shame.'

By now we're on the par three sixth and, after we've both found the green, I ask Jim what club he'd used as I was unclear about the exact yardage.

'A five iron – and I bet you used something like a seven,' he says. 'Aye. You see there's not much point in asking me things like that. I don't play the same game as everyone else seems to.'

And he's right. Using a thirty-year-old set of clubs called Swilcans – obviously after the famous burn and bridge on the Old Course – that used to be made in the town,

Jim never looks at yardages and always takes more club than anyone else would.

'I hit soft shots,' he explains. Taking more club and hitting it softly, of course, keeps the ball low – precisely the game needed to do well on a windy seaside links.

Walking up the seventh fairway a little later, we return to the subject of the Old Course and one of Jim's favourite stories about Hell Bunker, the notorious, cavernous hazard on the fourteenth hole.

'It wasn't during one of my tours. I was just out one Sunday evening for a walk and I noticed these guys in suits standing round the bunker. One of them was standing on the top edge, another had a bag and was actually in the bunker and pointing to a spot under the front face, and there was a third one taking pictures. "Is that where your ball was yesterday?" I asked the guy in the bunker. They were Americans. "Oh no," he says. "You see, my brother died recently," and he takes an urn out of the bag to show me. "I'm just looking for a place in Hell I can put him that he can't get out of."'

Nice family – I'm amazed they were allowed to scatter ashes on the course, I say.

'Oh, it's not exactly encouraged, but it comes back to that thing about it being public land,' says Jim. 'There's a big list of bye-laws for the links, but I don't think it mentions spreading ashes. I know you're not allowed to land a plane though.'

We've halved everything since the first, but my par at the short eighth hole is enough to move two ahead after more trouble off the tee for Jim, who is still insisting it will be the twelfth before he plays properly.

'I don't agree with all these whin bushes they planted,' says Jim. 'I don't think it's right on a course meant for high handicappers – it slows down the play.' Then, making a quick check to ensure the coast is clear and turning to face the nearest bush, he adds, 'Mind you, it's quite handy for people who've got weak bladders. Excuse me while I bless this bush.'

As we play the holes around the turn, Jim relates some of the history of the links. Stories like the so-called 'Rabbit Wars', when rabbit farmers won control of the land from the bankrupt town council in the late eighteenth century and sparked off twenty years of often bloody competition between golfers, rabbits and their keepers for the links. Then there was the fact that the course (you'll appreciate it only became the 'Old Course' when they built a new one in 1895) was originally twenty-two holes – eleven out and back and playing the same holes twice – but in 1764 the golfers decided the first/last four holes were too short and should be made into two holes. The total fell from twenty-two to eighteen and that has been the standard length for courses ever since.

Perhaps Jim's paying too much attention to his history and not enough to his golf, because by the time we reach the eleventh tee he is three down. At 442 yards with a slight dogleg left, it would make a testing par four, but this is the Strathtyrum for high handicappers so it is a par five. I hit a nice solid drive and Jim carves another one way right. Despite a couple of dry, sunny days, the thick rough is still damp underfoot.

'Don't get your feet wet for nothing,' Jim says to me, as I wade in to help him find his ball. 'I'll just give it a quick look.'

And that's what he does. Less than thirty seconds later he concedes not only the loss of the ball, but the hole as well. As he's pulling another ball from his pocket, I ask him why he's so cavalier about golf balls.

'I've a garage full of them. I've played golf since I was seven and I'm now sixty-five. Ask me how many golf balls I've bought.'

'How many?'

'None. Never bought a golf ball in my life. I just find them – and if you live in St Andrews you can find a hell of a lot of golf balls.'

So, £110 for unlimited golf on any St Andrews links course, £12 for Kingsbarns, thirty-year-old clubs and no need to buy golf balls.

'Aye, I know,' laughs Jim. 'Leaves more money for the bar, doesn't it?'

Four up, but now we are on the twelfth – time for Jim's game to kick in – and sure enough his slow, full swing finally sends the ball straight down the fairway. He then finds the green with a solid iron. Only the fact that it is a roller-coaster of a green – and not, it has to be said, in the best of condition – stops him safely two-putting for par. But I've done exactly the same, so at least he's stopped the rot with a half in five.

'Maybe you should play eleven holes before you start a match,' I suggest.

'Ah, wouldn't work. My game would adjust, believe me.'

This reminds me of a bloke I once played with. Every time he did something wrong, he would hiss, 'Gordon!' through gritted teeth. Golfers often reprimand themselves like that, but this was confusing because the guy's name was Brian. 'Yes, I call my game Gordon,' he told me. 'And, in case you hadn't noticed, Gordon's a bastard.'

Although not such an extreme case, Jim was still doing

that thing a lot of us do – talking about our game as a separate entity, like it has a life and a mind of its own.

The thirteenth is another par three, this time of about 143 yards. My seven-iron finds the front trap, while Jim bounces once on the green then over the back. Although I get nowhere near the hole with my bunker shot, Jim takes three hacks to get out from an awful lie. After I roll my first putt close, Jim picks his ball up and we head to the next tee with me dormie five. A relapse of blocking his irons right puts Jim in the worst place to try and chip back on to the fourteenth green, but he makes a magnificent job of it. Unfortunately for him, I've almost driven the green and a dink and two putts later I am the victor by six and four.

Over the closing holes it comes as little surprise to me – and absolutely none to Jim – that he plays beautifully. He finds the fairways on fifteen and sixteen, and the green on the par three seventeenth to par everything until the last. The eighteenth comes as a bit of a shock on this course – a genuinely tough par four with a couple of tracks cutting the fairway, a copse of trees to the right, thick rough down the left and a sloping green well guarded with bunkers.

Jim undoes all his good work with a wild lash into the trees, but I have to say – no really, I do – that my own drive is a peach. The two tracks meet at a corner that forms the apex of the fairway before you turn slightly left to approach the green and my ball is three feet behind the apex on a lovely wee patch of springy grass. As I walk up to the spot, it dawns on me that this was my final drive of the trip – and if you were to put a plaque in the ground saying, 'This is position a,' it would be right under my ball. Maybe it is the tears in my eyes or the lump in my throat, but I then hook it into the rubbish, hack out and three-putt for a double bogey. My final score on my final round is an underwhelming thirteen over par eighty-two, but – Jim and I shake hands and check our watches – under three hours. Marvellous.

'I'm afraid all I can offer you is a bridie,' says John Stewart.

That, I say, will hit the spot nicely.

Jim and I have popped in after our round for a quick chat with John, who works for the Links Trust, in an office that sometimes doubles as the starter hut for the Strathtyrum and Balgove courses. I had not thought of asking for lunch, but the offer of the bridie is very welcome, and the thing itself, once heated in the microwave, is absolutely delicious.

'A Mitchell's?' Jim asks John.

'Of course.'

'Tragic that, wasn't it?'

'Terrible.'

I have a mouth full of bridie and am getting slightly concerned. What exactly is so terrible about Mitchell's bridies?

'Oh, they're fine,' says Jim. 'It's just Murray Mitchell, the butcher . . . Dreadful, wasn't it, John? What a waste.'

'Dead?' I ask, having tried to swallow respectfully. 'An accident, long illness?'

'No, he just gave up golf,' says Jim, as John shakes his head in sorrow. 'A scratch golfer and he just gave up like that.'

That is St Andrews – a golf town to its core. It's the only place where you can get notices in the papers about a local banker's promotion to, say, Montrose and it reads like an obituary: 'Sandy Wilson will be a great loss to the town. He played off three.'

John is a mine of information on the trust, the plans for the seventh course and the history of St Andrews. Understandably, he spends a deal of time defending the trust's use of its powers and revenue.

'What a lot of locals don't appreciate is that it is actually in the original Links Act that visitors have rights to play golf as well as residents,' he says. 'We have to try to balance that with the tee-time schedules and at the moment it is roughly sixty-forty in favour of the locals, but try telling them that.'

Jim just smiles.

It is a great way to while away an afternoon, talking to two guys steeped in the history and love of the game, but home is just across the Firth of Forth and I can hear it calling from here. As we leave, John makes an interesting observation about golfers in St Andrews.

'Ever wondered why you don't get any champions from here any more? I don't think people in St Andrews are as good at golf as they should be and that's because it's too easy to play. If you're rubbish there's always tomorrow, but if you can't play so often and it costs you a fortune for the privilege, you're going to concentrate on your game, aren't you?'

I'm sure he didn't mean it as an argument for increasing the price of the season ticket, but Jim gives him a good-natured scowl across the bows just in case.

Conscious of my desire to get back on the road, Jim nevertheless offers me a quick drink in his club. The New Club, founded in 1902, is one of the town's five golf clubs (all non-course-owning), which includes the R&A and the ladies' clubs, St Rules and St Regulus. It has a clubhouse on the Links, the road that runs up the side of the eighteenth hole of the Old Course, and a chance to wet the whistle in this venerable watering hole is not to be missed. After a quick tour, including pointing out Murray Mitchell, the *former* golfing butcher, on the list of club champions, Jim gets a couple of half pints and sits me down at the window.

Well done Chris, I tell myself as I lean back, glass in hand – you've gone in search of the affordable, democratic, non-restrictive, public heart of golf in Britain and you've ended up sitting here in the wood-panelled bar of a men-only club, your leather armchair looking out over the R&A and the famous closing hole of one of the most expensive courses in the country.

Deciding it will do for an ironic twist at the end, I refrain from asking Jim searching questions about mixed memberships and the like. Instead, I bring up the Samuel Johnson question.

Jim looks out on a four-ball making their final approaches to the eighteenth with the late afternoon sun at their backs. 'No, I never tire of this place. Even when I'm not playing golf, I come down here and walk the West Sands at least twice a week,' he says. 'It's just a magical setting. There is so much history here, it never fails to give me a thrill just to look out on the Old Course.'

It certainly is an inspiring view – and a very civilised way to enjoy it. I could get used to this.

In fact, I bet the R&A over there has got some quality lounging facilities. Maybe I'll drop by on my way home and see if any of the old boys will put me up for membership . . . Oh, that's right – I don't have a tie.